R. code in Back

MW01121367

Grammar

and the

Chinese
ESL Learner

Grammar
and the
Chinese
ESL Learner

A LONGITUDINAL STUDY
ON THE ACQUISITION OF
THE ENGLISH ARTICLE SYSTEM

YONG LANG

CAMBRIA
PRESS

Amherst, New York

Requests for permission should be directed to:
permissions@cambriapress.com, or mailed to:
Cambria Press
20 Northpointe Parkway, Suite 188
Amherst, NY 14228

Library of Congress Cataloging-in-Publication Data

Lang, Yong, 1954-
    English grammar and the Chinese ESL learner : a longitudinal study on the
acquisition of the English article system / by Yong Lang.
        p. cm.
    Includes bibliographical references and index.
    ISBN 978-1-60497-670-0 (alk. paper)
1.   English language—Study and teaching—Chinese speakers. 2.   English
language—Ability testing. 3.   Second language acquisition. I. Title.

    PE1130.C4L28 2010
    428.3'4951—dc22

2009051346

To my wife, Weiwei Yang,
and son, Langtian Lang

TABLE OF CONTENTS

LIST OF FIGURES

LIST OF TABLES

Language learning is doubtless the greatest intellectual feat any one of us is ever required to perform.
                                                    —Leonard Bloomfield

To have another language is to possess a second soul.
                                                    —Charlemagne

PREFACE

This study was completed in 1998. There has been a substantial amount of research on the acquisition and use of the English article system from a wide spectrum of theoretical perspectives since the new millennium. Some of the new perspectives and theories in linguistics, psychology, and child language acquisition have been applied to exploring the acquisition process and uses of English articles. The noticeable patterns of article use by speakers of a particular first language (abbreviated L1) have been further investigated, described, and documented. This has been the case, among others, for Chinese (Lardiere, 2004; Leung, 2001; Lu, 2001; Robertson, 2000; White, 2008), Finnish and Swedish (Jarvis, 2002), Japanese (Kaku, 2006), Persian (Geranpayeh, 2000), Polish (Ekiert, 2004), Russian and Korean (Ionin, Ko, & Wexler, 2008), Serbian (Trenkic, 2002), Syrian Arabic (Sarko, 2008); Tai and French (Pongpairoj, 2007), Turkish (White, 2003), and Vietnamese (Thu, 2005). Different types of articles have also been more thoroughly studied individually, as in the case of the definite article *the* (Liu & Gleason, 2002), the indefinite article *a(n)* (Ekiert, 2007), and the zero and null articles (Master, 2003). Variability in article uses has been studied among second language (L2) learners (Avery & Radišić, 2007), across different text types (Wolf & Walters, 2001), and across different contact varieties of English (Sand, 2004). New pedagogies for English articles have been exploited and experimented (Master, 2002).

Persistent interest in the study of the acquisition and uses of English articles is due to the following factors. First, it is a known fact that L2 learners of English often have continual difficulty in the use of articles until the very late stages of acquisition. More often than not, they do not ever reach native-like levels of performance. Misuse of articles is often used as an evidence of long-lasting non-native performance. Secondly, the acquisition of English articles has been attested to be a notoriously difficult process in terms of semantic features, syntax-morphology interfaces, syntax-pragmatics interfaces, and meaning-form connections. This is especially the case for L2 learners whose native languages do not have an article system or have a different article system. Thirdly, the L2 acquisition of English articles can serve as a mirror to reflect the general processes of L2 acquisition. As a consequence, the following important questions can be directly or indirectly addressed:

- Is the interlanguage (IL) grammar constrained by Universal Grammar (UG) or not?
- What is the role of L1 transfer?
- Are there systematic and staged developments in IL?
- What might be the determining factors if there is variability in IL?
- What is the metalinguistic knowledge that L2 learners employ in learning a new language?
- What are the sources of difficulties in second language acquisition (SLA)?
- What are the sources of fossilization in SLA?
- How do frequency effects interact with other aspects of SLA processes?
- Does language depend on thought or is the reversal true?

A fourth factor concerns pedagogy and the role of instruction in SLA. As noted by Whitman (1974), "the article in English has always been considered one of the most formidable problems to overcome in teaching English grammar to foreigners" (p. 253). A colleague of mine, who has taught courses in English Grammar at the college level for almost 30 years, has concurred with Whitman's observation by telling me that "when and how to use English articles is indeed the most difficult question to answer in my grammar class during my entire academic career" (personal communication with Edward Heckler, February 18, 2009). Teachers are often at a loss when facing L2 learners' requests for simple and straightforward rules for English articles, and when facing L2 learners' random use of English articles. For many English teachers, "effectively teaching the article system to their students often remains an illusive goal" (Butler, 2002, p. 452). Hence, there is a pressing need to exploit and develop an effective and efficient pedagogy that can facilitate L2 learners' acquisition of English articles.

The accepted position of treating English articles as the head of Determiner Phrases (DPs) in the generative perspective and tradition has also contributed to inspire further studies on the acquisition and uses of English articles. In traditional grammar, content words play a much more important role than function words. Content words can project to phrases so that we have Noun Phrases (NPs), Verb Phrases (VPs), Adjective Phrases (APs), and Adverb Phrases (AdvPs). In contrast, function words, as their name suggests, simply perform grammatical functions in forming sentences, and in creating structural relationships into which the content words may fit. They cannot project to phrases and assume the role as the head of phrases. New perspectives in generative linguistics propose that functional categories such as complementizers and auxiliaries can also project to the phrasal level. Therefore, complementizers, serving as the syntactic head of a full clause, project to Complementizer Phrase (CP), and auxiliaries project to Inflection Phrase (IP), which constitutes the extended projection of the lexical head, the verb.

Following this line of reasoning, Abney (1987) observed that there are many similarities between nominal domains and clausal domains.

In order to capture the parallel, he extended the arguments made by a number of scholars (see Szabolcsi, 1983/84) and proposed that DP is the maximal category projected by the class of determiners. In DP, the determiner (D) is a functional head that selects a NP as its complement just as an auxiliary, instead of a verb, is the head of an IP. In other words, while an inflection (INFL) selects the VP, a D selects the NP. DP is the functional superstructure of the NP just like IP, which is the functional superstructure of the VP. Abney's proposal is known as the DP hypothesis, which contributes to drawing a parallelism between the syntactic structure of noun phrases and that of the sentence. The DP structure can be tree-diagramed as the following:

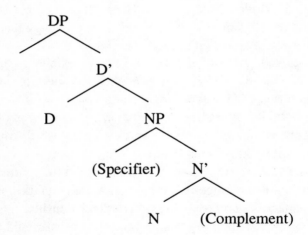

With this new position, articles, serving as the head of DP instead of the specifier of NP, have gained a new status in grammar. Whether or not articles and their features can be accessible to L2 learners has become a new focus in studies of second language acquisition. Thus, the study of the acquisition of articles, to a certain extent, has taken on greater importance than earlier studies.

SOURCES OF DIFFICULTIES

Research to date has yielded a variety of explanations for possible sources of L2 learner difficulties in the acquisition and uses of English articles. These sources of difficulties can be generally grouped under L1 influence, factors related to L2 learners and L2 learning processes, and L2 complexities.

L1 Influence

Following the summary by Avery and Radišić (2007), the effects of L1 influence on article acquisition can be reflected as syntactic deficit, phonological deficit, syntactic mismatch, or semantic mismatch.

Syntactic Deficit

If a language has no article system, this may result in a syntactic deficit in the acquisition of English, which has an article system. As Hawkins and Chan (1997) proposed in their Failed Functional Features hypothesis, "divergence from native-speaker representations is an effect of the inaccessibility of features of functional categories in second language acquisition" (p. 187).

According to this hypothesis, functional categories like articles that are not present in the L1 remain inaccessible to learners acquiring an L2. As a result, learners will either transfer L1 options to express semantic notions encoded in the L2 article system or develop an IL grammar for articles that is not compatible with either L1 or L2. In either case, "learners may, in fact, only adopt the surface morphophonological forms but have a syntactic representation that is incompatible with the L2" (Avery & Radišić, 2007, p. 2). Thus, Chinese L2 learners of English, whose native language lacks the category of DP, can be seen as having a syntactic deficit.

Phonological Deficit

Difficulties in the acquisition of English articles may result from a lack of similar prosodic structures in the L1. As Goad and White (2004) predicted in their Prosodic Transfer hypothesis,

> if the L1 does not permit certain kinds of prosodic representations as required by the L2, then second language speakers will have

difficulties in representing such morphology in the outputs of the phonological component of the interlanguage grammar. (p. 122)

Goad and White argued that the prosodic structure required for the representation of English articles is a free clitic, which is a bound element joined directly to the level of the phonological phrase. Not all languages have the prosodic structure for free clitics. Instead, they may have the prosodic structures for affixal clitics (adjuncts to phonological words) and/or internal clitics (incorporated into phonological words). As a consequence, those learners whose first language lacks the structure for free clitics will encounter problems in the acquisition of English articles. In other words, they will have difficulty in prosodically representing articles in spoken production since there are no prosodic structures available in their L1 to accommodate articles in the L2.

Syntactic Mismatch

A mismatch in syntactic structures may also be a source of difficulties. Language differences in topic and subject prominence have been argued to play a role in the acquisition of English articles. In linguistics, the topic (or theme) represents what is being talked about, and the comment (rheme) refers to what is being said about the topic (see Li & Thompson, 1981). Topic or theme generally precedes comment or rheme. In more topic-prominent languages such as Chinese and Korean, the topic-comment or theme-rheme organization of a sentence is predominant over the subject-object organization of a sentence. In other words, once a noun is introduced into the discourse in the post-verbal, comment/rheme position, its existence is established when it moves to the pre-verbal, topic/theme position (see Jung, 2004). Thus, topic position is in a way already semantically marked as definite. As reported in Robertson (2000), L2 learners tend to omit more articles in topic positions if their L1 is a topic-prominent language.

Semantic Mismatch

If the L1 has an article system in place, there is a strong possibility of some kind of mismatch in how the two article systems divide the labor in terms of notions such as definiteness, specificity, and partitivity. For instance, as Katz and Blyth (2007) pointed out, the French article system is markedly different from its English counterpart in terms of forms and functions. In French, the form of the article can vary according to the grammatical gender, number, or case of its noun. Hence, it is understandable that French learners of English have to remap their L1 article system with the English article system.

Semantic mismatch can also be reflected in the difference between the L1 and the L2 with respect to how the notion of definiteness and indefiniteness is encoded in the L1 and the L2. As summarized by C. Lyons (1999), based on his cross-linguistic studies, definiteness exists in some form of either simple definite or complex definite in all languages. English has a free form article *the* to encode definiteness, which is a straightforward way of expressing definiteness. Quite differently, Arabic has a prefixal article and Icelandic has a suffixal article to function as the definiteness marker attached to the head noun. There are also instances of mixed free form and affixal article systems. Apart from these direct ways of encoding definiteness, there are other languages that have less direct ways to do so. For instance, some languages have a prepositional or postpositional object marker which only occurs with "definite" object noun phrases, while other languages use word order, stress or context to signal definiteness. Thus, L2 learners have to adjust their L1 semantics to match the L2.

Factors Related to L2 Learners and Learning Processes

It can be argued that SLA is fundamentally different from first language acquisition (FLA) especially in terms of the ultimate attainment, the access to UG, the cognitive maturity, the input, as well as the impact of age and affective factors. Some of the major differences between SLA and FLA can be summarized in the following table, adapted from Ellis (1994, p. 107).

It has been reported that functional categories like articles are subject to a critical period after which it is very difficult for articles to be acquired by L2 learners. In other words, the age factor may account for at least one of the difficulties in the acquisition of English articles, and

TABLE 1. Differences between SLA and FLA.

	FLA	SLA
Overall success	Success is guaranteed. Learning a first language is about as natural to humans as walking upright.	Complete success is very rare; only about 5% of L2 learners have absolute success.
Variation	There is little variation among L1 learners with regard to overall success or the path they follow.	L2 learners vary in both their degree of success and the path they follow.
Goals	The goal is target language competence.	L2 learners may be content with less than target language competence.
Fossilization	Fossilization is unknown in child language development.	The L2 fossilizes at some point short of the knowledge of the native speakers.
Intuitions	Children develop clear intuitions regarding what is a correct and an incorrect sentence.	L2 learners are often unable to form clear grammaticality judgments.
Instruction	Children do not need formal lessons to learn their L1, so FLA is more in the sense of acquisition in natural settings.	L2 learners generally need formal instruction to learn the target language, so SLA is more in the sense of learning in formal settings.
Negative evidence	Children's errors are not typically corrected; correction is not necessary for acquisition.	Correction is generally viewed as helpful and, by some, as necessary.
Affective factors	Success is not influenced by personality, motivation, attitudes, and so forth.	Affective factors play a major role in determining proficiency.
Previous knowledge	There is none.	There is already an established L1.

Source. Ellis (1994, p. 107).

account for L2 learners' fossilization in the acquisition process of English articles. As proposed by Hawkins and Chan (1997),

> the virtual, unspecified features associated with the initial state of functional categories like C, Agr, D, and which determine parametric differences between languages, are available in that form

only for a limited period in early life. Exposure to samples of language during that critical period fixes the values of the features and associates them with particular morphophonological realizations. Beyond the critical period the virtual, unspecified features disappear, leaving only those features encoded in the lexical entries for particular lexical items. (p. 216)

Though there is no consensus, it has been widely reported that the L2 proficiency level affects L2 learners' use of English articles (see, among others, Liu & Gleason, 2002; Robertson, 2000). A higher accuracy rate in using English articles has been observed when the L2 learners' proficiency level increases.

Other factors that are unknown or have no roles in FLA, and that have an impact on L2 learners' use and acquisition of English articles, include the complexity of the task (Pongpairoj, 2007), instructional help (Nassaji & Swain, 2000), variability (Robertson, 2000), fossilization (White, 2003), metalinguistic knowledge (Butler, 2002), age (Zdorenko & Paradis, 2008), and native language effects (Gass & Mackey, 2002).

L2 Complexities

The English article system, though frequently used, is complex, obscure, and non-salient. It is ambiguous in the sense that it is based on a complex set of abstract distinctions that are arbitrarily mapped onto the surface forms of indefinite, definite and zero articles. Master (2002) identified the following three sources of difficulties in the acquisition and use of the English article system in terms of L2 complexities:

(1) the articles, which include the words *a*, *an*, *the*, and ∅, the invisible zero/null article, are among the most frequently occurring function words in the language…, making continuous conscious rule application difficult over an extended stretch of discourse; (2) function words are normally unstressed and consequently very difficult if not impossible for a NNS to discern, thus affecting the availability of input in the spoken mode; and (3) the article system stacks multiple functions onto a single morpheme, a considerable burden for the learner, who generally looks for a

one-form-one-function correspondence in navigating the laby-
rinth of any human language until the advanced stages of acquisition. (p. 332)

L2 complexities can also be reflected in the learning and use of so
many rules for English articles. It is, in fact, one of the most difficult
challenges and one of the most frustrating experiences for L2 learners. The difficult challenge lies in the fact that L2 learners have to learn
many rules about English articles. As demonstrated in *A Practical English Grammar* (Zhang, 1978), one of the most popular English grammar
books used in China, a whole chapter is devoted to articles. The chapter
consists of 26 sections (5 sections more than those in the chapter on
nouns). From those 26 sections, about 40 or more different rules can be
derived. Quirk, Greenbaum, Leech, and Svartvik (1985) went even further. In their influential book *A Comprehensive Grammar of the English
Language*, 47 sections in 33 pages were spent on article usage. L2 learners also feel extremely frustrated because all rules for English articles
have exceptions. Numerous rules go hand in hand with as many exceptions. Some of the rules that govern article usage are so subtle, complex,
and idiosyncratic that only years of experience with the language might
enable L2 learners to understand and apply those rules. In many cases,
even years of experience with the language and advanced proficiency
in the language cannot help them to understand and explain simple
cases such as why *the* is used in *The Ohio State University*, but not used
in *Ohio University* and *Michigan State University*. In other words, there
are no simple and golden rules for English articles.

In addition, there are still theoretic disputes on the property of definiteness. As summarized by Guella, Déprez, and Sleeman (2008), definiteness can be based on uniqueness/maximality, anaphoric properties,
familiarity, or the situational use of the definite DPs (saliency), or based
on the presupposition of the speaker and the hearer regarding the existence of a unique individual in the context denoted by the NP. Epstein
(2002) argued that no previous analysis is empirically satisfactory since
the focus is only on the referential function of the article and no analysis

can account for all uses of the definite article in English. Epstein cited the following quotes as a further basis for his argument:

a) "It is not in fact possible to specify a single function of the definite article which will apply in all areas of English grammar" (Du Bois, 1980, p. 208).

b) "Neither the uniqueness nor the familiarity approach have yet succeeded in providing a satisfactory account of all uses of definite descriptions" (Poesio & Vieira, 1998, p. 189).

c) "No one has shown conclusively that a version or mutation of either identifiability or inclusiveness accounts adequately for all definite uses" (C. Lyons, 1999, p. 274).

ACQUISITION SEQUENCES AND USAGE PATTERNS

In regards to the acquisition sequences and usage patterns of English articles by L2 learners, it has been consistently observed that L2 learners acquire the features of articles incrementally or learn to use certain functions of a particular article first. For the definite article *the*, the incremental acquisition can be demonstrated in the following natural order in terms of the accuracy rate (see, among others, Leung, 2001; Liu & Gleason, 2002; Pongpairoj, 2007; White, 2003),

use with singular nouns → use with plural and mass nouns

use with non-generic nouns → use with generic nouns

use in 'Art + N' context → use in 'Art + Adj + N' context

the situational use → the textual use → the structural use → the cultural use

In the case of the indefinite article, it has been reported that the deletion rate is higher when the article precedes a mass noun than when it precedes a count noun. It has also been noted that the highest accuracy in indefinite contexts is for existential sentences (see, among others, Robertson, 2000).

Though debatable and controversial (see the next section), there are a number of findings to indicate that L2 learners of English are significantly more accurate in using the definite article than in using the indefinite article, and a natural acquisition order of the definite article *the* before the indefinite article *a(n)* can be observed regardless of L1 background (see, among others, Lardiere, 2004; Zdorenko & Paradis, 2008). To account for this acquisition sequence, Lardiere (2004) suggested that the definite article is categorized as featurally less complex than the indefinite article since the definite article does not need to take number and the count/mass distinction into account. In other words, L2 learners of English have to identify at least one additional semantic feature in order to use the indefinite article appropriately.

REFLECTION

A review of the current research literature reveals many contradictory findings and results. For instance, some findings (Ionin et al., 2008) supported the Fluctuation hypothesis, which predicts that L2 learners fluctuate between the two settings of the Article Choice Parameter until the input leads them to set this parameter to the appropriate value, while other findings (Hawkins et al., 2006; Snape, Leung, & Ting, 2006) argued against the Fluctuation hypothesis.

To give another instance of contradictory findings, Avery and Radišić (2007) concluded that the acquisition of the indefinite article lags behind the definite article. In contrast, Ekiert (2007) drew the conclusion from her studies that the learner appears to be more successful with the marking of indefiniteness than definiteness.

Contradictory findings might be the result of the following. First, a variety of distinct theoretical perspectives is used—generative school, functional grammar, and cognitive theories, to name just a few. Even within the same theoretical framework, different positions might be taken. For instance, different positions in the generative school can be noticed regarding the L2 initial state, subsequent grammars during development, as well as the final state. The various approaches to the operation of UG and the role of the L1 are summarized by White (2000, p. 148) in the following table:

TABLE 2. Summary of claims on UG availability and transfer.

	Full Transfer/ Partial Access	No Transfer/ Full Access	Full Transfer/ Full Access	Partial Transfer/ Full Access	Partial Transfer/ Partial Access
Initial state	L1	UG	L1	UG	Parts of UG and L1
Grammar development	UG principles (via L1)	UG principles	UG principles	UG principles	(Some) UG principles
	L1 parameter settings (+ local adjustments)	L2 parameter settings	Parameter resetting from L1 → L2/Ln	Parameter resetting from L1 → L2	Parameters associated with functional features remain unspecified
	Possibility of "wild" grammars	No wild grammars	No wild grammars	No wild grammars	Locally wild grammars
Final state	L1 (+ local adjustments) L2 not attainable	L2	Ln (L2 possible but not inevitable)	L2 (Ln)	L2 not attainable

Source. White (2000, p. 148).

Second, the very concept of "article-less language" may not mean the same thing for languages that have no article system. *Less* may mean *none, without, completely different,* or *in the process of article emergence.* In other words, article-less languages vary in possible equivalent forms, in possible emergence of new article forms, and in ways to encode semantic notions like definiteness, specificity, and partitivity. A noticeable case in point is Chinese, a language often lumped together with other article-less languages such as Czech, Finnish, Hindi, Indonesian,

Japanese, Korean, Polish, Russian, and Serbian. Findings from a recent study (Chen, 2004) have, however, indicated that the Chinese numeral *yi* (one) is in the process of being grammaticalized as an equivalent to the English indefinite article *a* since it can serve all the major functions that *a* can play. It can be argued that *yi* (one) has "reached the endpoint of grammaticalization into an indefinite article" (p. 1177).

Third, different methodological approaches are employed. Some studies are longitudinal, while others are pseudo-longitudinal or cross-sectional. Mingled with different methodological approaches are different tasks used to elicit data: fill-in-the-blank task, forced-choice elicitation task, multiple-choice cloze task, multiple-choice insertion task, referential communication task, translation task, acceptability judgment task, grammaticality judgment task, story-telling task, and informal interview, to name a few. The data collected can also vary in emphasis on spontaneous or non-spontaneous production, individual, group, or corpus data, and written or spoken data.

It appears that the lack of conclusive answers in many areas of SLA research is nothing new. The myriad inconclusive or contradictory findings clearly show nothing but that second language acquisition is a very complicated process. Amidst the inconclusive or contradictory findings, the following generalizations, however, could be drawn regarding the acquisition and use of English articles by L2 learners.

Staged Development

There are natural orders for acquiring the English article system and for acquiring each individual type of article. A series of discrete stages L2 learners go through can be identified and described.

Incremental Process

The acquisition of semantic features of a particular article takes place incrementally rather than all at once. In other words, L2 learners acquire certain features or functions of a particular article first before acquiring its other features or functions.

Observable Variability

L2 learners vary in their level of success and paths in acquiring English articles. They also vary in their strategies and linguistic resources used to acquire English articles. Furthermore, their variable use is heavily influenced by context of the situation and a variety of other factors.

Effects of L1 Transfer

L1 plays an important role in the acquisition of articles. Similarities between the L1 and the L2 in the article system may facilitate L2 acquisition of English articles while differences between the two may cause difficulties in the article acquisition. Research findings have constantly indicated that L2 learners of English whose native language has an article system perform much better than those whose native language does not have an article system.

Age Factor

Compared with adult L2 learners, child L2 learners do much better in acquiring English articles, regardless of their L1 background.

Multiple Sources of Difficulties

The L2 acquisition of English articles is a complex and difficult process. The complexity and difficulty lie in various sources rather than in just one source.

In sum, significant progress has been made in the research of the acquisition and use of English articles by L2 learners. It still remains a challenge, however, to tackle and solve the puzzles as to why English articles are among the first words to be learned, but are among the last words to be acquired; and why English articles are among the most frequently used words and among the simplest words in spelling, but are among the most formidable grammatical issues to teach.

REFERENCES

Abney, S. (1987). *The English noun phrase in its sentential aspect.* Unpublished doctoral dissertation, Massachusetts Institute of Technology, Cambridge, MA.

Avery, P., & Radišić, M. (2007). Accounting for variability in the acquisition of English articles. In A. Belikova, L. Meroni, & M. Umeda (Eds.), *Proceedings of the 2nd Conference on Generative Approaches to Language Acquisition North America (GALANA)* (pp. 1–11). Somerville, MA: Cascadilla Proceedings Project.

Butler, Y. G. (2002). Second language learners' theories on the use of the English articles: An analysis of the metalinguistic knowledge used by Japanese students in acquiring the English article system. *Studies in Second Language Acquisition, 24*(3), 451–480.

Chen, P. (2004). Identifiability and definiteness in Chinese. *Linguistics, 42*(6), 1129–1184.

Du Bois, J. W. (1980). Beyond definiteness: The trace of identity in discourse. In W. L. Chafe (Ed.), *The pear stories: Cognitive, cultural, and linguistic aspects of narrative production* (pp. 203–274). Norwood, NJ: Ablex.

Ekiert, M. (2004). Acquisition of the English article system by speakers of Polish in ESL and EFL settings. *Teachers College, Columbia University Working Papers in TESOL & Applied Linguistics, 4*(1): Retrieved October 6, 2008, from http://journals.tc-library.org/index.php/tesol/article/view/42/49.

Ekiert, M. (2007). The acquisition of grammatical marking of indefiniteness with the indefinite article *a* in L2 English. *Teachers College, Columbia University Working papers in TESOL & Applied Linguistics, 7*(1): Retrieved October 6, 2008, from http://journals.tc-library.org/index.php/tesol/article/view/265/224.

Ellis, R. (1994). *The study of second language acquisition*. Oxford: Oxford University Press.

Epstein, R. (2002). The definite article, accessibility, and the construction of discourse referents. *Cognitive Linguistics, 12*(4), 333–378.

Gass, S. M., & Mackey, A. (2002). Frequency effects and second language acquisition. *Studies in Second Language Acquisition, 24*(2), 249–260.

Geranpayeh, A. (2000). The acquisition of the English article system by Persian speakers. *Edinburgh Working Papers in Applied Linguistics, 10*, 37–51.

Goad, H., & White, L. (2004). Ultimate attainment of L2 inflection: Effects of L1 prosodic structure. In S. Foster-Cohen, M. S. Smith, A. Sorace, & M. Ota (Eds.), *EUROSLA Yearbook* (Vol. 4) (pp. 119–145). Amsterdam: John Benjamins Publishing Company.

Guella, H., Déprez, V., & Sleeman, P. (2008). Article choice parameters in L2. In R. Slabakova, J. Rothman, P. Kempchinsky, & E. Gavruseva (Eds.), *Proceedings of the 9th Generative Approaches to Second Language Acquisition Conference (GASLA 2007)* (pp. 57–69). Somerville, MA: Cascadilla Proceedings Project.

Hawkins, R., & Chan, C. Y.-H. (1997). The partial availability of Universal Grammar in second language acquisition: The 'failed functional features hypothesis'. *Second Language Research, 13*(3), 187–226.

Hawkins, R., Al-Eid, S., Almahhboob, I., Athanasopoulos, P., Chaengchenkit, R., Hu, J., Rezai, M., Jaensch, C., Jeon, Y., Jiang, A., Leung, Y.-K. I., Matsunaga, K., Ortega, M., Sarko, G., Snape, N., & Velasco-Zárate, K. (2006). Accounting for English article interpretation by L2 speakers. In S. H. Foster-Cohen, M. Medved Krajnovic, & J. Mihaljevi´c Djigunovi´c (Eds.), *EUROSLA Yearbook* (Vol. 6) (pp. 7–25). Amsterdam: John Benjamins Publishing Company.

Ionin, T., Ko, H., & Wexler, K. (2008). The role of semantic features in the acquisition of English articles by Russian and Korean speakers.

In J. M. Liceras, H. Zobl, & H. Goodluck (Eds.), *The role of formal features in second language acquisition* (pp. 226–268). New York: Lawrence Erlbaum Associates.

Jung, E. H. (2004). Topic and subject prominence in interlanguage development. *Language Learning, 54*(4), 713–738.

Kaku, K. (2006). Second language learners' use of English articles: A case study of native speakers of Japanese. *Cahiers Linguistiques d'Ottawa/ Ottawa Papers in Linguistics, 34*, 63–74.

Katz, S. L., & Blyth, C. S. (2007). *Teaching French grammar in context: Theory and practice*. New Haven, CT: Yale University Press.

Jarvis, S. (2002). Topic continuity in L2 English article use. *Studies in Second Language Acquisition, 24*(3), 387–418.

Lardiere, D. (2004). Knowledge of definiteness despite variable article omission in second language acquisition. In A. Brugos, L. Micciulla, & C. E. Smith (Eds.), *Proceedings of the 28th Annual Boston University Conference on Language Development* (pp. 328–339). Somerville, MA: Cascadilla Press.

Leung, Y.-K. I. (2001). The initial state of L3A: Full transfer and failed features? In X. Bonch-Bruevich, W. Crawford, J. Hellerman, C. Higgins, & H. Nguyen (Eds.), *The Past, Present, and Future of Second Language Research: Selected Proceedings of the 2000 Second Language Research Forum* (pp. 55–75). Somerville, MA: Cascadilla Press.

Li, C., & Thompson, S. (1981). *Mandarin Chinese: A functional reference grammar*. Berkeley: University of California Press.

Liu, D.-L., & Gleason, J. L. (2002). Acquisition of the article *the* by nonnative speakers of English: An analysis of four nongeneric uses. *Studies in Second Language Acquisition, 24*(1), 1–26.

Lu, C. F.-C. (2001). The acquisition of English articles by Chinese learners. *Second Language Studies, 20*, 43–78.

Lyons, C. (1999). *Definiteness*. Cambridge: Cambridge University Press.

Master, P. (2002). Information structure and English article pedagogy. *System, 30*, 331–348.

Master, P. (2003). Acquisition of the zero and null articles in English. *Issues in Applied Linguistics, 14*(1), 3–20.

Nassaji, H., & Swain, M. (2000). A Vygotskian perspective on corrective feedback in L2: The effect of random versus negotiated help on the learning of English articles. *Language Awareness, 9*(1), 34–51.

Poesio, M., & Vieira, R. (1998). A corpus-based investigation of definite description use. *Computational Linguistics, 24*, 183–216.

Pongpairoj, N. (2007). Asymmetric patterns of English article omissions in L2A. In C. Gabrielatos, R. Slessor, & J. W. Unger (Eds.), *Papers from the Lancaster University Postgraduate Conference in Linguistics & Language Teaching (LAEL PG 2006)* (Vol. 1) (pp. 103–119). Lancaster, England: Department of Linguistics and English Language, Lancaster University.

Quirk, R., Greenbaum, S., Leech, G., & Svartvik, J. (1985). *A comprehensive grammar of the English language*. London: Longman Group Ltd.

Robertson, D. (2000). Variability in the use of the English article system by Chinese learners of English. *Second Language Research, 16*(2), 135–172.

Sand, A. (2004). Shared morpho-syntactic features in contact varieties of English: Article use. *World Englishes, 23*(2), 281–298.

Sarko, G. (2008). Morphophonological or syntactic transfer in the acquisition of English articles by L1 Speakers of Syrian Arabic? In R. Slabakova, J. Rothman, P. Kempchinsky, & E. Gavruseva (Eds.), *Proceedings of the 9th Generative Approaches to Second Language Acquisition Conference (GASLA 2007)* (pp. 206–217). Somerville, MA: Cascadilla Proceedings Project.

Snape, N., Leung, Y.-K. I., & Ting, H.-C. (2006). Comparing Chinese, Japanese, and Spanish Speakers in L2 English article acquisition: Evidence against the Fluctuation hypothesis? In M. G. O'Brien, C. Shea, & J. Archibald (Eds.), *Proceedings of the 8th Generative Approaches to Second Language Acquisition Conference (GASLA 2006)* (pp. 132–139). Somerville, MA: Cascadilla Proceedings Project.

Szabolcsi, A. (1983/84). The possessor that ran away from home. *The Linguistic Review, 3*, 89–102.

Thu, H. N. (2005). *Vietnamese learners mastering English articles*. Unpublished doctoral dissertation, University of Groningen, Groningen, the Netherlands.

Trenkic, D. (2002). Form-meaning connections in the acquisition of English articles. In S. H. Foster-Cohen, T. Ruthenberg, & M. L. Poschen (Eds.), *EUROSLA Yearbook* (Vol. 2) (pp. 115–133). Amsterdam: John Benjamins Publishing Company.

White, L. (2000). Second language acquisition: From initial to final state. In J. Archibald (Ed.), *Second language acquisition and linguistic theory* (pp. 130–155). Malden, MA: Blackwell Publishers Inc.

White, L. (2003). Fossilization in steady state L2 grammars: Persistent problems with inflectional morphology. *Bilingualism: Language and Cognition, 6*, 129–141.

White, L. (2008). Different? Yes. Fundamentally? No. Definiteness effects in the L2 English of Mandarin speakers. In R. Slabakova, J. Rothman, P. Kempchinsky, & E. Gavruseva (Eds.), *Proceedings of the 9th Generative Approaches to Second Language Acquisition Conference (GASLA 2007)* (pp. 251–261). Somerville, MA: Cascadilla Proceedings Project.

Whitman, R. (1974). Teaching the article in English. *TESOL Quarterly, 8*, 253–262.

Wolf, Y., & Walters, J. (2001). Definite articles in the context of literary and scientific writings. *Journal of Pragmatics, 33*, 965–967.

Zdorenko, T., & Paradis, J. (2008). The acquisition of articles in child second language English: fluctuation, transfer, or both? *Second Language Research, 24*(2), 227–250.

Zhang, D.-Z. (1978). *A practical English grammar*. Beijing: The Commercial Press.

Acknowledgments

I am deeply indebted to Dr. Keiko Samimy of the Ohio State University for her patient guidance and elucidatory advice while I conducted the research on which this book is based. Sincere and heartfelt gratitude also goes to Dr. Alan Hirvela, who, both as a knowledgeable professor and as an unforgettable friend, has provided me with an unfailing source of help, encouragement, and guidance for my academic studies as well as for my personal life. Similar gratitude should be extended to Dr. Galal Walker, who has provided me not only with moral support and invaluable encouragement, but also with scholarship to complete my research.

I am very grateful to Dr. Donald Winford and Dr. Charles Hancock for their valuable and insightful comments on the early draft; to Dr. Elizabeth Bernhardt, Dr. Diane Birckbichler, Dr. Diane Belcher, Dr. Michael Riley, and Dr. Laurel Richardson, for their help in shaping my view of second language acquisition; to Weiping Yang and Zhiying Lu for their help in collecting the data; and to Kelly Dickhof, a neighbor and a friend, for her devotion during interviews of the informant and for proofreading every transcript.

I owe a large debt of thanks to Dr. Edward Heckler and Dr. Glenn A. Martínez, my colleagues at the University of Texas-Pan American, for their remarkable generosity in reading and commenting on the early draft of this book. Dr. Paul Richardson has been a very attentive, helpful, and gracious editor from Cambria Press, and for his invaluable advice and guidance, I will always be thankful. I want to give Toni Tan of Cambria Press a special thanks for her belief in my work and her help in leading this work to publication. I would also like to acknowledge here my gratitude to the editors of Cambria Press and the anonymous reviewers for all the constructive comments and suggestions. However, I must add that I alone should be held to account for any faults in this book.

Last but not the least, my thanks go to my parents, Saili Zeng and Yaowen Lang, and my parents-in-law, Suyun Tang and Zuohua Yang, for their unwavering support. Besides myself, the persons who have done most to see this project through have been my wife, Weiwei Yang, and my son, Langtian Lang. I want to express my deepest gratitude for their love, concern, support, and encouragement all these years that provided me with the stability and desire to complete this project, and it is to them that I dedicate this book.

Grammar

and the

Chinese
ESL Learner

CHAPTER 1

THE PROBLEM

INTRODUCTION

Sequencing and acquisition are, to a certain extent, intertwined with each other and cannot be separated since sequencing is an important element inherent in the acquisition process of a second language. It shows that in the process of acquiring a second language (L2), learners always progress step-by-step along identifiable stages in mastering specific grammatical structures or linguistic elements (R. Ellis, 1994). For instance, L2 learners have been consistently observed to master the grammatical form of *Verb + ing* before the grammatical form of *Verb + ed*. Another example is that the acquisition sequence of interrogatives for English as a Second Language (ESL) learners, as summarized by Larsen-Freeman and Long (1991), can be classified into the following four stages: Stage 1. Rising intonation, as in *He work today?*; Stage 2. Uninverted WH (+/– aux.), as in *What he (is) saying?*; Stage 3. Overinversion, as in *Do you know where is it?*; and Stage 4. Differentiation, as in *Does she like where she lives?*

It is generally the case that learners cannot reach a later stage if they have not passed through the previous stage(s) (R. Ellis, 1989; Pavesi, 1986). As a result, successful learning of a second language can only be accomplished by following the natural developmental sequences rather than violating their orders. This characteristic of second language acquisition (SLA) is best captured in Pienemann's (1984) Teachability hypothesis, which expounded that "an L2 structure can be learnt from instruction only if the learner's interlanguage (IL) is close to the point when this structure is acquired in the natural setting" (p. 201). In other words, L2 learners have to be prepared and ready for the new rule, and ready in the sense that they are at a stage where all the required preceding rules have already been learned or acquired.

The investigation of acquisition sequences in the learner's language has been motivated by the desire to describe the learner language in its own right, as a system of rules that learners constructed and repeatedly revised. Since the 1970s, studies of SLA have in part focused on the examination of the learner's linguistic output as an independent natural language called IL (Corder, 1978; Selinker, 1972). As opposed to Contrastive Analysis of the 1950s and 1960s and Error Analysis of the 1970s, IL is no longer viewed as a collection of errors or a dependent linguistic system derived from the learner's native or target language, but rather as an independent linguistic system in its own right. With the identification of acquisition sequences, one of the most important claims to have emerged in the field of SLA is that L2 acquisition proceeds in a regular and systematic fashion. In other words, the learner's language exhibits common accuracy orders and developmental sequences (Larsen-Freeman & Long, 1991).

Although in the past three decades a number of acquisition sequences have been identified and a number of influential theories or hypotheses in SLA such as Krashen's (1982) Natural Order hypothesis and the Multidimensional model by Meisel, Clahsen, and Pienemann (1981) have been proposed based on the discovery of those acquisition sequences, studies of acquisition sequences are limited to a few linguistic elements such as commonly used morphemes, negation, interrogation, and word order

(Cook, 1993; R. Ellis, 1994; Larsen-Freeman & Long, 1991). In a sense, research on the nature of systems in IL cannot claim to be successful until all the acquisition sequences in IL have been clearly isolated and identified. There is an urgent need, therefore, to further explore and discover the new acquisition sequences exhibited in phonological, morphological, syntactic, semantic and discourse structures. In addition, most of the acquisition sequences identified to date are quite language specific. As a corollary, they lack generalizability or universality. A related problem is that identified developmental sequences are often linked with learners of some specific linguistic backgrounds. Further research aimed at confirming those discovered acquisition sequences to learners with different language backgrounds needs to be carried out.

STATEMENT OF THE PROBLEM

It has been observed that "the article in English has always been considered one of the most formidable problems to overcome in teaching English grammar to foreigners, and its misuse is one of the most evident grammatical signs that a person is not a native speaker of English" (Whitman, 1974, p. 253). As claimed by Robberecht (1983), the English article system is "one of the notorious problem areas that foreign learners of the language are faced with" (p. 61). Quite ironically, the English article system is one of the most frequently used linguistic systems in the English language. In one of the widely used word frequency counts (Carroll, Davies, & Richman, 1971), the definite article ranks first while the indefinite article ranks fourth. In a word-frequency analysis based on the Birmingham corpus, a well-known language corpus which consists of 18 million words of text, *the* is found to be the most frequently used word while *a* is ranked as the fifth most frequently used word. It has been found in the corpus that *the* and *a* together with *of, and, to, in, that, it, I*, and *was* account for 23% of all English text (Taylor, 1990, p. 23). As further calculated by Berry (1991), the articles account for almost every 10th word in English if one adds the percentage frequency of the definite article and the indefinite article together. Berry's finding has been supported by Nation and Waring (1997), who concluded that *the* "occurs so frequently that about 7% of the words on a page of written English and the same proportion of the words in a conversation are repetitions of the word *the*" (pp. 8–9). The English article system is also a complex syntactic phenomenon both from the linguistic point of view (Chomsky, 1962; Christophersen, 1939; Hewson, 1972; Quirk, Greenbaum, Leech, & Svartvik, 1985) and from the viewpoint of language learning (Celce-Murcia & Larsen-Freeman, 1983; Grannis, 1972; Master, 1995). Because of its frequent use, its multifaceted nature and its potential to reflect the complexity as well as the systematicity involved in the process of SLA, the acquisition or the acquisition sequence of the English articles has been the focus or part of the focus of a number of important studies documented in the current research literature of SLA (see Bailey, Madden, & Krashen, 1974; Chaudron & Parker, 1990; Dulay & Burt, 1974; Gorokhova, 1990; Hakuta, 1976; Huebner, 1983; Lee, Cameron, Linton, & Hunt, 1994; Master, 1988; Parrish, 1987; Thomas, 1989a, 1989b; Sharon, 1993; among others). Research to date has reported the following: (1) the definite article *the* is acquired before *a(n)* (Thomas, 1989a); (2) the acquisition sequence of the article system is in the order of *the*, *a(n)* and zero article for learners whose native languages have an article system (Gorokhova, 1990; Master, 1988); and (3) the acquisition sequence of the article system is in the order of zero article, *the* and *a(n)* for learners whose native languages have no article system (Master, 1988).

Although there have appeared no findings that challenge these proposed sequences so far, several issues relating to these sequences still remain unsettled and call for further research. First, these sequences need to be tested against learners with different language backgrounds for their validity and universality. The baseline data of Chinese ESL learners, for example, is useful in this regard since there is no article system in Chinese. Moreover, in the current literature there is little longitudinal data available concerning Chinese-speaking children's acquisition of English articles. Second, the proposed sequences often use *a(n)* as a cover term to combine *a* and *an*. This clearly implies that *a* and *an* are acquired at the same time. However, without convincing explanations, more empirical data and further research are needed to justify such a claim. Third, research has shown that the acquisition of each individual type of article might pass through several stages as in the case of the definite article *the*. Lee et al. (1994), for instance, observed that the developmental sequence of the English definite article for L2 learners undergoes a referential place-holding phase and a referential substitution phase before it is fully acquired. However, the possible stages for the indefinite article *a(n)* and the zero article still remain unclear. Fourth, due to the complexity and the confusion involved in identifying the non-use of any article and the use of the zero article, research to date has not given enough attention to the acquisition process of the zero article. And lastly, noun phrases, the most important linguistic environment for articles, have not been given enough description, with the consequence that one can only see trees but not the forest. As an attempt to address those issues, the present study investigates one Chinese child's longitudinal acquisition of the English articles.

SIGNIFICANCE OF THE PROBLEM

> *Nothing can be certain until second language acquisition has been studied in tangible case histories or until empirical evidence has been obtained.*
>
> —Hatch (1978, p. 10)

The discovery of acquisition sequences has contributed to making SLA an independent field of inquiry, since demonstrating the existence of an L2 sequence of acquisition proves that there is a point to developing SLA research separately from the study of first language (L1) and L2, as well as from L1 acquisition (Cook, 1993). It helps to establish the fact that the ILs of L2 learners are valid and unique objects of study. Moreover, it provides a way of showing how learners acquire or learn a language. As R. Ellis (1994) pointed out, the discovery of "the existence of developmental sequences is one of the most important findings in second language research to date" (p. 21). With the identification and recognition of those developmental sequences, there is now a general acceptance in the field of the SLA research that the acquisition of an L2 grammar, like the acquisition of a native language grammar, occurs in sequences or stages and that "much of language acquisition is in fact sequence learning" (N. Ellis, 1996, p. 91).

However, those previously discovered general developmental sequences should be verified for learners in different situations and with differing language backgrounds. Moreover, the understanding of the process of SLA is still far from complete. There is a need to search for new developmental sequences and to refine the currently discovered ones in order to augment the knowledge base of SLA and to impact the current and future language pedagogy. An in-depth description and analysis of one Chinese ESL learner's acquisition process with regard to English articles, which is lacking in the current research literature on SLA, will contribute to this understanding and augmentation.

From a pedagogical viewpoint, the study of the acquisition sequence of the English articles is also worthwhile. There are two well-known paradoxes related to the articles in English. One paradox, as described by Kaluza (1981), is that

> while presenting one of the most difficult problems to foreigners (e.g. the Poles, Russians, and Japanese find it strange even to justify the existence of this part of speech, absent in their article-less languages), they are never taught to the native speakers of English because of their obviousness. (p. 7)

Hence, it is highly significant in terms of both theory and pedagogy to reveal the acquisition process of English articles in L1 as well as in L2, and to find a better way to obtain and explain this "obviousness."

Another paradox is related to the fact that while the articles *a* and *the* constitute two of the most frequently used words in the English language, they are, however, among the most difficult linguistic elements to learn for learners of English, especially for those learners whose native language lacks the article system. It has been reported that ESL learners who are Chinese-speaking adults as well as Chinese-speaking children exhibit difficulty in mastering the English articles both in classroom settings and in natural English-speaking environments (Aaronson &

Ferres, 1987; Johnson & Newport, 1989; Lee et al., 1994; Liao, 1985; Taylor & Taylor, 1990). It has also been reported that article usage is the number one teaching problem of ESL teachers (Celce-Murcia & Larsen-Freeman, 1983), and language instructors often wonder where learners' difficulties lie in learning articles and how to teach articles to those learners whose native languages have no article system (Greene, 1957). The discovery of the acquisition sequence incorporated with the possible strategies used by learners will provide insights for language instructors in search of effective ways of teaching English articles and will enhance their ability to assist learners in the acquisition of this difficult syntactic phenomenon.

IMPORTANT FINDINGS

Research to date has yielded the following important findings regarding the acquisition or acquisition sequence of English articles:

1. The developmental sequence of the English article system for second language learners whose native languages have the article system is in the order of *the*, *a(n)*, and zero article (Gorokhova, 1990; Master, 1988).
2. The developmental sequence of the English article system for ESL learners whose native languages lack the article system is in the order of the zero article, *the* and *a(n)* (Master, 1988).
3. L2 learners acquire the definite article *the* before *a(n)* (Chaudron & Parker, 1990; Thomas, 1989a).
4. The developmental sequence of the English definite article for Chinese ESL learners will undergo a referential place-holding phase and a referential substitution phase before it is fully acquired (Lee et al., 1994).
5. L1 learners acquire *a(n)* before *the* (Leopold, 1949).
6. The developmental sequence of the English article system for first language learners is in the order of *a(n)*, *the*, and the zero article (Zehler & Brewer, 1982).

7. The first stage of the acquisition of articles for L1 learners is characterized by the use of the indefinite and/or definite article(s) for specific referents, and zero article for both non-specific referents and naming (Cziko, 1986).

8. Beginning learners are speculated to have a three-way division between a definite article for presupposed-specific NP, an indefinite article for asserted-specific NP, and a zero form for non-specific NP (Bickerton, 1981, 1984).

9. Low proficiency L2 learners use articles significantly more often in front of specific NPs than high-proficiency L2 learners (Adamson, 1988).

10. L2 learners systematically use different articles to realize different functions at different levels of their language proficiency (Huebner, 1983).

11. L2 learners are most accurate in tasks that have been designed to require least attention to form (Tarone, 1985; Tarone & Parrish, 1988).

RESEARCH QUESTIONS

Based on those important findings regarding the acquisition of English articles and on the problems stated previously, the following research questions were designed to present the major areas of inquiry that are explored in this study. The central research question for this study was: Are the acquisition sequences of the English articles documented in L2 research literature applicable to a Chinese ESL learner?

The related research questions included the following:

1. What is the acquisition sequence of English articles as shown in the performance data of a Chinese ESL learner?
2. What are the acquisition stages for the definite article *the*?
3. What are the acquisition stages for the indefinite article *a*?
4. What are the acquisition stages for the indefinite article *an*?
5. What are the acquisition stages for the zero article?

6. What are the general features of noun phrases in the IL of a Chinese ESL learner?
7. What syntactic locations are associated with the correct use of different types of articles?
8. What types of article errors are committed by a Chinese ESL learner?
9. What syntactic locations are associated with the misuse of different types of articles?
10. What semantic functions of articles are used by a Chinese ESL learner?
11. What is the general relation between articles, article-related determiners, and other types of determiners?
12. What is the ratio of articles to noun phrases?
13. What is the specific relation between different types of articles and their respectively related determiners?
14. What strategies might a Chinese ESL learner use in the acquisition of the English article system?
15. How might L1 influence L2 in the acquisition of articles?

DEFINITION OF THE TERMS

Acquisition: A continuum ranging from the first appearance of a specific feature to the accurate use of that feature shown in the participant's performance data.

Acquisition sequence: The stages of acquisition through which a learner passes in acquiring specific grammatical structures. In this study, this term has the same meaning as "developmental pattern" (R. Ellis, 1994), which includes "developmental order" (R. Ellis) or "acquisition order" (Larsen-Freeman & Long, 1991) and "developmental sequence" (R. Ellis; Larsen-Freeman & Long).

Article system: A linguistic system consisting of the definite article *the*, the indefinite articles *a* and *an*, and the zero article ∅.

Definite article: A NP-initial determiner realized as *the* and used to mark a noun phrase as definite in meaning:

1. Who? *The man* in the brown coat?
2. How do you like *the tea*?

Indefinite article: A NP-initial determiner realized as *a* or *an* and used generally to mark a singular countable noun phrase as indefinite in meaning:

1. Chris approached me carrying *a dog*.
2. I guess I should buy *a new car*.

Variable: An abstract linguistic unit realized by two or more variants. For this study, four variables of the informant's article system were recognized and identified as THE, A, AN, and ∅, which are actualized by different variants in the forms of *the*, *a*, *an*, or ∅.

Variant: An actualized linguistic form of the variable.

Zero: Zero is an abstraction, symbolized by *0*, representing a gap where there could theoretically be, or in comparable grammatical contexts there is, some sound, syllable, or word. The concept of zero is used as a way of making rules more comprehensive and more "regular" than they would otherwise be.

Zero article: A NP-initial determiner realized as ∅ and used to mark an uncountable noun or a plural count noun phrase as indefinite in meaning:

1. *Fruit* flourishes in the valley.
2. They were covered with *dust*.

BASIC ASSUMPTIONS

Several assumptions guided this study. They were:

1. The informant is a typical Chinese learner of English as a second language.

2. The informant remains accessible for the duration of this study.
3. The informant's use of the English articles exhibits at least some sequence of development when one examines samples of his language utterances.

LIMITATIONS

Several limitations for the present study can be speculated as follows:

1. Generalizations from any empirical study to a larger population of learners should always be made with extreme caution, let alone a study with a single informant. As Fasold (1975) correctly pointed out, "impressive results from one analysis can be accepted only tentatively until they are replicated by another set of data" (pp. 37–38). With this in mind, it would be premature to accept the results obtained from the present study as something more than an initial examination of how English articles are acquired by Chinese ESL learners.
2. The data collected within a specified time frame for a longitudinal study can only reflect a part of the acquisition process.
3. The learning environment of the present informant was in the American context. This is different from those ESL learners who learn English in the Chinese context.
4. Audio-taping equipment may have inhibited the informant's use of English even after he was accustomed to its presence.

CHAPTER 2

BACKGROUND STUDY

INTRODUCTION

The acquisition of the English article system has been a subject of inquiry for linguists, psychologists, child language specialists, and second language acquisition (SLA) researchers; the system probably owes its wide appeal to the fact that the articles are important in a wide variety of discourse processes and in the interaction of linguistic and nonlinguistic knowledge, and to the fact that they are very frequently used while at the same time difficult to learn.

Articles belong to the closed class of function words in English. Taylor and Taylor (1990) classified articles as prototypical function words because they have all the characteristics of function words. They "play syntactic roles, belong to a closed class, are highly frequent, are monosyllabic, have little semantic content, are not used alone in complete utterances, are unstressed in normal use, and are redundant and predictable" (p. 89). However, there are some problems with this characterization of articles. For one thing, not all researchers agree that articles contain little semantic content. Berry (1991) argued that articles do convey additional information to the text since the omission of an article or the misuse of articles will, in many cases, produce disastrous consequences. For instance, the utterance *He's uneducated man* may well be understood as *an educated man*. For another instance, the meaning and implication in the utterance *I'm looking for a wife* is quite different from that of *I'm looking for the wife*. Pica (1983a) concluded, in her investigation of native speakers' use of articles in exchanges involving the requesting and the giving of directions, that "even though participants spoke in grammatically correct utterances, communication broke down when articles were used in reference to items in one participant's experience but not in another's" (p. 231). In other words, the correct and appropriate use of articles may be crucial for successful communication by showing what assumptions the speaker makes about the listener.

The misuse or inappropriate use of articles may cause a breakdown of communication. This shows from one perspective the importance and significance of studying the use of articles. From another angle, it can be noted that what has attracted researchers are the functions articles fulfill. One of the essential functions of the articles is to mark specific/non-specific reference both extralingusitically and by intralinguistic cross-reference. As suggested by Maratsos (1976),

> The indefinite and definite articles, *a* and *the*, do not seem like an auspicious place to study the semantic knowledge of young children. They are not semantic or syntactic building blocks of a language, like nouns, verbs, or adjectives, or even markers for tense. Yet they draw on and demand of the speaker mastery of referential systems of surprising complexity. They demand of the child, should he be born into a community that employs them, the formulation of correspondingly sophisticated semantic systems. (p. 1)

Researchers' interest in studying the acquisition or the use of articles is also closely related to the fact that articles are difficult to learn and teach even though they are very frequently used. It has been noted that article misuse often persists even for very highly proficient learners of English. As observed by Karmiloff-Smith (1979), "interestingly enough, foreigners with a near perfect command of, say, French or English, can often be detected as non-native speakers solely on the basis of their faulty article usage" (p. 23). Hence, finding an efficient way to teach and learn the English article system is of great pedagogical significance.

In short, what has motivated researchers in studying the acquisition and learning of English articles is the desire to reveal the interaction between linguistic and nonlinguistic knowledge, to reveal the process of acquiring the referential system, to reveal the process of acquiring a complicated linguistic system, and to reveal the strategies used to learn something frequently used yet difficult to master.

FIRST LANGUAGE ARTICLE ACQUISITION STUDIES

Studies of the first language (L1) acquisition of English have provided some evidence about when and how children start to acquire the article system along with other grammatical elements. Leopold (1939, 1949) made a careful record of the speech development in English and German of his daughter, Hildegard. He kept a diary in great detail and without interruption from Hildegard's eighth week until the end of her seventh year. It was observed that the indefinite article *a* occurred when Hildegard was 2:1 years old while the definite article *the* occurred when she was 2:4 years old. In other words, the indefinite article was found to occur earlier than the definite article in her speech even though they both were first used at the age of 2. Leopold (1949) also compared his results with those of a number of other studies regarding the time when articles began to occur in child speech. The times when articles began to be used were observed as 1:9 in Ament's 1912 survey of the history of child-research, as 1:11 in Gregoire's 1933 study of two children; as 2:2–3 in Preyer's 1882 careful and detailed observations of his own son during his first 1000 days; as 2:8 in Cohen's 1925 selected observations of three children; and as age 4 in Bergmann's 1919 selective record of his two children's language development over 10 years. As evident from those research findings, children begin to acquire the use of articles around the age of two to three years.

Brown (1973) was the first to study, systematically and longitudinally, the acquisition of English morphemes, among them the articles *a* and *the*. Brown observed that children in the early stages of first language acquisition appear to leave out grammatical morphemes rather than lexical morphemes, producing sentences such as *Here bed*, *Chair broken*, or *Not dada*. In other words, the content words (mainly nouns, verbs, and adjectives) are used much more frequently in the early stage speech while, in sharp contrast, the function words such as inflections, auxiliaries, prepositions, articles, and the copula "are used seldom or not at all" (p. 249). Brown characterized the early stage of children's speech as telegraphic for the very reason that "the sentences the child makes are like adult telegrams in that they are largely made up of nouns and verbs...and in that they generally do not use prepositions, conjunctions, articles, or auxiliary verbs" (p. 75). Grammatical morphemes or function words gradually appear in children's sentences over a period of time. Brown accordingly investigated the emergence of 14 grammatical morphemes in Eve, Adam, and Sarah, three selected American children between the ages of 18 to 44 months old. Two hours of their speech were recorded every month and were analyzed to see how many times per recording each morpheme occurred in "obligatory contexts," occasions in which a native speaker is obliged to use particular morphemes in the sentence. The child was regarded as having acquired a morpheme when it was supplied correctly in over 90% of obligatory contexts for three consecutive recordings; the separate points at which each morpheme was acquired were put in sequence to determine an order of acquisition. The orders for each of the three children were then averaged to identify a common sequence for their first language acquisition. Brown found that although each of the children developed at an individual rate, the acquisition of 14 grammatical morphemes in English for those three children was invariant in the following order: Present progressive *-ing* (as in *He is sitting down*) → Preposition *in* (as in *The mouse is in the box*) → Preposition *on* (as in *The book is on the table*) → Plural *-s* (as in *The dogs ran away*) → Past irregular *-ed* (as in *The boy went home*) → Possessive *-s* (as in *The girl's dog is big*) → Uncontractible copula *be* (as in *Are they boys or girls?*) → Articles *a/the* (as in *He has a book*) → Past regular *-ed* (as in *He jumped the stream*) → 3rd person regular *-s* (as in *She runs very fast*) → 3rd person irregular *-s* (as in *Does the dog bark?*) → Uncontractible auxiliary *be* (as in *Is he running?*) → Contractible copular *be* (as in *That's a spaniel*) → Contractible auxiliary *be* (as in *They're running very slowly*).

As shown in the aforementioned acquisition pattern, *a* and *the* are treated as one linguistic element under the cover term of *a/the*. According to Brown,

> One cannot always tell from the transcriptions whether a specific object not previously referred to in speech was in the focus of attention for speaker and listener and so whether the child should use *a* or *the* in mentioning it. One cannot always tell whether a part-whole context is implied: thus when Eve said *I'm a Mommy* was she simply placing herself in a set in which case she spoke correctly or was she assigning herself a role in a pretend-family in which case she ought to have said *the*. (p. 350)

For this reason, Brown "lumped together all contexts requiring either *a* or *the* and established a single acquisition point for articles."

Among the 14 grammatical morphemes, the acquisition of articles is in the eighth place. Brown concluded that both grammatical and semantic complexity were major determinants of the order in which the morphemes were acquired, but that the two were probably interrelated and neither could be isolated as the sole determinant of the acquisition order. Brown's study is significant for the language learning theory, which states that all children learn the various grammatical features of English in a similar order.

The same order of morphemes that Brown discovered was also obtained in de Villiers and de Villiers's (1973) cross-sectional study of 21 English-speaking children between the ages of 16 to 40 months. As stated by de Villiers and de Villiers, "the correlations obtained between the two studies approach the magnitude of those found among the three children in Brown's longitudinal study" (p. 272). de Villiers and de Villiers suggested that the order of acquisition might be best predicted by some combination of syntactic and semantic complexity, frequency of these forms in the parents' speech, and perceptibility in the speech.

Generally speaking, children seem to have fully mastered the use of the article system by the age of nine (Warden, 1976). Yet the period between two and three years appears to be the most crucial for article acquisition since this is the time period when children start acquiring articles, as shown in Leopold's studies. Moreover, children appear to have differentiated the dimension of specific versus non-specific reference with some precision around age of three. As Brown (1973) observed, "children somewhere between the ages of 32 and 41 months, roughly three years, do control the specific/non-specific distinction as coded by the articles" (p. 355). During this period, it has been observed that children often tend to overuse the definite article *the*. To find a way to explain this phenomenon, Maratsos (1976) conducted the first major experimental study of child acquisition of the articles and investigated the use and understanding of the articles by three- and four-year-old children through a story-telling task and a set of tasks consisting of various games. He found that both the three- and the four-year-old children could make the contrast between *the* as specific and *a* as non-specific in certain specified contextual features. When the object in question was specific to the child (speaker) but not to the listener, however, the three-year-old children substituted the definite article for the indefinite article. Maratsos concluded that the younger children could understand and apply the basic rules for article usage, but their usage was for the most part egocentric (Piaget, 1926) in that they did not consider the listener's lack of knowledge about something they already knew.

Walden (1976) came to the same conclusion drawn by Maratsos. He studied children of three to nine years old, as well as adults, and compared the usage of the indefinite article with that of the definite article. He found that both adults and children used the indefinite article correctly for naming objects. The children, however, unlike the adults, frequently used the definite article rather than the indefinite article for introducing a new referent, and their referring expressions were for the most part definite. Walden also attributed this incorrect use of the definite article to the children's egocentric viewpoint.

Zehler and Brewer (1982), however, argued against the egocentric point of view for its inadequacy in explanation. They suggested that the inappropriate use of *the* results from an overextension of a principle of shared knowledge found in adult article use, rather than the child's inability or failure to consider the listener's perspective. Zehler and Brewer obtained data from both adults and two age groups of children. The age range of the younger group of children was 2:4 to 2:11, and the age range of the older group of children was 3:0 to 3:5. Zehler and Brewer developed a new classification of English article usage by including a total of eight representative article usage categories based on three general usage types: introduction/anaphoric reference, context frame reference, and generic reference. According to Zehler and Brewer, in introduction/anaphoric usage, the articles are used either to introduce a new topic into the discourse or to make anaphoric reference back to a previously mentioned referent. In context frame usage, article selection is based on knowledge of typical objects and events without previous specific linguistic or nonlinguistic introduction of the referent. In generic usage, the articles are used to indicate reference to knowledge of conceptual classes and membership in these classes.

Zehler and Brewer counted and examined the definite article *the*, the indefinite article *a*, as well as the zero article in their data. They found an acquisition sequence of the article system in the following identifiable stages: Stage I was characterized by the initial use of *a* and null. Stage II featured the beginning of the use of *the*. Stage III was represented by the overuse of *the*. The overuse of *the*, however, was recognized only in the context-nonspecific category and after correct *the* usage had become stable as demonstrated in the accomplishment of 50% of accuracy. This led Zehler and Brewer to conclude that the overuse of *the* is not due to egocentrism, but rather due to the nature of the article system.

Karmiloff-Smith (1979), in a different approach, considered the articles as part of a broader system of determination. Karmiloff-Smith divided the functions of the articles into two major categories of descriptor and determinor. The determinor function, according to Karmiloff-Smith, can be further subdivided into five functions: deictic reference, exophoric reference, non-specific reference, anaphoric reference, and generic reference. The deictic reference means that the speaker uses an indexical definite referring expression together with paralinguistic markers such as gaze, head motion, and finger pointing (e.g. *Give me the pencil* in a context where several pencils are present, but an indexical gesture at the moment of uttering the determiner enables the addressee to identify the referent). The exophoric reference implies a distance between the speaker and his utterance. It involves the choice made by the speaker of a definite referring expression when a referent is the only member of its class in the current extra-linguistic setting, and the choice of an indefinite referring expression when the referent is one of several identical ones (e.g. *The boy pushed the red car* vs. *The boy pushed a car*). Exophoric reference thus means the speaker takes into account the relationship between objects in the extralinguistic setting, rather than the speaker's subjective involvement with an object upon which the speaker is focusing all of his or her attention. Non-specific reference is close to the generic function. However, whereas the generic use of the articles involves a conceptualized reference with no concrete instantiation as in the example *The tiger/a tiger is an animal*, non-specific reference implies any non-particular member of a class as in the case of *Give me a cigarette*. The generic use of articles indicates a collected whole, as shown in the example *The cigarette is a danger to health*. The anaphoric reference involves intralinguistic procedures. It implies substitution and reference back to a previously mentioned antecedent, as shown in the following: *I saw a pretty girl near your house. Do you know the girl?*

Based on the findings of 16 experiments, Karmiloff-Smith suggested that the acquisition of the indefinite article could be categorized into the following stages: schwa-form → nominative function → numeral function → non-specific function → generic function. As demonstrated in this sequence, the indefinite article is initially used as part of a procedure for naming, that is, in its appellative or nominative function. Karmiloff-Smith noticed that young children never made the error of using the definite article for this function.

Karmiloff-Smith also proposed that the acquisition of the definite article could be identified into the following stages: schwa-form → deictic function → exophoric function → anaphoric function → generic function. As revealed in this sequence, the definite article from the outset has quite a distinct function. It is used by the child deictically to draw attention to the referent that is the focus of attention.

The numeral function of the indefinite article and deictic function of the definite article appear to be related to the historical development of the indefinite and the definite articles. According to J. Lyons (1975, 1977), the definite article and the demonstratives are historically linked. The definite article in English is derived from the Old English neutral demonstrative pronoun *þæt*, which split to produce *the* and the weak non-contrastive *that*. Both these words can be used determinatively to situate a referent in context. *The* indicates specificity of object, while *that* adds context to the noun.

The indefinite article, however, derives from the Old English *an*, which served as either *a* or the numeral *one*. Today these two forms are virtually interchangeable, although there are circumstances where *a* is preferred. For example, with the use of an idea contrary to that expected, *a* is the form used as shown in the following dialogue:

A: *There's a/one man.*
B: *No, it isn't a man; it's a lady.*

So, historically speaking, the indefinite article is not part of a contrastive system with the definite article, but the latter is more closely related to the demonstratives.

Based on this kind of historical fact, scholars such as Karmiloff-Smith (1979) and Garton (1983) suggested strongly that the use of demonstratives *this*, *that*, *these*, and *those*, as well as the use of the numeral *one* should also be described whenever the acquisition of articles is studied.

Looking at the inner creativity of the human mind, Bickerton (1981, 1984) proposed the Language Bioprogram hypothesis, which holds in part that learners have a natural sensitivity to specificity and non-specificity of reference. Bickerton argued that children are biologically programmed to make the specific/non-specific distinction in acquiring a new language since this distinction is marked in all creole languages by the use of articles. Bickerton predicted "when a substantial body of early child language is properly examined, there will be found to be a significant skewing in article placement, such that a significantly higher percentage of articles will be assigned to specific-reference NP, while zero forms will persist in non-specific environments longer than elsewhere" (p. 154). Based on Bickerton's hypothesis and seven studies related to the acquisition of articles (Bresson, 1974; Brown, 1973; Emslie & Stevenson, 1981; Garton, 1983; Karmiloff-Smith, 1979; Maratsos, 1976; Warden, 1976), Cziko (1986) proposed a four-stage sequence in the L1 acquisition of articles. Stage I is characterized by the use of the indefinite and/or definite article(s) for specific referents, and zero article for both non-specific referents and naming. Stage II is marked by the use of the indefinite article for non-specific referents, and the definite article for specific referents regardless of whether they are presupposed. Stage III is identified by an increase in the correct use of the indefinite article for specific, non-presupposed referents, with a concomitant decrease in the correct use of the definite article for specific, presupposed referents. Stage IV is featured by the correct use of the definite and indefinite articles.

In sum, the acquisition of the English article system has been investigated quite extensively in L1 studies. Various criteria and research methodologies have been proposed and experimented. Obtained findings have indicated clearly that the English article system is acquired sequentially, and, moreover, the different uses of each individual article are acquired at different stages.

STUDIES OF L2 ACQUISITION SEQUENCES IN GENERAL

Larsen-Freeman and Long (1991) summarized one of the major principles governing interlanguage (IL) development as follows: "ILs exhibit common accuracy orders and developmental sequences" (p. 81). This principle is based on the premise that there are inherent orders and developmental sequences in the learner language, and that those orders and developmental sequences are largely systematic and identifiable. This principle has been supported by findings from morpheme studies and studies of the acquisition of a number of syntactic structures.

Early empirical evidence of the existence of L1-neutral developmental sequences was provided by the so-called "morpheme studies," which established the existence of a common acquisition order for a subset of English grammatical morphemes. Dulay and Burt (1973) adapted Brown's approach to SLA research. Their participants were 151 Spanish-speaking children aged six to eight learning English in the United States. Samples of speech were collected by means of the Bilingual Syntax Measure, an instrument designed to elicit a range of grammatical structures by asking the learners 33 questions about a series of seven cartoon pictures. After eight grammatical morphemes supplied in the obligatory contexts were scored, it was found that the participants exhibited accuracy orders in the following way: plural -s → -ing → copula be → auxiliary be → the/a → irregular past → 3rd person -s → possessive -s.

The finding of a common morpheme order was confirmed, again using the Bilingual Syntax Measure, with 60 Spanish-speaking children and 55 Chinese-speaking children, by Dulay and Burt (1974), and with 73 Spanish-speaking and non-Spanish-speaking adults by Bailey, Madden, and Krashen (1974).

Reviewing over a dozen English as a second language (ESL) morpheme studies available at the time, Krashen (1977) postulated the following "natural order": the group consisting of -ing, plural -s and copula be → the group consisting of auxiliary be and the articles the/a → the group consisting of irregular past → the group consisting of regular past, 3rd person singular and possessive -s. Krashen argued that it was more meaningful to discuss acquisition in terms of a hierarchy of morphemes in groups than individual morphemes since each group constituted a clear developmental stage and the morphemes within each group were acquired at more or less the same time.

Despite the discovery of some acquisition orders, the morpheme studies have also been subjected to some severe criticism. One obvious problem with this line of research is that the findings are specific to English and have not been replicated with other languages except Spanish. In addition, they can be generalized only to languages that have both bound and free grammatical morphemes with identical meanings. The findings cannot, however, be applied to languages, such as Chinese, that have no morphological component to the grammar. Another problem is the heterogeneity of the morphemes that are involved. As Maratsos (1983) put it, those morphemes do not belong to any coherent structural category. The morphemes selected for study are a mixture of bound and free morphemes, as in the case of 3rd person -s and copula verb *be*. While the former is a bound morpheme, the latter is a free morpheme.

To remedy the problem of heterogeneity, researchers have shifted their focus to some independent homogeneous linguistic elements or systems. This is evident in studies of relative pronouns, negation, interrogatives, and word order rules.

Felix and Hahn (1985) proposed that various semantic features of pronouns are acquired in the following sequence: emergence of 1st person and *he* or *you* to represent all other persons → number is recognized → occurrence of 3rd person → gender is distinguished.

A quite similar sequence was suggested by Lightbown and Spada (1990) for possessive pronouns among French learners of English: Stage I is characterized by the use of definite articles in place of possessive pronouns, as in *She reads the book*; Stage II is featured with the use of a generalized possessive pronoun for all persons, genders, and numbers, as in *She reads your book*; Stage III is represented by the use of a single 3rd person possessive pronoun, which is overgeneralized, as in *She reads his book*; Stage IV is marked by the differentiated use of possessive pronouns with some possessed nouns but continued errors with human nouns, as in *She reads her book to his brother*; Stage V is notable for the correct use of possessive pronouns with all nouns, as in *She reads her book to her brother*.

Syntactic structures selected for study included interrogatives, negatives, relative clauses, and word orders. As summarized by Larsen-Freeman and Long (1991), the developmental sequence for interrogatives in ESL can be identified into the following stages: Stage 1. Rising intonation, for example, *He work today?*; Stage 2. Uninverted WH (+/-aux.), for example, *What he (is) saying?*; Stage 3. Overinversion, for example, *Do you know where is it?*; and Stage 4. Differentiation, for example, *Does she like where she lives?*.

As for negatives, Cancino, Rosansky, and Schumann (1978) investigated six Spanish speakers learning English and discovered a common developmental sequence of frequency for four stages: Stage I: "no + X," as in *No this one*; Stage II: "don't + V," as in *My dad no have job*; Stage III: "aux-neg," as in *I can't play the guitar*; and Stage IV: "analyzed don't," as in *She doesn't drink beer*.

The acquisition of relative clauses has also been extensively investigated. Schumann (1980) examined the development of relative clauses in five Spanish-speaking learners of English. He found that relative clauses used to modify the object of a sentence were acquired before relative clauses used to modify the subject of a sentence. In terms of the use of relative pronouns, the following sequence was observed: Omission (as in *I got a friend speaks Spanish*) → Substitution with a personal pronoun (as in *I got a friend he speaks Spanish*) → Proper use (as in *I got a friend who speaks Spanish*).

Based on a number of earlier studies, Keenan and Comrie (1977) suggested an accessibility hierarchy for relative clauses. In a linguistic hierarchy, the related grammatical structures or functions are ordered in such a way that the presence of one structure or function implies the presence of all the structures or functions higher in the hierarchy. This provides an ordering from the most accessible to the least accessible for relative clauses according to the grammatical function of the relative pronoun, as shown in the following table.

TABLE 3. The accessibility hierarchy of relative clauses.

Rank Order	Function	Example
1.	Subject	The man who gave me the book ...
2.	Direct object	The place that she visited ...
3.	Indirect object	The student whom he gave the book ...
4.	Object of preposition	The house that they live in...
5.	Genitive	The woman whose handbag he stole ...
6.	Object of comparison	The man that I am richer than ...

Source. Adapted from Cook (1993, p. 140).

Some support has been found to correlate this accessibility hierarchy with second language (L2) learners' performance. Gass (1979), for instance, found that the easiest position to relativize was that of subject while the most difficult to relativize was that of object of comparison. The only exception was the genitive, which was observed in terms of accuracy next to Subject, but before Direct object, Indirect object, and Object of comparison.

One of the most impressive developmental patterns documented in SLA research literature is related to word orders. A clear developmental pattern of the acquisition of German word order rules emerges from a large number of studies as follows: Canonical order → Adverb preposing → Verb separation → Inversion → Verb-end (Pienemann, Johnston, & Brindley, 1988).

Johnston and Piernemann (1986) tested the predictions generated by the model on the acquisition of English by migrant workers in Australia and found evidence to support them. They used implicational scaling on data collected cross-sectionally to establish the hierarchy of stages, shown as follows: Stage I: Single words; formulas as in *Dad home.*, *My name is John Smith.*; Stage II: SVO; plural marking as in *I eat rice.*, *I have books.*; Stage III: Do-fronting; adverb preposing; neg. + V as in *Do you understand me?*, *Yesterday I go to school.*, *She no coming today.*; Stage IV: Pseudo-inversion; yes/no inversion; V + to + V as in *Where is my purse?*, *Have you car?*, *I want to go.*; Stage V: 3rd person -s; 2nd person -do as *He works in a factory.*, *You do not understand.*; and Stage VI: Question-tag; adverb-VP as in *He's Polish, isn't he?*, *I can always go.*

Overall, learners' IL development provides evidence for some common acquisition sequences. Research to date has shown a natural acquisition order of some commonly used morphemes, and some development sequences for relative pronouns, negation, interrogatives, and word order rules.

SECOND LANGUAGE ARTICLE ACQUISITION STUDIES

In the so-called morpheme studies, the definite article and the indefinite article were regarded as one morpheme under the cover term of *the/a*. Under this line of studies, the acquisition of articles was often studied side by side with that of other morphemes. In other words, articles were not treated as an independent system. It was soon discovered, however, that articles themselves are acquired gradually and systematically with identifiable sequences or stages.

Hakuta (1976) conducted a longitudinal study of a Japanese girl learning English as a second language. This Japanese girl was observed over a period of 60 weeks, from the age of 5:4, which was five months after her exposure to English began, until the age of 6:5. Spontaneous speech was recorded once every two weeks. Extending Brown's method of the attainment of the 90% criterion in the obligatory context, Hakuta scored for what he called errors of commission (supplying articles in nonobligatory contexts), as opposed to errors of omission (not supplying articles in obligatory contexts). He found a large number of errors of commission in his analysis. This suggests that a learner may recognize the form of an article before recognizing its function. He also found that *the* was acquired before *a* by his informant.

Andersen (1977) discussed the performance of 89 first-year university students in the use of English articles. All his participants were native speakers of Spanish. In an innovative way, Andersen identified the following four articles: *a*, the indefinite article; *the*, the definite article; $\emptyset_1$, the absence of an article or other determiner in English in those contexts where Spanish requires a definite article; $\emptyset_2$, the absence of an article or other determiner in English in those contexts where there is also no article or other determiner in Spanish. It is clear from this classification that Andersen separated *a(n)* from *the*; moreover, he considered the $\emptyset$ article as a full article consisting of two subsets, namely $\emptyset_1$ and $\emptyset_2$. From his data, Andersen was able to find the following: (a) most of the participants performed quite well with *the* in obligatory contexts, but their performance with *a* ranged from almost 0% up to 10%; (b) the indefinite article *a* was frequently omitted in contexts where it is omitted in Spanish and *one* was often used where *a* is required; and (c) the participants performed well when the articles are the same in both English and Spanish (i.e., $\emptyset_2$) but not so well when the articles are different in the two languages (i.e., $\emptyset_1$). Based on those findings, Andersen concluded that "wherever English and Spanish both require the definite article or do not permit an article (*the* and $\emptyset_2$) the subjects perform well. When Spanish and English require different articles (*a* and $\emptyset_1$) considerable variability is evident and many of the errors seem to be interference errors" (p. 72).

Yamada and Matsuura (1982) investigated article usage in Japanese students. Although they looked for target-like usage rather than a non-target IL system, the study was an improvement on earlier work in that the articles were broken down into separate tallies for *a(n)*, *the*, and $\emptyset$. In general, Yamada and Matsuura found that the overall difficulty order (easiest to most difficult) for intermediate level Japanese ESL students was *the* $\rightarrow$ *a(n)* $\rightarrow$ $\emptyset$, whereas the difficulty order for advanced level Japanese ESL students was *the* $\rightarrow$ $\emptyset$ $\rightarrow$ *a(n)*.

It is not difficult to see that the studies done by Hakuta, Andersen, and Yamada and Matsuura were more or less based on Brown's criterion paradigm, which was criticized by Bickerton (1981) as the tendency "to look to the goal, rather than the path, to ask 'What has the child acquired?' rather than 'How has he acquired it?'" (p. 143).

In an effort to abandon this criterion paradigm, Huebner (1983) conducted a longitudinal study. His lone participant was a Hmong refugee from Laos learning ESL in an untutored setting. The participant, in his early twenties, had never had any formal instruction in English. The data collection began within a few weeks of his arrival in Hawaii. The data were collected on an average of every three weeks for one year. Huebner developed a system of analysis that accounted for article use in all prenominal positions. Using Bickterton's (1981) proposed universal features of referentiality (Specific Referent) and (Assumed Known to Hearer), Huebner divided environments for articles according to whether the noun phrase on which the article was dependent was used referentially or nonreferentially [±Specific Referent] ([±SR]), and whether or not that the noun phrase was identifiable by the listener [±Assumed Hearer's Knowledge] ([±HK]). These two binary features varied independently, yielding a "semantic wheel," or more accurately speaking, four cross-classified environments for articles as shown in the following table.

TABLE 4. Semantic wheel for noun phrase reference.

Features	Environment	Articles	Example
[–SR+HK]	Generic NP	a, the, ∅	A rat is larger than a mouse. The whale is becoming extinct. ∅ Fruit flourishes in the valley.
[+SR+HK]	Definite NP	the	Close the door, please.
[+SR–HK]	Indefinite NP	a, ∅	I have a car. She cleaned the floor with ∅ water.
[–SR–HK]	Nonspecific indefinite NP	a, ∅	I guess I should buy a new car. I need ∅ money.

Source. Adapted from Huebner (1983, p. 133).

In regard to the use of the definite article, Huebner uncovered a pattern of development consisting of four main stages. In the first stage, the participant was observed to use the definite article to mark those noun phrases that had the features of [+ Specific Referent, + Hearer's Knowledge]. The exception was the case of a clear noun-phrase topic. Huebner (1983) reasoned that "if a noun phrase is clearly a topic, as indicated by its position in the sentence, the listener already knows it is [+ HK]. There is no need to mark it twice" (p. 142). In the second stage, the definite article was found to mark all noun phrases including the nondefinite or nonspecific ones. In other words, NP environments were "flooded" with the definite article "da." In the third stage, "da" was dropped from [– Specific Referent, – Hearer known] environments. So at this point, the placement of the definite article was most prominent in referential, specific NP environments. In the fourth stage, "da" was further dropped from [+ Specific Referent, – Hearer known] environments and was only used to mark those noun phrases that had the feature of [+ HK]. From stage four on, the participant produced the definite article in a target-like manner. Huebner (1983) concluded that the acquisition process for the definite article in general "consisted of using the form in virtually all environments before gradually eliminating it from the 'incorrect' environments" (p. 147).

Master (1988) conducted a pseudo-longitudinal analysis of article usage by 20 ESL learners with five different native language backgrounds: three with no article system (Chinese, Japanese, and Russian) and two with article systems (Spanish and German). Among those 20 participants, 9 were males and 11 were females. The age range was from 13 to 93 years. The length of time in the United States ranged from 3 weeks to 32 years. The IL level of each participant was determined by the negation criteria and classified into four stages, namely basilang, low-mesolang, mid-mesolang, and high-mesolang, which corresponded to the following stages in the development of negation: (i) *no(t)* + verb, (ii) unanalyzed *don't*, (iii) auxiliary + negator, and (iv) analyzed *don't*. Twenty tape-recorded informal interviews were used as the data source. In this study, both *a* and *an* were counted as correct, even if *a* was incorrectly used before a vowel sound, as in *a apple*. Additionally, due to the low occurrence of proper nouns, the investigation was confined to the use of articles with common nouns. The data were analyzed to measure accuracy and usage. In terms of accuracy, the acquisition sequence for learners whose native languages had no article system was found to be $\varnothing \rightarrow the \rightarrow a$, while the acquisition sequence for learners whose native langauges had article systems appeared to be $the/\varnothing \rightarrow a$.

Thomas (1989a) conducted a cross-sectional study of *a(n)*, *the*, and the null article in the speech of 30 adult L2 learners, who represented 9 native languages: 5 with articles (Greek, Spanish, Italian, French, and German) and 4 without articles (Japanese, Chinese, Korean, and Finnish). The average length of the participants' residence in English-speaking countries was 10 months, with a range from 2 to 30 months. They were attending ESL classes at five different levels in a large urban university. A picture-description task was devised to elicit their performance data. The analysis of the data showed that the accurate control of *the* occurred before that of *a*, which was significantly delayed, and that the most common source of errors in both *a* and *the* contexts among L2 learners across different proficiency levels was overgeneralization of $\varnothing$, or equivalently, failure to use any article.

Gorokhova (1990) conducted a cross-sectional study of 70 adult Spanish-speaking learners of English enrolled in four different levels of the ESL program at the Institute for Bilingual Studies in Hudson County Community College. These learners, with ages ranging from 19 to 44 years old, came from 10 different countries in Latin America: Honduras, El Salvador, Colombia, Panama, Puerto Rico, Chile, Dominican Republic, Peru, Ecuador, and Cuba. A structured open-ended interview consisting of questions for participants and 12 pictures for description was designed to elicit the participants' article usage in various contexts. The transcripts of the interviews as well as the participants' written journals and answers on an oral placement test were used as the data source. Based on the analysis of these data, it was found that the article signals were acquired in an order of *the*, *a*, and zero article. This developmental sequence, as suggested by Gorokhova, can be manifested in five stages. In Stage I, speakers only have *the* and use it with visible referents and important contextual referents. Stage II is featured by the addition of the indefinite article *a*, which is used with less important referents and with small visible referents.

Stage III is a transitional stage where students have more awareness of the linguistic discourse. Stage IV is marked by new systemic values for *the* and *a*, which are based on discourse and thus are closer to those in Standard English. In Stage V, the last signal ∅ (zero article) is acquired.

Lee et al. (1994) conducted an 18-month longitudinal study to examine the acquisition of English articles by three 6-year-old, second language-learning children whose native language was Chinese. Starting from their third month in Canada, the children were interviewed individually once a month. Brown's coding scheme and an extended coding scheme were used in scoring the corpora of the children's responses to a Syntax Elicitation Task. The researchers' main interest was when English articles were acquired. Specifically, they explored the possibility of using *one* and *this/ that/these/those* as placeholders respectively for *a(n)* and *the* in the process of acquiring English articles. They observed that their participants tended not to use *one* for those occasions where the indefinite article is required. However, they did find that those three children's use of the definite article developed through an unmarked phase (no appearance of *the*), a referential place-holding phase (frequent use of *this/that* or *these/those*), a marked phase (correct use of *the*), and a referential substitution phase (dominant use of *this/that* or *these/those*) before the definite article was fully acquired.

Representative L2 research on the acquisition of English articles, as previously described, shows that various methods have been used to identify and describe acquisition sequences of English articles. Most notable was the use of Brown's (1973) obligatory occasion analysis and Huebner's (1983) semantic wheels. Regarding Brown's scheme, several extended and modified versions have been designed in order to achieve better results. This includes Hakuta's (1976) classification of errors of commission (supplying articles in non-obligatory contexts) as opposed to errors of omission (not supplying articles in obligatory contexts), Andersen's (1977) Group Range extending Brown's 90% criterion to 80% criterion and 70% criterion, and Lee et al.'s (1994) use of the extended coding scheme of the subcategories of *a*-overuse and *the*-overuse.

Two other extended versions of Brown's scheme are also worth mentioning. One is Pica's (1983b) target-like use (TLU) analysis. According to this analysis, morphemes are first scored for correct use in obligatory contexts. The score obtained then becomes the numerator of a ratio that includes in its denominator the sum of both the number of obligatory contexts for suppliance of the morpheme and the number of non-obligatory contexts in which the morpheme is supplied inappropriately. The formula for TLU analysis of morphemes can be illustrated as the following:

$$TLU = \frac{n \text{ correct suppliance in obligatory contexts}}{(n \text{ obligatory contexts} + n \text{ suppliance in non-obligatory contexts})} \times 100$$

By using this method, Pica (1985), in her study of 18 participants under three different conditions of the target language exposure, found the following acquisition pattern of the article *a*: greater TLU of *a* first appears in isolated units, then emerges in noun complements and direct objects, and finally occurs in noun objects of prepositions.

The other extended version is Parrish's article matrix, which can be illustrated in the following table.

TABLE 5. Parrish's article matrix.

	Article Required in Target Language		
	Definite	**Indefinite**	$\varnothing$
Form Supplied by the Learner			
Definite Article			
Indefinite Article			
$\varnothing$			
Quantifiers			
Demonstratives			
Total			
Percent Correct			

Source. Parrish (1987, p. 372).

What was innovative in Parrish's scheme was the inclusion of Quantifiers and Demonstratives as well as the overuse of articles. Comparing the results derived from the use of this scheme, Brown's scheme, and Huebner's scheme in analyzing one informant's performance data, Parrish concluded that the first scheme is more adequate to uncover the processes underlying IL development than the latter ones.

As shown in the aforementioned review, the article system has been extensively studied from both L1 and L2 perspectives. In summary, research in L1 has produced four representative views concerning the acquisition sequence of English articles. The first view implies that the definite article and indefinite articles are acquired at the same time. This view can be best demonstrated in morpheme order studies such as Brown (1973) and de Villiers and de Villiers (1973), which have simply shown that articles *a/the* are acquired after present progressive *-ing*, preposition *in*, preposition *on*, plural *-s*, past irregular *-s*, possessive *-s*, and uncontractible copula *be*, but before past regular *-ed*, 3rd person regular *-s*, 3rd person irregular, uncontractible auxiliary *be*, contractible copular *be*, and contractible auxiliary *be*. No information has been provided to indicate whether *a(n)* is acquired before *the* or after *the*.

The second view holds that *a(n)* is acquired before *the*. The representative studies that reflect this viewpoint are those conducted by Leopold (1949) and Zehler and Brewer (1982).

The third view, as represented by Karmiloff-Smith's (1979) study, holds that the different functions performed by articles are acquired in a sequenced way. The acquisition of the indefinite article can be identified into the following stages: schwa-form → nominative function → numeral function → non-specific function → generic function. By comparison, the acquisition of the definite article can be identified into the following stages: schwa-form → deictic function → exophoric function → anaphoric function → generic function.

The fourth view is derived from Bickerton's (1981) Language Bioprogram hypothesis, which holds that the human mind has a three-way division between a definite article for presupposed-specific NP, an indefinite article for asserted-specific NP, and a zero article for non-specific NP.

Based on this theoretical framework and seven L1 studies, Cziko (1986) proposed a four-stage hypothesis of the acquisition of articles, character-ized by a) the use of the indefinite and/or definite article(s) for specific referents, and the zero article for both non-specific referents and nam-ing; b) the use of the indefinite article for non-specific referents, and the definite article for specific referents whether or not they are presupposed; c) an increase in the correct use of the indefinite article for specific, non-presupposed referents, with a concomitant decrease in the correct use of the definite article for specific, presupposed referents; and d) the correct use of the definite and indefinite articles.

Comparable research on the acquisition or use of articles by L2 learn-ers has appeared only relatively recently. There have been contrastive studies about articles: English versus Slavic in Kaluza (1963), English versus Persian in Jafarpur (1979), and English versus Arabic in Al-Johani (1982). Similarly, pedagogical analyses of the article system can be found in Hok (1970), Grannis (1972), McEldowney (1977), and Master (1990). There have also been descriptions of the use of English articles by learners of a particular L1, as in the cases of Kharma (1981) for Arabic; Yamada and Matsuura (1982) for Japanese; Agnihotri, Khanna, and Mukherjee (1984) for Hindi and Punjabi; and Liao (1985) for Chinese. In the context of variation research, evidence has been found showing that variation on article selection and use can be affected by task (Tarone, 1985; Tarone & Parrish, 1988), by semantic function of noun phrase (Huebner, 1983), by interlocutor (Young, 1986), by planning condition (Crookes, 1989), and by different levels of the target-language proficiency (Huebner, 1983).

Compared with the L1 acquisition order of morphemes, evidence has been found showing that in L2 acquisition, articles *a/the* (in the same group with auxiliary) are acquired after the group consisting of *-ing*, plu-ral, and copular; and before the group consisting of irregular past as well as the group consisting of regular past, 3rd person singular, and posses-sive *-s* (Krashen, 1977).

As for the acquisition sequence of articles, research findings have quite consistently suggested that *the* is acquired before *a(n)* (Andersen, 1977; Chaudron & Parker, 1990; Crookes, 1989; Gorokhova, 1990; Hakuta,

1976; Huebner, 1983; Lee et al., 1994; Master, 1988; Parrish, 1987; Shannon, 1995; Thomas, 1989a). As one of the best representatives of the current SLA research into the acquisition sequence of articles, Master (1988) proposed the acquisition sequence of *zero article → the → a(n)* for those learners whose native languages have no article system and *the/zero article → a(n)* for those learners whose native languages have an article system.

It is quite evident from the aforementioned review that even though L2 research is heavily influenced by L1 research methodology, the suggested L1 acquisition sequences of English articles are quite different from those sequences proposed in the L2 context. One typical example is that the indefinite article is often considered to be acquired earlier than the definite article in one's first language. However, in sharp contrast, the definite article has been quite consistently observed to be acquired earlier than the indefinite article in L2 settings. It can also be noted that the research focused on L2 has shifted from comparing articles in different languages, to treating the articles as one of the morphemes, to considering the articles as a separate linguistic system with its own developmental sequence.

CHAPTER 3

PROCEDURES

CASE STUDY METHODOLOGY

> *A true picture of article acquisition should be based on longitudinal studies.*
>
> —Master (1988, p. 9)

The present study was a longitudinal case study that involved observing and investigating the development of article performance in the spontaneous speech of a nine-year old Chinese boy. A few words about case study methodology seem necessary at this juncture since misconceptions about this methodology do exist and people often doubt the value of a case study, especially a single-case study. Moreover, it is important to understand why such an approach is an appropriate methodology for this dissertation research.

Case study, as defined by Yin (1984), is "an empirical inquiry that investigates a contemporary phenomenon within its real-life context" (p. 22). It "typically involves observing the development of linguistic performance, usually the spontaneous speech of one subject, when the speech data are collected at periodic intervals over a span of time" (Larsen-Freeman & Long, 1991, p. 11). According to Yin, case study is "the preferred strategy when 'how' or 'why' questions are being posed, when the investigator has little control over events, and when the focus is on a contemporary phenomenon within some real-life context" (p. 13). In addition to this, case study methodology has the advantages of detailed and comprehensive description, psycholinguistically coherent investigation (Larsen-Freeman & Long), hypothesis generation, and theory testing.

Case study, even single-case study, is not something new in the field of the second language acquisition (SLA) research. In fact, some very influential and widely quoted studies documented in the research literature of the field have used the methodology of single-case study. For instance, Halliday's (1975) influential theory of three-phase acquisition process in terms of language functions is derived from his study of one child, Nigel. Based on the observation and analysis of the language development of this child, Halliday proposed that in Phase I, there is a one-to-one form/ function correspondence. A child uses the language to perform the following seven functions, namely, Instrumental ("*I want*"); Regulatory ("*do as I tell you*"); Interactional ("*me and you*"); Personal ("*here I come*"); Heuristic ("*tell me why*"); Imaginative ("*let's pretend*"); and Informative ("*I've got something to tell you*"). In Phase II, a one-to-one form/function correspondence is no longer an adequate system for the encoding of meaning because the functional basis of the child's language becomes more general and abstract, and because the functions begin to combine in the same utterance. Phase III sees the adult-like language system. In other words, the child has moved from the Phase I position of "function equals use," through a transition Phase II in which the functions become more generalized, to Phase III, in which they have developed into the three-function system of the adult language, in which each utterance combines ideational, interpersonal. and textual meanings.

Other well-known examples of single-case studies include Schumann's (1975, 1978) Pidginization hypothesis and Acculturation model, which are based on his studies of Alberto, a 33-year-old working-class Costa

Rican; Huebner's (1983) notion of developmental patterns of interlanguage (IL), which is based on his study of Ge, a young adult Hmong speaker acquiring English in a natural setting without formal instruction; Bailey's (1980) insights on learning strategies, which are based on the diary study of her own experience as a student of French; and Schmidt's (1983) challenge to Krashen's Monitor model and Schumann's Acculturation model, which is based on his study of Wes, a highly successful Japanese artist living in Honolulu who had access to massive amounts of comprehensible input over many years of exposure to English and had stabilized far short of native-like norms in most aspects of grammatical morphology, despite the fact that his affective profile was for the most part very positive.

Cases such as these have shown clearly that single-case study methodology, if used appropriately, is an effective method for conducting research. However, the most important criterion here is appropriateness. As Larsen-Freeman and Long (1991) stated, "it should not be a case of choosing between the qualitative and quantitative paradigms nor among extant methodologies, but rather of designing a research methodology which possesses the optimal combination of attributes to address the research question under consideration" (p. 45). In other words, the research question should determine the choice of the method.

For the present study, the central research question was: Are the suggested acquisition sequences of the English articles applicable to a Chinese, beginning English as a second language (ESL) learner? The single-case study methodology appears to be an appropriate one and can address this research question. As pointed out by Yin (1994), one of the important rationales for using a single-case methodology is that the single case selected and studied can represent a typical sample in testing a well-constructed theory.

> The theory has specified a clear set of propositions as well as the circumstances within which the propositions are believed to be true. To confirm, challenge, or extend the theory, there may exist a single case, meeting all of the conditions for testing the theory. This single case can then be used to determine whether a theory's

> propositions are correct or whether some alternative set of explanations might be more relevant. In this manner...the single case can represent a significant contribution to knowledge and theory-building. Such a study can even help to refocus future investigations in an entire field. (pp. 38–39)

This describes the aim of the present study, which was designed to test the established acquisition sequences of the English articles and to learn whether some alternative set of explanations might be more relevant in the case of a Chinese ESL learner.

Also, because of the following concerns, the single-case methodology was chosen for the present study. First, a thorough investigation is needed to determine whether a hesitation sound or an indefinite article is used. A common problem often encountered in cross-sectional studies of the acquisition or use of English articles is the difficulty of making a distinction between the hesitation sound and the indefinite article in the speech samples (Master, 1988; Shannon, 1995), as shown in the following utterance:

The pleasure is uh/a very precious experience for me.

This difficulty has forced researchers to discard those instances where it is unclear whether a given sound represents an article or a hesitation morpheme (Thomas, 1989a), or even served as part of the reason for excluding indefinite articles in a study (Shannon, 1995). However, this problem can be easily solved if the single case methodology is employed. If necessary, the sole informant can be frequently and conveniently consulted concerning what he or she is actually speaking. As a result, the accuracy or the quality of the data can be ensured.

Second, an in-depth understanding of a single case is needed to clarify the following issues related to the acquisition of English articles: the acquisition of the indefinite articles *a* and *an*; the difference between the use of the zero article and non-use of any article; the relationship between articles and other related determiners. These important issues cannot be thoroughly dealt with in cross-sectional studies, as reflected in the current L2 research literature.

In summary, even though the lack of generalizability of findings from single-case longitudinal studies cannot be overlooked, the single-case methodology can be justified for the present study that attempted to test an established theory by tracing a Chinese ESL learner's changes in patterns of English articles over time and by exploring some neglected issues related to the study of the use or acquisition of English articles from a second language perspective.

INFORMANT

The informant for this longitudinal study was a 9-year-old Chinese male, who arrived in the United States on December 10, 1995, and started school in Columbus, Ohio on January 5, 1996. Before coming to the United States, he had not learned any English at school. Students in China generally start learning English in middle school. However, he had a student tutor who coached him in spoken English twice each week for the two months before leaving China. Each session lasted about one hour.

Upon entering school in Columbus, Ohio, he entered the fourth grade. While attending regular classes at school, he had a daily ESL class, which usually lasted about 50 minutes. The ESL class was reduced to twice each week when he entered the fifth grade. In the ESL class, the instructor focused on his spoken English and the reading problems he encountered in the regular class. The instructor would normally assign him some homework after each class and ask him to keep a dialogue journal in English.

At home, he spoke only Chinese with his parents. However, they would help him understand the school assignments and tell him some words or expressions if necessary.

ANECDOTE TO THE COLLECTION OF THE FIRST DATA

Ever since this child arrived in the United States, the present researcher observed very closely how he learned English and recorded any noticeable progress he made. Attempts had been made to conduct interviews in

English between him and his parents before September 28, 1996. However, due to interference caused by the familiarity of family relations, the attempted interviews failed to yield useful data because Chinese was used most of the time during the interviews. On the one hand, the child felt embarrassed to speak English with his parents because Chinese was the only language used among family members for communication at home. On the other hand, whenever he had difficulty expressing himself in English, he would turn to Chinese. As the interviews revealed, he could not express himself consistently in English. The impression he gave to the researcher from those attempted interviews was that he had just learned some English words and expressions. It appeared that more time was needed for him to develop his English language proficiency. Also, a lesson learned from those unsuccessful interviews was that it was better for the interviewer to be a native speaker of English. This could serve as a measure to avoid the interference of familiar family relationships and inauthentic contexts for speaking in English.

At the end of June 1996, six months after his arrival in the United States, the child was still observed to be speaking very little English. His mother, who was very worried about his English, even suggested hiring an English tutor for him. However, the child did not want a tutor. His parents then suggested that he attend summer classes or camps during the long July-to-September summer vacation. Again, this child turned down the suggestion for the very reason that he could not understand and communicate with others in those classes or camps. Therefore, during this long vacation, he stayed at home and spent most of his time with his grandparents, who came to the United States to visit him and who knew little English.

When school started at the end of September 1996, the researcher thought that he could not wait any longer to collect spoken data, since this child had already stayed in the United States for nine months. From the point of view of second language acquisition, that was indeed not a short period of time. An interview was scheduled between a native speaker and this child. The researcher believed that, at the very least, some information could be collected at this time since the child would have no way to use his Chinese if he talked with a native speaker who had no knowledge of Chinese. The first set of data in the present study was the product of this interview.

When listening to the recording of this interview, the informant's mother and grandparents could not believe that he could communicate so fluently in English with a native speaker at this stage. The researcher also felt surprised about his informant's sudden jump in learning to speak English, failed to find an adequate theory to explain this phenomenon in the process of second language acquisition, and regretted being deceived by his "careful observation," which had resulted in a failure to make recordings of some possible earlier learning processes involved in acquiring English articles.

DATA COLLECTION

Data were collected during the 13 months from September 1996 to September 1997 in Columbus, Ohio. The data collected were in the form of interview transcripts. The dates of the interview sessions are listed in the following table.

TABLE 6. Data collection schedule.

Tape	Date
1	9/28/1996
2	10/5/1996
3	10/13/1996
4	10/23/1996
5	11/2/1996
6	11/30/1996
7	12/8/1996
8	12/16/1996
9	1/12/1997
10	1/19/1997

(continued on next page)

TABLE 6. (*continued*)

Tape	Date
11	2/2/1997
12	2/16/1997
13	3/2/1997
14	3/16/1997
15	4/1/1997
16	4/29/1997
17	5/27/1997
18	6/29/1997
19	7/27/1997
20	8/31/1997
21	9/28/1997

As shown in the table, the interviews were conducted one to three times each month in the first eight months, and once each month in the remaining five months. More interviews were conducted during the first few months for the sake of describing some possible subtle changes in the early acquisition processes, as suggested by some researchers (Hatch, 1978). However, such subtle changes regarding the use of articles were not very obvious after a careful examination, so the speech samples collected within the same month were combined into one data set and the entire collection of data was reorganized and indexed as shown in the following table, where the corresponding exposure time of the informant to English in the American context was also included.

Each interview session lasted from 20 to 30 minutes. To avoid the possible negative effect caused by a non-native speaker interlocutor, as mentioned previously, the interlocutor was a native speaker of English. The informant knew that he was being audio-taped. He also knew that the purpose of the audio-taping was to examine his progress in learning English. However, he did not know the true nature of why he was being audio-taped. In other words, he did not know that this was the researcher's

TABLE 7. Reorganization of the data.

Data Set No.	Original Tape No.	Exposure Time to English
1	1	9 months
2	2, 3, 4	10 months
3	5, 6	11 months
4	7, 8	12 months
5	9, 10	13 months
6	11, 12	14 months
7	13, 14	15 months
8	15, 16	16 months
9	17	17 months
10	18	18 months
11	19	19 months
12	20	20 months
13	21	21 months

dissertation research, which focused on his acquisition of the English articles. The concern here was simply for soliciting his natural speech without paying any special attention to the use of the English articles. So, for him, each interview session was just a practice session for his oral English. To motivate his participation, both the researcher and the interviewer frequently advised the informant that practice makes perfect and the best way to learn to speak English is to talk with a native speaker. After each session, he usually received some general positive comments from his native speaker partner such as, "You've made some great progress," "You can speak English very well now," and "You speak much, much better than the last session." As it turned out, the informant enjoyed each of these sessions and often continued his talking with the interviewer even when the investigator told him that the time was up.

The interviews were conducted either at the informant's home or in the interviewer's house. Topics ranged from school life and daily activities to the narration of experiences. Before each interview, the investigator would normally provide the interviewer with a list of some recent events in which the informant had participated. To assure the quality of the data, a transcript was made within one week after each interview and proofread by the interviewer. The interviewee also listened to the tape while checking the transcript together with the investigator. The complete corpus of speech transcriptions is located in Appendix C.

RECORDING EQUIPMENT

The interviews were recorded using an AIWA HS-J505 FM/AM Auto-Reverse Stereo Cassette tape recorder with a freestanding microphone. The cassettes used were professional quality 60-minute tapes, usually Sony HF tapes. Generally, the recorder was placed on the table with no attempt made to conceal it. The investigator usually sat somewhere out of sight to take notes.

DATA ANALYSIS

The analysis consisted of three steps, namely a qualitative index of the data in Non-numerical Unstructured Data Indexing Searching and Theory-building (NUD.IST) version 3.0.4d (for various features of this program, see Appendix A: Overview of the Software Program of NUD. IST), a quantitative examination in the Statistical Package for the Social Sciences (SPSS) version 7.5 (for various features of this program, see Appendix B: Overview of the Software Program of SPSS), and a discussion of the findings against the research questions.

During the qualitative index stage, every noun phase occurring in the data was carefully scrutinized to determine how the informant had used or misused articles. With the facilitation of the software program of NUD. IST version 3.0.4d, every noun phrase was indexed with the following information: grammatical category; grammatical function; grammatical structure; the presence or absence of the article; if present, the type of article used, its appropriateness and its semantic function; if absent, the use of the determiners *this/that*, *these/those*, *some* or *one*, or some other types of determiners. A coding frame had been pilot-studied and designed in the following way:

FIGURE 1. Tree diagram of the coding frame.

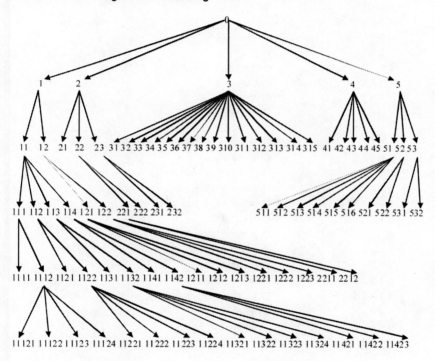

As shown in figure 1, the coding system can be displayed in the form of a tree diagram. Each number in figure 1 represents a node in the tree. The name and definition for each node or each number are shown in table 8, while each ending node or number is further illustrated in table 9, where the dash indicates the absence of the instance in the data.

The coding frame, as demonstrated in figure 1 and explained as well as illustrated in tables 8 and 9, provided a template for coding all the noun

TABLE 8. Name and definition for each coding node.

Node/Number	Name	Definition
0/Root	My Project: Articles	
1	Appearance	
1 1	Present	Presence of articles
1 1 1	*the*	
1 1 2	*a*	
1 1 3	*an*	
1 1 4	∅	Zero article
1 1 1 1	Correct (*the*)	
1 1 2 1	Correct (*a*)	
1 1 3 1	Correct (*an*)	
1 1 4 1	Correct (∅)	
1 1 1 2 1	Overuse *the* to *a*	
1 1 1 2 2	Overuse *the* to *an*	
1 1 1 2 3	Overuse *the* to ∅	
1 1 1 2 4	Overuse *the* to non-use	
1 1 2 2 1	Overuse *a* to *the*	
1 1 2 2 2	Overuse *a* to *an*	
1 1 2 2 3	Overuse *a* to ∅	
1 1 2 2 4	Overuse *a* to non-use	
1 1 3 2 1	Overuse *an* to *the*	
1 1 3 2 2	Overuse *an* to *a*	
1 1 3 2 3	Overuse *an* to ∅	
1 1 3 2 4	Overuse *an* to non-use	
1 1 4 2 1	Overuse ∅ to *the*	
1 1 4 2 2	Overuse ∅ to *a*	
1 1 4 2 3	Overuse ∅ to *an*	
1 2	Absent	Absence of articles
1 2 1	Determiner	
1 2 1 1	*this-that; these-those*	*the*-related determiner
1 2 1 2	*some*	∅-related determiner
1 2 1 3	*one*	*a/n*-related determiner
1 2 2	Other Determiner	Other types of determiners
1 2 2 1	Quantifier	
1 2 2 2	Possessive	

(*continued on next page*)

TABLE 8. (*continued*)

Node/Number	Name	Definition
1 2 2 3	*Wh-determiner*	
2	NP Type	Noun phrase type
2 1	Proper	Proper noun phrase
2 2	Common	Common noun phrase
2 2 1	Countable	Countable noun phrase
2 2 1 1	Singular	Singular countable noun phrase
2 2 1 2	Plural	Plural countable noun phrase
2 2 2	Uncountable	Uncountable noun phrase
2 3	Pronoun	Pronoun phrase
2 3 1	Personal	Personal pronoun phrase
2 3 2	Other	Other types of pronoun phrase
3	NP Function	Function of a noun phrase in a sentence
3 1	S	Subject
3 2	DO	Direct object
3 3	IO	Indirect object
3 4	PC	Prepositional complement
3 5	SC	Subject complement
3 6	OC	Object complement
3 7	EC	Existential complement
3 8	ADV	Adverbial
3 9	CONJ	Conjunct
3 10	PREM	Premodifier
3 11	POSM	Postmodifier
3 12	APPO	Apposition
3 13	ABS	Absolute
3 14	EXCL	Exclamation
3 15	VOC	Vocative
4	NP Structure	Internal structure of a noun phrase

(*continued on next page*)

TABLE 8. (*continued*)

Node/Number	Name	Definition
4 1	Head	Without any determiner and modifier
4 2	DH	determiner(s) + head
4 3	(D)MH	(determiner(s)) + premodifier + head
4 4	(D)HP	(determiner(s)) + head + postmodifier
4 5	(D)MHP	(determiner(s)) + pre-modifier + head + postmodifier
5	Semantic Meaning	
5 1	*the*	*the*
5 1 1	Earlier Mention	Identity established by the prior utterance
5 1 2	Postmodification	Identity established by the postmodification
5 1 3	Unique Object	Identifying the object or group of objects as the only one that exists or has existed
5 1 4	Specified Order	Identity established by a specified order or rank in a set
5 1 5	Given Setting	Identity established by a given setting
5 1 6	Generic	Referring to what is general or typical for a whole class of objects
5 2	*a(n)*	*a* and *an*
5 2 1	Individual	Referring to an indefinite individual entity
5 2 2	Generic	Referring to what is general or typical for a whole class of objects
5 3	∅	Zero article
5 3 1	Parti-generic	Referring to an indefinite amount of the genus
5 3 2	Toto-generic	Referring to the whole genus

TABLE 9. Illustration for each ending node.

Ending Node	Description	Exemplification
1 1 1 1	Correct Use of (*the*)	Mine in my class is *the* biggest one. [D3]
1 1 2 1	Correct Use of (*a*)	He get *a* small one like that big. [D2]
1 1 3 1	Correct Use of (*an*)	Half *an* hour for recess and half *an* hour for Academic Assist. [D12]
1 1 4 1	Correct Use of (∅)	There's ∅ water in there. [D3]
1 1 1 2 1	Overuse of *the* to *a*	And there are people, there are houses, and there is *the* road. [D10]
1 1 1 2 2	Overuse of *the* to *an*	…remember when *the* airplane start? [D11]
1 1 1 2 3	Overuse of *the* to ∅	We can save money and buy *the* food. [D13]
1 1 1 2 4	Overuse of *the* to non-use	…my aunt um she-she is in *the* um Ja-Japan. [D2]
1 1 2 2 1	Overuse of *a* to *the*	…he saw a mouse. [D3]
1 1 2 2 2	Overuse of *a* to *an*	Yeah, we have *a* ice-cream party. [D3]
1 1 2 2 3	Overuse of *a* to ∅	----
1 1 2 2 4	Overuse of *a* to non-use	I can do some like I use *a-a* um something to go up your hand. [D2]
1 1 3 2 1	Overuse of *an* to *the*	----
1 1 3 2 2	Overuse of *an* to *a*	----
1 1 3 2 3	Overuse of *an* to ∅	----
1 1 3 2 4	Overuse of *an* to non-use	----
1 1 4 2 1	Overuse of ∅ to *the*	And we study um like ∅ United States is-is called what. [D2]
1 1 4 2 2	Overuse of ∅ to *a*	So on next Wednesday in the afternoon we have ∅ Halloween party. [D2]
1 1 4 2 3	Overuse of ∅ to *an*	I'm not ∅ old man. [D12]
1 2 1 1	*this-that; these-those*	*That* guy was funny. [D10]

(*continued on next page*)

TABLE 9. (*continued*)

Ending Node	Description	Exemplification
1 2 1 2	*some*	…then we can drink *some* water. [D2]
1 2 1 3	*one*	Then *one* mouse is coming. [D3]
1 2 2 1	Quantifier	He-he saw there are *many* games in there. [D3]
1 2 2 2	Possessive	I don't know *its* name. [D2]
1 2 2 3	*Wh-determiner*	*Which* choice may have better result? [D4]
2 1	NP Proper	We don't know *Christmas*. [D2]
2 2 1 1	NP Singular Countable	No, they never write me *a letter*. [D10]
2 2 1 2	NP Plural Countable	We need write *some notes* every day. [D2]
2 2 2	NP Uncountable	I have some trouble. [D4]
2 3 1	NP Personal Pronoun	*I* don't know. [D3]
2 3 2	NP Other Pronoun	*What*'s *this* for? [D2]
3 1	NP as Subject	Sometimes *we* need do something. [D2]
3 2	NP as Direct Object	You need *some money*. [D3]
3 3	NP as Indirect Object	My mom give *me* one dollar. [D2]
3 4	NP as Prepositional Comp	We took that turkey to *some friend's house*. [D3]
3 5	NP as Subject Comp	His name is *Willy*. [D2]
3 6	NP as Object Comp	And but we call them *Jeff, Stan, and Jess*. [D13]
3 7	NP as Existential Comp	But there're *something* you can't found in the book. [D2]
3 8	NP as Adverbial	But *one day* there're many people are coming want see what he do. [D2]
3 9	NP as Conjunct	Always there is a ace, *one jack*, and *two kings*. [D11]
3 10	NP as Premodifier	I borrow that in the *Upper Arlington* library. [D2]

(*continued on next page*)

TABLE 9. *(continued)*

Ending Node	Description	Exemplification
3 11	NP as Postmodifier	----
3 12	NP as Apposition	And this-this small children *he-he* like that. [D2]
3 13	NP as Absolute	No, *a place*. [D12]
3 14	NP as Exclamation	He is tall, *man*. [D12]
3 15	NP as Vocative	Come on, *Willy!* [D2]
4 1	Head	*I* think so. [D10]
4 2	Determiner(s) + Head	It's *a lake*. [D10]
4 3	(Determiner(s)) + Premodifier + Head	I didn't get *a big one*. [D2]
4 4	(Determiner(s)) + Head + Postmodifier	Oh, that's *the day* that we go to, you know, Lane Avenue. [D10]
4 5	(Determiner(s)) + Premodifier + Head + Postmodifier	She got like as *long hair* as yours. [D13]
5 1 1	Earlier Mention *(the)*	Um you know yesterday I told you where I go in Washington... *The* place is? [D5]
5 1 2	Postmodification *(the)*	...beside *the* side of Washington. [D5]
5 1 3	Unique Object *(the)*	...this is *the* Capitol Hill. [D5]
5 1 4	Specified Order *(the)*	So she is like *the* best one because she go to many place. [D5]
5 1 5	Given Setting *(the)*	Where is *the* map? [D5]
5 1 6	Generic *(the)*	...told you how to be how to do *the* magic. [D2]
5 2 1	Individual *(a(n))*	Then he just have *a party* for his birthday. [D2]
5 2 2	Generic *(a(n))*	----
5 3 1	Parti-generic *(∅)*	So we need ∅ money to get a card. [D5]
5 3 2	Toto-generic *(∅)*	And ∅ girls...grow up very quick. [D2]

phrases and articles occurring in the data corpus. Following is an example of actual coding that was taken from the data corpus stored in the computer.

But
you
(1 2)   /appearance/absent
(2 3 1)   /np category/pronoun/personal
(3 1)   /np function/S
(4 1)   /np structure/Head
know on the on
the land
(1 1 1 1)   /appearance/present/the/correct
(2 2 2)   /np category/common/uncountable
(3 4)   /np function/PC
(4 4)   /np structure/(D)HP
(5 1 2)   /semantic meaning/the/postmodification
out there, there are
shops.
(1 1 4 1)   /appearance/present/∅/correct
(2 2 1 2)   /np category/common/countable/plural
(3 7)   /np function/EC
(4 2)   /np structure/DH
(5 3 1)   /semantic meaning/∅/parti-generic

In this coding frame, consideration was given to:

1. *The occurrence of all the forms of English articles and determiners*

Four forms of English articles were recognized and identified in this coding frame, namely *the*, *a*, *an*, and ∅ (zero article). In this way, *a* and *an* were treated separately instead of treating them as *a(n)*. Also, the zero article was recognized as an independent type of article. Treating and recognizing articles like this was one measure taken in the present study for the purpose of remedying the neglect of the acquisition process involving the zero article and the possible separate acquisition processes for *a* and *an*, a tendency evident in SLA research literature relating to the acquisition process of English articles. In addition to the recognition of these forms, three other forms of determiners were also identified as article-related. Those three forms of determiners were *this/that-these/those*, *some*, and *one*. The rationale for including those determiners was based on some modern linguistic theories which suggested that *this/that* and *these/those* are historically linked to *the* (J. Lyons, 1975, 1977), *some* and the zero article can be used interchangeably in certain contexts (Leech & Svartvik, 1975; Quirk et al., 1985), and "*one* may be regarded as a stressed form of the indefinite article" (p. 65). To provide a complete picture of the determiners occurring before the noun phrases, all other determiners that were neither included in the category of Article nor included in the category of Article-related Determiner were identified in the category of Other Determiner, with three subcategories under the titles of Quantifier, Possessive, and Wh-determiner, respectively. In this way, all the determiners occurring before noun phrases were categorized and analyzed.

2. *The linguistic environment*

English articles can only occur before noun phrases. Furthermore, "*the* and *a* have no function or lexical meaning independent of the noun they precede" (Kaluza, 1981, p. 12). For these reasons, noun phrases have to be carefully described since they serve as the linguistic environment for the occurrence or absence of articles. In this coding frame, noun phrases were described from three different aspects in terms of the types they belonged to, the functions they played in a sentence, and the internal structures they possessed. To be consistent, those three different aspects were all related to grammar. In other words, they were grammatical types, grammatical functions, and grammatical structures. Within the node of NP Type, noun phrases were classified into three types, namely Proper Noun Phrase, Common Noun Phrase, and Pronoun Phrase, even though they are generally classified into two types, namely proper noun phrase and common noun phrase. Pronoun phrase was treated as a separate node because it is one unique type of common noun phrase that does not require the use of any form of article. As shown in the coding frame, Common Noun Phrase has been further divided into Countable and Uncountable, with Countable being subdivided into Singular and Plural.

The proposed fifteen functions played by noun phrases were based on the present author's research findings from the Lancaster-Leeds Treebank, a language corpus which is believed to reflect and represent the modern British English (see Lang, 1989). One possible advantage to indexing the current data with these fifteen functions was that some comparisons could be made, if needed, at a later stage of the research.

The coding scheme for noun phrase structure was based on Quirk et al.'s (1985) description of noun phrases and Haan's (1987) theoretical framework for English noun phrase structures. The bracket in "determiner(s)" means the possibility of the occurrence of several determiners at one time, as in the case of *all the* *students*, where two determiners are used.

3. *Semantic functions*

The use of articles embodies different semantic functions in different contexts in discourse. Hence, it is inadequate to study English articles without considering the semantic or discourse functions they play in discourse. As Hatch (1990) correctly pointed out, "definite and indefinite articles and pronouns cannot be accurately studied apart from the discourse framework in which they occur (since these forms depend on the role of the noun phrase within a particular discourse)" (p. 699). To reflect this feature of articles, each entry for a correctly used article was further indexed with the specific semantic function it carried in the discourse.

Based on the Brown (1973) matrix for the definite article, Celce-Murcia and Larsen-Freeman's (1983) 10 circumstances under which a definite article may have specific reference for the speaker and the hearer alike, and Leech and Svartvik's (1975) communicative functions of the definite article, the semantic functions of the definite article *the* were classified into the categories of Earlier Mention, as in *Tom bought a TV and a radio, but he returned the radio*; Postmodification, as in *The wines of France are the best in the world*; Unique Object, as in *The sun is red*; Specified Order, as in *Look at the last sentence*; Given Setting, as in *I wrote some words on the blackboard*; and Generic, as in *The tiger is in danger of becoming extinct*.

As for the indefinite articles *a* and *an*, their semantic functions were classified into two major categories, respectively called Individual, as in *I got a new car*, and Generic, as in *A tiger is a beautiful animal*.

According to Hewson (1972, p. 120), an examination of zero article usage in English revealed that there are two main types of the zero article. In Christophersen's or Jespersen's terms, one is called parti-generic, which refers to an indefinite amount of the genus, as seen in the examples *we are going to have ∅ tea soon, there is still ∅ frost in the ground*, and *they ate ∅ ices*. The other is called toto-generic, which refers to the whole genus occurring everywhere and at all times, as in the examples *∅ time is ∅ money, ∅ lead is heavier than ∅ iron*, and *∅ thoughts are sometimes difficult to put into ∅ words*. This frame for the classification of the zero article was used in indexing the semantic functions carried by the zero article in the present study.

4. *The accuracy as well as the usage of English articles*

In regard to the acquisition of a linguistic item, there are two different theoretical positions existing in the field of SLA. One position holds that acquisition can only be measured in terms of accuracy, say 85 or 90% of the accurate use of the target linguistic item in performance data. The percentage is arbitrary since there is no consensus on a fixed percentage. The arbitrary percentage indicates, however, the target linguistic item is acquired when it is used accurately 85 to 95% of the time. The other position holds that learners' IL should be described in its own right and the emphasis should be put on the acquisition process rather than on the final product. As a result of this second position, acquisition can be regarded as the first appearance of a specific linguistic item.

As pointed out by R. Ellis (1994), each of these two positions has its own weakness. While the first position fails to treat learners' IL as an independent and dynamic system, the second position fails to acknowledge the fact that the target linguistic accuracy is the ultimate goal of language acquisition. To avoid these weaknesses, the position held here is a compromise between these two theoretical positions. Acquisition has been understood in this study as a continuum ranging from the first appearance of a specific linguistic item to the accurate use of that item shown in the informant's performance data. In order to reflect this middle-ground position, this study investigated the acquisition of articles in terms of correctness or approximation to the target as well as in terms of the learner's usage without regard to accuracy or the target. The information related to accuracy in the use of English articles can be shown in such nodes as Correct and Overuse. In other words, the following questions were asked concerning the informant's use of articles: Is the use of the article correct? Is the article overused? If overused, what type of overuse occurs? In what kind of context or linguistic environment is it located? Regarding the learner usage, the coding scheme ensured that all uses of articles by the learner could be easily retrieved for further analysis.

This coding frame, on the whole, provided a convenient tool to describe the informant's use, correct use, and misuse of the English articles in various noun phrase environments.

In the quantitative examination stage, the indexed data were first exported into the software program of SPSS version 7.5. The statistical trend related to the following three types of information regarding the informant's use of English articles was then calculated. The first type of information targeted the description and analysis of the general context for articles. In other words, the general use of noun phrases across the different data sets was the primary focus. Specifically, this included how noun phrases in different categories were used across different data sets, how noun phrases with different grammatical functions were used across different data sets, and how noun phrases with different internal structures were used across different data sets. The second type of information dealt with the informant's accuracy in using articles. Brown's (1973) scheme, Pica's (1985) scheme, and a revised scheme designed by the researcher were all employed to examine the acquisition sequences of articles. To obtain results from different angles, the correct use and the incorrect use of English articles in specific NP environments across different data sets were further analyzed. Specifically, this included the statistical calculation of the following: correct use of *the* with different types of NP across different data sets; correct use of *a/n* with different types of NP across different data sets; correct use of *zero article* with different types of NP across different data sets; correct use of *the* with NP Function across different data sets; correct use of *a/n* with NP Function across different data sets; correct use of *zero article* with NP Function across different data sets; incorrect use of *the* with different types of NP across different data sets; incorrect use of *a/n* with different types of NP across different data sets; incorrect use of *zero article* with different types of NP across different data sets; incorrect use of *the* with NP Function across different data sets; incorrect use of *a/n* with NP Function across different data sets; incorrect use of *zero article* with NP Function across different data sets; semantic function of *the* across different data sets; semantic function of *a/n* across different data sets; and semantic function of *zero article* across different data sets. The third type of information was about the learner's usage of articles. Included in this type of information were the correlation between articles and article-related determiners, between articles and other types of determiners, between articles and noun phrases, and usage patterns related to different types of articles.

In the third stage of the analysis, various findings were examined against various research questions.

PRINCIPLES FOR DETERMINING THE TOKENS OF ARTICLES

In order to understand the informant's IL article use, every NP phrase, every determiner, and every article were identified and coded. In other words, all NPs were examined as possible environments for articles, all determiners were checked as some form of article companion, and all articles were scrutinized. Each occurrence of NPs or determiners was counted as one token of a NP or determiner except in the case of repetition. However, this was not always the case with articles. The scrutinizing of every article did not mean that every article occurring in the data was counted as a token. The following were some guiding principles used for determining whether an article was counted as a token in this study:

1. ***Repetition was not counted***

As reflected in the data, an article was sometimes repeated without any intervening material, for example,

> *the-the-the* second teacher [D4]

> Like read *a-a* story and answer the question. [D1]

In such cases, only one token of *the* or *a* was counted.

2. *If several articles were used together, only the last one was counted*

In the case of combined use of different articles, only the last one was counted as a token while the previous one was not counted. In instances such as the following

> …he did some-something in *the a-a* can. [D3]

> Remember *the a* fat man? [D3]

a was counted as a token while the underlined *the* was not counted. This principle was actually suggested by the informant, who made it clear to the researcher that what came last was the article he really wanted to use. In other words, the combined occurrence of different articles reflected his attempt to choose what he considered the correct article in the specific linguistic context.

3. *Idiomatic use of a was not counted*

A little bit and *a lot of* were two idiomatic expressions frequently used by the informant, as shown in the following two examples:

> There just *a little bit* 4th grade. [D1]

> I borrow *a lot of* movies. [D8]

In such cases, *a* was not counted as a token of the indefinite article *a* in the present study. Instead, *a little bit* and *a lot of* were treated as instances of Quantifier in the present coding scheme.

4. *If used as a hesitation sound, the or a was not counted*

When *a* and *the* were used as meaningless hesitation sounds, they were not counted as the use of articles. This was the case with the following two examples

> *Give a um someone um excuse.* [D7]

> *Copy from the like a paper.* [D7]

in which the underlined *a* and *the* were not counted as tokens of articles. The differentiation between articles as hesitation sounds and articles in their real sense was indeed one of the advantages to having the informant proofread the transcript and reflect on his own speech.

5. *The environment for the zero article was carefully delimited*

How can the zero article be counted? How can a distinction between the use of the zero article and non-use of any article be made? These were two of the toughest questions the present study had to answer. Unfortunately, little help could be obtained in this regard from the review of the previous L2 research on the use or acquisition of English articles. The main problem with a good deal of previous research was that the use of the zero article was, more often than not, either regarded as a synonym for non-use of any article or simply excluded from the study. This tendency to blend the zero article and the absence of articles is clearly revealed in the following statements and illustrations aimed at defining the zero article

a) "a $\emptyset$ article is used when such differentiation [of one referent from other referents] is not required for the hearer to successfully understand the message being communicated" (Gorokhova, 1990, p. 89).

b) $\emptyset_1$, the absence of an article or other determiner in English in those contexts where Spanish requires a definite article; and $\emptyset_2$, the absence of an article or other determiner in English in those contexts where there is also no article or other determiner in Spanish (Andersen, 1977, p. 50).

c) The zero article is "the null article, or absence of an article, represented by the symbol $\emptyset$…Like the indefinite article *a* (or *an*), the zero article is a convention needed to make generic statements" (Odlin, 1994, p. 332).

To illustrate, Gorokhova (p. 90) used the examples of *He went to $\emptyset$ bed early* (went to sleep on whatever bed), *He went $\emptyset$ home* (his home), *$\emptyset$ Einstein died in $\emptyset$ Princeton* (only one possible referent), and *$\emptyset$ Water boils at 212°F* (any and all water); while Andersen (p. 51) presented *Then she goes to $\emptyset$ school, $\emptyset$ Saturday I cleaned my house, What do you think* *about* $\varnothing$ *politics?* as instances of $\varnothing_1$ and *He is giving $\varnothing$ food to the animals* as an example of $\varnothing_2$.

As shown in these examples, there is no difference between the zero article and the absence of an article or non-use of any article. In this line of reasoning, the zero article occurs before an abstract noun, a proper noun, a common noun in the set phrase, and even an adverb derived from a noun.

In an attempt to make a distinction between the zero article and non-use of any article, the present study followed Chalker's (1995) definition and treated the zero article as a form of article occurring only "before an uncountable noun or a plural countable noun when either is used with an indefinite meaning. Thus $\varnothing$ alternates with *a/an* (used before a singular count noun) in a paradigmatic relationship, e.g. $\varnothing$ *food*, $\varnothing$ *vegetables*, *a cauliflower*" (p. 262). In concord with this definition, uncountable noun phrases and plural countable noun phrases were recognized as two environments for the possible occurrence of the zero article. If Gorokhova's and Andersen's examples were still used, only the following three could be chosen as the tokens of the zero article: $\varnothing$ *Water boils at 212°F*; *What do you think about $\varnothing$ politics?*; and *He is giving $\varnothing$ food to the animals*. Other examples appearing in the aforementioned illustration were simply considered as instances of non-use of any article in this study.

Apart from these two environments, a third environment for the zero article was stipulated as follows: if *the*, *a*, or *an* does not appear in the obligatory context, a token of the overuse of the zero article will be counted. In other words, the failure to use *the*, *a*, or *an* in the obligatory context was considered as the overuse of the zero article to *the*, *a*, or *an* in this study. The rationale behind this principle was that overuse is a general feature of the learner's IL (R. Ellis, 1994; Huebner, 1983; Master, 1987) and the only way to capture the overuse of the zero article is the location where its variants or other forms of articles are required. Using Thomas's (1989a) words, "perhaps more realistically... 'overgeneralization of $\varnothing$'" should be regarded as the equivalent of "failure to use any article" (p. 349).

In addition to these principles for determining the tokens of articles mentioned previously, attention was also paid to putting each noun or determiner into the appropriate category where it belonged. For instance, a difference for the word *one* was recognized and identified among the following three examples: *one o'clock, one person, one of my friends*. The *one* in *one o'clock* was coded as Quantifier, the *one* in *one person* was coded as Article-related Determiner, while the *one* in *one of my friends* was coded as Other Pronoun.

CODING RELIABILITY FOR ARTICLE TOKENS

When the researcher finished coding articles in the transcription, two educated, native speakers of English were consulted regarding the appropriateness of the coding. The purpose of bringing in two native speakers of English was, on one hand, that the researcher himself was not a native speaker of English, hence his judgment about the informant's correct or incorrect use of articles, and about what article should be used in certain occasions might not be accurate. On the other hand, this was, as Guy (1993) suggested, to apply "a check on the tightness of the definitions and the possible bias or inattentiveness" of the researcher (p. 227).

Reliability testing demonstrated a rate of inter-rater reliability at 83%. In cases where there was a difference in view between two consultants, a third native speaker of English was consulted.

CHAPTER 4

RESULTS AND DISCUSSION

INTRODUCTION

The analyses that follow were based on approximately 10 hours of speech data collected during the 13-month period mentioned earlier, resulting in a 154-page (single-spaced) corpus of transcriptions, and encompassing 7,602 tokens of noun phrases, 817 tokens of the definite article *the*, 408 tokens of the indefinite article *a*, 2 tokens of the indefinite article *an*, 376 tokens of the zero article, 1,136 tokens of other determiners, and 81 index markers within five coding categories. The data were subjected to three separate but related analyses. The first analysis investigated the general use of noun phrases in terms of their syntactic categories, functions, and structures across different data sets. The second analysis specified the acquisition sequences of the English articles as well as the syntactic locations associated with the correct and the incorrect use of the English articles by using the accuracy criterion. The third analysis presented the article usage in relation to other determiners and noun phrases as well as the usage patterns associated with different types of articles. It should be pointed out that the percentage figures in the tables presented in this chapter were naturally rounded to the first decimal point, due to space limitations. The rounding explains why the figures of 100.0 in the "total" rows do not always agree completely with the individual entries.

GENERAL USE OF NOUN PHRASES

In this section, tables display the analysis of the general use of noun phrases across different data sets in terms of their grammatical categories, grammatical functions, and internal structures. The purpose of this analysis was to present the linguistic contexts in which articles were used by the informant.

Noun Phrase Types

As described in chapter 3, all the noun phrases in the present data corpus were classified into the categories of Proper Noun Phrase, Pronoun Phrase and Common Noun Phrase. Pronoun Phrase was further classified into Personal Pronoun Phrase and Other Pronoun Phrase. Common Noun Phrase was further classified into Uncountable Noun Phrase and Countable Noun Phrase, which was subdivided into Singular Countable Noun Phrase and Plural Countable Noun Phrase. Table 10 and table 11 report the distribution of different types of noun phrases across different data sets. In the tables, Proper stands for "Proper Noun Phrase," Uncoun for "Uncountable Noun Phrase," Propers for "Personal Pronoun Phrase," Proothe for "Other Pronoun Phrase," Singula for "Singular Countable Noun Phrase," and Plural for "Plural Countable Noun Phrase."

As shown in tables 10 and 11, a general tendency of the ranking order based on either the absolute frequency or the relative frequency can be diagrammed as follows: Personal Pronoun Phrase > Singular Countable Noun Phrase > Other Pronoun Phrase > Proper Noun Phrase > Uncountable Noun Phrase > Plural Countable Noun Phrase. The first three types of noun phrases, namely Personal Pronoun Phrase, Singular Countable Noun Phrase, and Other Pronoun Phrase were remarkably consistent in maintaining the ranking order as the most frequently used, the second most

TABLE 10. NP types across different data sets.

	Data 1	Data 2	Data 3	Data 4	Data 5	Data 6	Data 7	Data 8	Data 9	Data 10	Data 11	Data 12	Data 13	Total
Proper	43	69	32	26	78	24	58	55	51	59	33	89	73	690
Uncoun	11	50	62	52	31	21	30	34	21	34	60	33	57	496
Propers	113	327	222	283	206	149	190	193	192	158	264	373	280	2950
Proothe	33	97	77	126	115	72	63	52	64	63	103	88	99	1052
Singula	90	216	185	155	154	156	136	119	127	94	168	245	110	1955
Plural	19	43	37	39	48	19	29	27	16	32	52	49	49	459
Total	309	802	615	681	632	441	506	480	471	440	680	877	668	7602

TABLE 11. Relative frequency of NP types across different data sets.

	Data 1	Data 2	Data 3	Data 4	Data 5	Data 6	Data 7	Data 8	Data 9	Data 10	Data 11	Data 12	Data 13	Total
Proper	13.9	8.6	5.2	3.8	12.3	5.4	11.5	11.5	10.8	13.4	4.9	10.1	10.9	9.1
Uncoun	3.6	6.2	10.1	7.6	4.9	4.8	5.9	7.1	4.5	7.7	8.8	3.8	8.5	6.5
Propers	36.6	40.8	36.1	41.6	32.6	33.8	37.5	40.2	40.8	35.9	38.8	42.5	41.9	38.8
Proothe	10.7	12.1	12.5	18.5	18.2	16.3	12.5	10.8	13.6	14.3	15.1	10.0	14.8	13.8
Singula	29.1	26.9	30.1	22.8	24.4	35.4	26.9	24.8	27.0	21.4	24.7	27.9	16.5	25.7
Plural	6.1	5.4	6.0	5.7	7.6	4.3	5.7	5.6	3.4	7.3	7.6	5.6	7.3	6.0
Total	100.0	100.0	100.0	100.0	100.0	100.0	100.0	100.0	100.0	100.0	100.0	100.0	100.0	100.0

frequently used, and the third most frequently used across every data set except in data 1, where Proper Noun Phrase appeared more frequent than Other Pronoun Phrase. The tendency of the heavy use of Pronoun Phrase and Countable Noun Phrase can be more clearly revealed if the categories of Personal Pronoun Phrase and Other Pronoun Phrase are lumped together into one category of Pronoun Phrase, and the categories of Singular Countable Noun Phrase and Plural Countable Noun Phrase into one category of Countable Noun Phrase, as shown in the following table

TABLE 12. Relative frequency of major NP types across different data sets.

	Data 1	Data 2	Data 3	Data 4	Data 5	Data 6	Data 7
Proper	13.9	8.6	5.2	3.8	12.3	5.4	11.5
Uncoun	3.6	6.2	10.1	7.6	4.9	4.8	5.9
Pron	47.2	52.9	48.6	60.1	50.8	50.1	50.0
Coun	35.3	32.3	36.1	28.5	32.0	39.7	32.6
Total	100.0	100.0	100.0	100.0	100.0	100.0	100.0

where the percentage of Pronoun Phrase used is 52.6 while that for Countable Noun Phrase is 31.8 among the total number of noun phrases. The consistently heavy use of Pronoun Phrase can at least significantly indicate:

1. the informant's interlanguage (IL) discourse at this stage was characterized by the frequent use of identified personal referents apart from two other general characteristics described by Larsen-Freeman and Long (1991) as "more oriented to the 'here and now'" (p. 122).
2. it might have been a strategy for the informant to avoid the use of articles or determiners. In other words, whenever possible, pronouns were used instead of articles or other determiners.
3. at least half of the noun phrases at this stage of the informant's IL did not require the use of any article or other determiner.

Noun Phrase Functions

Generally speaking, noun phrases can function syntactically as Subject, Direct Object, Indirect Object, Prepositional Complement, Subject Complement, Object Complement, Existential Complement, Adverbial, Conjunct, Premodifier, Postmodifier, Apposition, Absolute, Exclamation, and Vocative. Table 13 and table 14 display the distribution of noun phrases with different syntactic functions across different data sets. The abbreviations used in the tables can be explained as follows: S = Subject,

Data 8	Data 9	Data 10	Data 11	Data 12	Data 13	Total
11.5	10.8	13.4	4.9	10.1	10.9	9.1
7.1	4.5	7.7	8.8	3.8	8.5	6.5
51.0	54.4	50.2	54.0	52.6	56.7	52.6
30.4	30.4	28.6	32.4	33.5	23.8	31.8
100.0	100.0	100.0	100.0	100.0	100.0	100.0

DO =Direct Object, IO = Indirect Object, PC = Prepositional Complement, SC = Subject Complement, OC = Object Complement, EC = Existential Complement, ADV = Adverbial, CONJ = Conjunct, PREM = Premodifier, POSM = Postmodifier, APPO = Apposition, ABS = Absolute, EXEL = Exclamation, and VOC = Vocative.

Table 13 and table 14 reveal the following findings:

1. The three most frequently used functions in the data are almost consistently in the ranking order of Subject, Direct Object, and Preposition Complement across different data sets.
2. Such functions as Object Complement, Premodifier, Postmodifier, Apposition, Exclamation, and Vocative do not appear in data 1. This might suggest that these functions were acquired by the informant at a later stage compared with other functions.

TABLE **13**. NP functions across different data sets.

	Data 1	Data 2	Data 3	Data 4	Data 5	Data 6	Data 7	Data 8	Data 9	Data 10	Data 11	Data 12	Data 13	Total
S	132	345	240	319	260	183	207	207	226	201	357	404	291	3372
DO	54	172	136	159	95	72	99	95	72	59	103	157	114	1387
IO	3	8	7	7	3	0	2	0	2	4	0	6	2	44
PC	56	127	85	94	86	51	63	78	74	57	83	131	96	1081
SC	21	27	34	45	67	31	39	16	34	38	56	55	32	495
OC	0	1	3	0	0	0	0	0	0	1	3	1	4	13
EC	24	16	27	9	10	6	4	4	6	15	12	3	7	143
ADV	5	8	14	12	12	18	9	6	15	6	12	18	19	154
CONJ	8	18	22	11	25	33	25	18	12	15	14	34	37	272
PREM	0	20	16	5	11	7	22	17	7	5	4	17	22	153
POSM	0	0	0	0	0	0	0	0	0	0	0	0	0	0
APPO	0	24	10	5	17	7	5	8	9	5	12	15	9	126
ABS	6	35	21	15	46	28	29	31	14	33	23	32	35	348
EXEL	0	0	0	0	0	5	2	0	0	0	0	1	0	8
VOC	0	1	0	0	0	0	0	0	0	1	1	3	0	6
Total	309	802	615	681	632	441	506	480	471	440	680	877	668	7602

TABLE 14. Relative frequency of NP functions across different data sets.

	Data 1	Data 2	Data 3	Data 4	Data 5	Data 6	Data 7	Data 8	Data 9	Data 10	Data 11	Data 12	Data 13	Total
S	42.7	43.0	39.0	46.8	41.1	41.5	40.9	43.1	48.0	45.7	52.5	46.1	43.6	44.4
DO	17.5	21.4	22.1	23.3	15.0	16.3	19.6	19.8	15.3	13.4	15.1	17.9	17.1	18.2
IO	1.0	1.0	1.1	1.0	0.5	0.0	0.4	0.0	0.4	0.9	0.0	0.7	0.3	0.6
PC	18.1	15.8	13.8	13.8	13.6	11.6	12.5	16.3	15.7	13.0	12.2	14.9	14.4	14.2
SC	6.8	3.4	5.5	6.6	10.6	7.0	7.7	3.3	7.2	8.6	8.2	6.3	4.8	6.5
OC	0.0	0.1	0.5	0.0	0.0	0.0	0.0	0.0	0.0	0.2	0.4	0.1	0.6	0.2
EC	7.8	2.0	4.4	1.3	1.6	1.4	0.8	0.8	1.3	3.4	1.8	0.3	1.0	1.9
ADV	1.6	1.0	2.3	1.8	1.9	4.1	1.8	1.3	3.2	1.4	1.8	2.1	2.8	2.0
CONJ	2.6	2.2	3.6	1.6	4.0	7.5	4.9	3.8	2.5	3.4	2.1	3.9	5.5	3.6
PREM	0.0	2.5	2.6	0.7	1.7	1.6	4.3	3.5	1.5	1.1	0.6	1.9	3.3	2.0
POSM	0.0	0.0	0.0	0.0	0.0	0.0	0.0	0.0	0.0	0.0	0.0	0.0	0.0	0.0
APPO	0.0	3.0	1.6	0.7	2.7	1.6	1.0	1.7	1.9	1.1	1.8	1.7	1.3	1.7
ABS	1.9	4.4	3.4	2.2	7.3	6.3	5.7	6.5	3.0	7.5	3.4	3.6	5.2	4.6
EXEL	0.0	0.0	0.0	0.0	0.0	1.1	0.4	0.0	0.0	0.0	0.0	0.1	0.0	0.1
VOC	0.0	0.1	0.0	0.0	0.0	0.0	0.0	0.0	0.0	0.2	0.1	0.3	0.0	0.1
Total	100.0	100.0	100.0	100.0	100.0	100.0	100.0	100.0	100.0	100.0	100.0	100.0	100.0	100.0

3. Among different types of object functions, Direct Object was more frequently used than Indirect Object. Among different types of complement functions, the ranking order based on frequency can be stated as Prepositional Complement > Subject Complement > Existential Complement > Object Complement. Among modification functions, Premodifier appeared earlier and was used more frequently than Postmodifier.

Noun Phrase Structures

Based on the internal structure, noun phrases in the present data were classified into five categories, namely Head, Determiner(s) + Head, (Determiner(s)) + Premodifier + Head, (Determiner(s)) + Head + Postmodifier, and (Determiner(s)) + Premodifier + Head + Postmodifier. Table 15 and table 16 report the distribution of noun phrases with different internal structures across different data sets.

Table 15 and table 16 demonstrate that the ranking of noun phrases with different structures by frequency was constantly ordered from simple noun phrases to complex noun phrases except in data 15 where the fourth type was used slightly more often than the third type. This finding suggests that the simpler the noun phrase was in its structure, the more frequently it was used, while in contrast, the more complex the noun phrase was in its structure, the less frequently it was used by the informant during the 13-month investigation. This tendency can be more clearly revealed if the first two types of noun phrases are lumped into the category of Simple Noun Phrase and the latter three types into the category of Complex Noun Phrase as shown in the following table, where "Simp" stands for Simple Noun Phrase and "Comp" for Complex Noun Phrase.

Table 17 clearly indicates that the informant used Simple Noun Phrases much more often than Complex Noun Phrases. While the former occupies a percentage of 89.4 among the total number of 7,602 noun phrases, the latter occupies a percentage of only 10.8. The statistical figures in the table, however, show no indication of a linear progression of the increased use of Complex Noun Phrase or the decreased use of Simple Noun Phrase across different data sets. This finding was quite contrary to

TABLE 15. NP structures across different data sets.

	Data 1	Data 2	Data 3	Data 4	Data 5	Data 6	Data 7	Data 8	Data 9	Data 10	Data 11	Data 12	Data13	Total
Head	176	470	354	448	383	285	306	307	291	281	407	561	450	4719
DH	92	234	208	201	194	121	126	127	120	108	202	204	139	2076
(D)MH	18	59	46	28	40	24	60	34	32	29	38	82	36	526
(D)HP	23	36	7	4	14	10	11	11	27	20	29	26	39	257
(D)MHP	0	3	0	0	1	1	3	1	1	2	4	4	4	24
Total	309	802	615	681	632	441	506	480	471	440	680	877	668	7602

TABLE 16. Relative frequency of NP structures across different data sets.

	Data 1	Data 2	Data 3	Data 4	Data 5	Data 6	Data 7	Data 8	Data 9	Data10	Data 11	Data 12	Data 13	Total
Head	57.0	58.6	57.6	65.8	60.6	64.6	60.5	64.0	61.8	63.9	59.9	64.0	67.4	62.1
DH	29.8	29.2	33.8	29.5	30.7	27.4	24.9	26.5	25.5	24.5	29.7	23.3	20.8	27.3
(D)MH	5.8	7.4	7.5	4.1	6.3	5.4	11.9	7.1	6.8	6.6	5.6	9.4	5.4	6.9
(D)HP	7.4	4.5	1.1	0.6	2.2	2.3	2.2	2.3	5.7	4.5	4.3	3.0	5.8	3.4
(D)MHP	0.0	0.4	0.0	0.0	0.2	0.2	0.6	0.2	0.2	0.5	0.6	0.5	0.6	0.3
Total	100.0	100.0	100.0	100.0	100.0	100.0	100.0	100.0	100.0	100.0	100.0	100.0	100.0	100.0

TABLE 17. Relative frequency of simple NP and complex NP across different data sets.

	Data 1	Data 2	Data 3	Data 4	Data 5	Data 6	Data 7	Data 8	Data 9	Data10	Data 11	Data 12	Data 13	Total
Simp	86.7	87.8	91.4	95.3	91.3	92.1	85.4	90.4	87.3	88.4	89.6	87.2	88.2	89.4
Comp	13.3	12.2	8.6	4.7	8.7	7.9	14.6	9.6	12.7	11.6	10.4	12.8	11.8	10.6
Total	100.0	100.0	100.0	100.0	100.0	100.0	100.0	100.0	100.0	100.0	100.0	100.0	100.0	100.0

TABLE 18. Frequency of correct and incorrect use of articles across different data sets.

	Data 1	Data 2	Data 3	Data 4	Data 5	Data 6	Data 7	Data 8	Data 9	Data 10	Data 11	Data 12	Data 13	Total
C the	26	83	39	44	52	69	43	31	59	37	99	104	52	738
I the	3	28	13	2	6	6	1	1	3	6	4	4	2	79
Total	29	111	52	46	58	75	44	32	62	43	103	108	54	817
C a	14	41	40	41	36	14	31	27	34	16	25	41	27	387
I a	1	1	4	3	1	1	0	4	1	2	3	0	0	21
Total	15	42	44	44	37	15	31	31	35	18	28	41	27	408
C an	0	0	0	0	0	0	0	0	0	0	0	2	0	2
I an	0	0	0	0	0	0	0	0	0	0	0	0	0	0
Total	0	0	0	0	0	0	0	0	0	0	0	2	0	2
C Ø	6	15	16	20	12	6	7	22	6	21	30	16	44	221
I Ø	12	22	11	8	12	9	13	12	15	14	7	12	8	155
Total	18	37	27	28	24	15	20	34	21	35	37	28	52	376

the expectation of the researcher, who assumed that more complex NPs would be used with the increased language proficiency level on the part of the informant.

ACQUISITION OF ARTICLES IN TERMS OF THE ACCURACY CRITERION

In this section, various tables display the analysis of the data from the perspective of the accuracy paradigm with the purpose of showing how the informant's use of articles approximated the standard use of articles on the part of native speakers. This section is divided into four parts: acquisition sequences of articles; article accuracy by syntactic categories and functions; article error by syntactic categories and functions; and semantic functions of articles.

Acquisition Sequences of Articles

This part of the section presents the informant's acquisition sequences of English articles from three perspectives in the accuracy paradigm, namely, Brown's scheme, Pica's scheme and a revised scheme designed by the researcher. However, before the analysis using these three schemes is presented, the distribution of correct use and incorrect use of articles as well as the relative frequency of correct use across different data sets are described.

Correct and Incorrect Use of Different Types of Articles

Table 18 reports the distribution of correct and incorrect use of different articles across different data sets. In the table, the capital letter "C" stands for correct use while the capital letter "I" represents incorrect use.

As shown in the table, the ranking by the absolute frequency is generally in the order of *the*, *a*, *zero article*, and *an*. While there was no instance of incorrect use found with *an*, the zero article, in contrast, appeared to be more frequently used incorrectly, compared with other types of articles. By dividing the number of correct uses by the total number of occurrences of each article, the percentage of correct use could be calculated, as shown in the following table.

TABLE 19. Percentage of correct use of articles across different data sets.

	Data 1	Data 2	Data 3	Data 4	Data 5	Data 6
the	89.7	74.8	75.0	95.7	89.7	92.0
a	93.3	97.6	90.9	93.2	97.3	93.3
an	0	0	0	0	0	0
Ø	33.3	40.5	59.3	71.4	50.0	40.0
Total	74.2	73.2	77.3	89.0	84.0	84.8

Table 19 indicates the following findings:

1. the indefinite article *an* was rarely used by the informant. However, when used, it was used correctly. In other words, it was never used incorrectly in the present data.
2. 100% of correct use also appeared with the indefinite article *a*, as demonstrated in data 7, data 12, and data 13. Yet, this is not the case with the definite article and the zero article. While the highest percentage of correctness for the former was 97.7, the highest percentage of correctness for the latter was only 84.6.
3. while there was no clear progression pattern shown for each individual article since a U-shaped pattern is normally presented, the "total" row, in contrast, reflected a clear pattern of progression, starting from over 70% (data sets 1–3), to over 80% (data sets 4–9), and to over 90% (data sets 11–13), with the only exception being the figure in data 10, which fell into the range of over 70%. This finding indicates that the informant used articles more correctly as language proficiency level and total exposure to English increased.

Acquisition Sequence: Brown's Scheme
Accuracy in this section was based on the standard notion of supplied in obligatory context (SOC). According to Brown (1973), SOC indicates

Data 7	Data 8	Data 9	Data 10	Data 11	Data 12	Data 13
97.7	96.9	95.2	86.1	96.1	96.3	96.3
100.0	87.1	97.1	88.9	89.3	100.0	100.0
0	0	0	0	0	100.0	0
35.0	64.7	28.6	60.0	81.2	57.1	84.6
85.3	82.5	83.9	77.1	91.7	91.1	92.5

the number of correct items divided by the number of environments of obligatory contexts in which the article should be used, and then multiplied by 100. The number of environments of obligatory contexts and the number of correct items in the present data are presented in table 20, where "NOC" stands for number of obligatory contexts while "NCU" is an abbreviation for number of correct uses of the article.

Using the figures in table 20, the SOC for each type of article across different data sets could be calculated by using Brown's formula, as described previously. The results are reported in table 21.

As shown in table 21, the informant had already acquired the zero article and the indefinite article *a*, since they both appear to be supplied in over 90% of obligatory contexts for three consecutive recordings or three consecutive data sets. The informant, in contrast, had not acquired the definite article *the* and the indefinite article *an*, as they both failed to reach the standard of occurring in over 90% of obligatory contexts for three consecutive recordings. The percentage figures for *the*, however, appeared much higher than those for *an*, which never went over 50% across different data sets. Hence, the acquisition sequence of articles for the present informant, according to Brown's scheme, can be specified as follows: *zero article → a → the → an*.

Acquisition Sequence: Pica's Scheme
It should be noted that one problem with Brown's scheme is its failure to account for the overuse of articles in non-obligatory contexts.

TABLE 20. Number of obligatory contexts and correct use for articles across different data sets.

	Data 1	Data 2	Data 3	Data 4	Data 5	Data 6	Data 7	Data 8	Data 9	Data 10	Data 11	Data 12	Data 13
NOC *the*	34	99	49	47	62	75	54	43	70	49	104	110	60
NCU *the*	26	83	39	44	52	69	43	31	59	37	99	102	52
NOC *a*	18	54	45	45	40	18	32	27	39	19	27	44	27
NCU *a*	14	41	40	41	36	14	31	27	34	16	25	41	27
NOC *an*	1	0	2	4	0	1	1	4	1	2	4	4	0
NCU *an*	0	0	0	0	0	0	0	0	0	0	0	2	0
NOC ∅	6	17	17	21	12	7	7	22	6	22	30	16	45
NCU ∅	6	15	16	20	12	6	7	22	6	21	30	16	44

TABLE 21. SOC for different types of articles across different data sets.

	Data 1	Data 2	Data 3	Data 4	Data 5	Data 6	Data 7	Data 8	Data 9	Data 10	Data 11	Data 12	Data 13
the	76.5	83.8	79.6	93.6	83.9	92.0	79.6	72.1	84.3	75.5	95.2	92.7	86.7
a	77.8	75.9	88.9	91.1	90.0	77.8	96.9	100.0	87.2	84.2	92.6	93.2	100.0
an	0	0	0	0	0	0	0	0	0	0	0	50.0	0
∅	100.0	88.2	94.1	95.2	100.0	85.7	100.0	100.0	100.0	95.5	100.0	100.0	97.8

For instance, in the following examples, *the* is not counted in Brown's scheme:

> *We can play that ball in the some place.* [D3]
>
> *Then we play the that game.* [D3]

As a remedy to this problem, Pica (1985) suggested a method for target-like use (TLU) analysis, which can be stated in a formula as follows:

$$TLU = \frac{\text{n correct suppliance in obligatory contexts}}{\text{(n obligatory contexts + n suppliance in non-obligatory contexts)}} \times 100$$

By using this formula, it was possible to describe the acquisition sequence of articles for the present informant from another perspective. The raw data are reported in table 22, where "NSN" stands for the number of suppliance in non-obligatory contexts.

Using the figures in table 22, the TLU for each article across different data sets could be calculated by using Pica's formula. The results are reported in table 23.

As shown in table 23, no article was used correctly over 90% of the time for three consecutive data sets. The indefinite article *a* is the only one that was used correctly over 90% of the time for two consecutive data sets. Figures in individual data sets show, however, that *a* reached 96.9% in data 7 while *the* reached 91.7% in data 11. In contrast, both *an* and ∅ never occurred correctly over 90% in any single data set. Compared with *an*, the zero article had a much higher percentage, showing over 80% in two data sets. As indicated by these findings, an acquisition sequence of English articles based on Pica's scheme might be specified as follows: *a → the → zero article → an*.

Acquisition Sequence: Revised Scheme

In both Brown's scheme and Pica's scheme, the count of obligatory occasions does not include those occasions where *this-that*, *these-those*, *one*, and *some* are used. However, as described in modern linguistic theories,

TABLE 22. Number of obligatory contexts, correct use, and overuse in non-obligatory contexts for articles across different data sets.

	Data 1	Data 2	Data 3	Data 4	Data 5	Data 6	Data 7	Data 8	Data 9	Data 10	Data 11	Data 12	Data 13
NOC the	34	99	49	47	62	75	54	43	70	49	104	110	60
NCU the	26	83	39	44	52	69	43	31	59	37	99	102	52
NSN the	3	28	13	2	6	6	1	1	3	6	4	4	2
NOC a	18	54	45	45	40	18	32	27	39	19	27	44	27
NCU a	14	41	40	41	36	14	31	27	34	16	25	41	27
NSN a	1	1	4	3	1	1	0	4	1	2	3	0	0
NOC an	1	0	2	4	0	1	1	4	1	2	4	4	0
NCU an	0	0	0	0	0	0	0	0	0	0	0	2	0
NSN an	0	0	0	0	0	0	0	0	0	0	0	0	0
NOC ∅	6	17	17	21	12	7	7	22	6	22	30	16	45
NCU ∅	6	15	16	20	12	6	7	22	6	21	30	16	44
NSN ∅	12	22	11	8	12	9	13	12	15	14	7	12	8

TABLE 23. TLU for different types of articles across different data sets.

	Data 1	Data 2	Data 3	Data 4	Data 5	Data 6	Data 7	Data 8	Data 9	Data 10	Data 11	Data 12	Data 13
the	70.3	65.4	62.9	89.8	76.5	85.2	78.2	70.5	80.8	67.3	91.7	89.5	83.9
a	73.7	74.5	81.6	85.4	87.8	73.7	96.9	87.1	85.0	76.2	83.3	93.2	100.0
an	0	0	0	0	0	0	0	0	0	0	0	50.0	0
∅	33.3	38.5	57.1	69.0	50.0	37.5	35.0	64.7	28.6	58.3	81.1	57.1	83.0

this/that and *these/those* are historically linked to *the* (J. Lyons, 1975, 1977), *some* and the zero article can be used interchangeably in certain contexts (Leech & Svartvik, 1975; Quirk et al., 1985), and "*one* may be regarded as a stressed form of the indefinite article" (p. 65). For this reason, some researchers (Parrish, 1987; Lee et al., 1995) suggested the inclusion of these determiners into the count of obligatory occasions. Based on these linguistic theories as well as on Brown's scheme and Pica's scheme, a revised scheme for target-like article usage (TLAU) was designed as follows: articles are first scored for correct use in obligatory contexts. The score obtained then becomes the numerator of a ratio which includes in its denominator the sum of the number of obligatory contexts for suppliance of the article, the number of non-obligatory contexts in which the article is supplied inappropriately or incorrectly, and the number of *this* (including *that*, *these*, and *those*) or *one* or *some*. These can be described in formulas in the following ways:

$$\text{TLAU }(the) = \frac{\text{n correct suppliance in obligatory contexts}}{(\text{n obligatory contexts} + \text{n suppliance in non-obligatory contexts} + \text{n }this)} \times 100$$

$$\text{TLAU }(a/n) = \frac{\text{n correct suppliance in obligatory contexts}}{(\text{n obligatory contexts} + \text{n suppliance in non-obligatory contexts} + \text{n }one)} \times 100$$

$$\text{TLAU }(\emptyset) = \frac{\text{n correct suppliance in obligatory contexts}}{(\text{n obligatory contexts} + \text{n suppliance in non-obligatory contexts} + \text{n }some)} \times 100$$

Table 24 reports the raw data while table 25 shows the results yielded with the use of those formulas.

As shown in table 25, the ranking of TLAU by the highest percentage for different articles was in the order of *a* (90%, data 13), $\emptyset$ (76.9%, data 11), *the* (73.4%, data 12), and *an* (50%, data 12). Although it appears that the informant only partially acquired the use of $\emptyset$, *the*, and *an* since none of them reached the general standard of over 90% in at least one data set, the acquisition sequence based on the ranking of TLAU can be described

TABLE 24. Number of obligatory contexts, correct use, overuse in non-obligatory contexts, and related determiner(s) for articles across different data sets.

	Data 1	Data 2	Data 3	Data 4	Data 5	Data 6	Data 7	Data 8	Data 9	Data 10	Data 11	Data 12	Data 13
NOC *the*	34	99	49	47	62	75	54	43	70	49	104	110	60
NCU *the*	26	83	39	44	52	69	43	31	59	37	99	102	52
NSN *the*	3	28	13	2	6	6	1	1	3	6	4	4	2
this	8	18	27	28	28	17	24	15	16	13	32	25	26
NOC *a*	18	54	45	45	40	18	32	27	39	19	27	44	27
NCU *a*	14	41	40	41	36	14	31	27	34	16	25	41	27
NSN *a*	1	1	4	3	1	1	0	4	1	2	3	0	0
one	1	16	12	6	7	5	3	0	2	2	9	3	3
NOC *an*	1	0	2	4	0	1	1	4	1	2	4	4	0
NCU *an*	0	0	0	0	0	0	0	0	0	0	0	2	0
NSN *an*	0	0	0	0	0	0	0	0	0	0	0	0	0
one	0	0	0	0	0	0	0	0	0	0	0	0	0
NOC Ø	6	17	17	21	12	7	7	22	6	22	30	16	45
NCU Ø	6	15	16	20	12	6	7	22	6	21	30	16	44
NSN Ø	12	22	11	8	12	9	13	12	15	14	7	12	8
some	10	25	25	10	5	0	3	6	0	0	2	3	5

TABLE 25. TLAU for different types of articles across different data sets.

	Data 1	Data 2	Data 3	Data 4	Data 5	Data 6	Data 7	Data 8	Data 9	Data 10	Data 11	Data 12	Data 13
the	57.8	57.2	43.8	57.1	54.2	70.4	54.4	52.5	66.3	54.4	70.7	73.4	59.1
a	70.0	57.7	65.6	75.9	75.0	58.3	88.6	87.1	81.0	69.6	64.1	87.2	90.0
an	0	0	0	0	0	0	0	0	0	0	0	50.0	0
Ø	21.4	23.4	30.2	51.3	41.4	37.5	30.4	55.0	28.6	58.3	76.9	51.6	75.9

or predicted according to this revised scheme as *a* → *zero article* → *the* → *an*.

Article Accuracy by Syntactic Categories and Functions

This part of the section presents the analysis of the syntax associated with the correct use of articles across different data sets. Syntax here means the grammatical categories of noun phrases and the grammatical functions of noun phrases.

Correct Use of the with Different Types of Noun Phrases

Table 26 and table 27 report the occurrence of *the* with different types of noun phrases across different data sets.

As shown in table 27, the correct use of *the* tended to be more frequently related to singular countable NPs, which constantly occupy the largest percentage among various types of noun phrases across different data sets. It can also be seen that there was an increased frequency of the correct *the* with plural countable NPs and uncountable NPs. This is evident in the row of Plural Countable NP, which starts with a percentage of 3.8 in data 1 and progresses to its highest percentage of 13.5 in data 13, and in the row of Uncountable NP, which starts with a percentage of 3.8 in data 1 and progresses to its highest percentage of 25.0 in data 13.

Correct Use of the with NP Functions

Table 28 and table 29 display various syntactic functions of noun phrases linked with the correct use of *the*. In the tables, "Other" is a cover term for those functions besides subject, complement, object and adverbial. These include such NP functions as conjunction, modifier, apposition, absolute, exclamation, and vocative.

As indicated in table 29, *the* was most frequently used with complement noun phrases even though the most frequent function of noun phrases in the whole data corpus was subject, as revealed in the previous section. This finding was constant across different data sets, where *the* with Complement occupied the largest percentage. The percentage figures in the row of Subject show that *the* appeared much lower in the late

TABLE 26. Correct use of *the* across different NP types in 13 data sets.

	Data 1	Data 2	Data 3	Data 4	Data 5	Data 6	Data 7	Data 8	Data 9	Data 10	Data 11	Data 12	Data 13	Total
Proper	2	6	6	0	12	4	1	1	5	2	3	3	3	48
Singular Coun	20	61	22	34	26	51	33	25	36	28	66	84	21	507
Plural Coun	1	5	3	3	4	8	2	0	0	1	12	9	7	55
Uncountable	1	11	4	6	5	2	2	4	8	5	16	5	13	82
Pronoun	2	0	4	1	5	4	5	1	10	1	2	1	8	44
Total	26	83	39	44	52	69	43	31	59	37	99	102	52	736

TABLE 27. Relative frequency of correct use of *the* across different NP types in 13 data sets.

	Data 1	Data 2	Data 3	Data 4	Data 5	Data 6	Data 7	Data 8	Data 9	Data 10	Data 11	Data 12	Data 13	Total
Proper	7.7	7.2	15.4	0.0	23.1	5.8	2.3	3.2	8.5	5.4	3.0	2.9	5.8	6.5
Singular Coun	76.9	73.5	56.4	77.3	50.0	73.9	76.7	80.6	61.0	75.7	66.7	82.4	40.4	68.9
Plural Coun	3.8	6.0	7.7	6.8	7.7	11.6	4.7	0.0	0.0	2.7	12.1	8.8	13.5	7.5
Uncountable	3.8	13.3	10.3	13.6	9.6	2.9	4.7	12.9	13.6	13.5	16.2	4.9	25.0	11.1
Pronoun	7.7	0.0	10.3	2.3	9.6	5.8	11.6	3.2	16.9	2.7	2.0	1.0	15.4	6.0
Total	100.0	100.0	100.0	100.0	100.0	100.0	100.0	100.0	100.0	100.0	100.0	100.0	100.0	100.0

TABLE 28. Correct use of *the* across different NP functions in 13 data sets.

	Data 1	Data 2	Data 3	Data 4	Data 5	Data 6	Data 7	Data 8	Data 9	Data 10	Data 11	Data 12	Data 13	Total
Subject	8	21	9	10	6	21	5	4	7	9	37	15	4	156
Complement	9	31	20	24	17	22	18	15	31	19	45	54	21	326
Object	8	20	6	8	17	15	15	8	9	3	8	17	15	149
Adverbial	0	0	1	0	1	0	2	0	4	1	1	8	4	22
Other	1	11	3	2	11	11	3	4	8	5	8	8	8	83
Total	26	83	39	44	52	69	43	31	59	37	99	102	52	736

TABLE 29. Relative frequency of correct use of *the* across different NP functions in 13 data sets.

	Data 1	Data 2	Data 3	Data 4	Data 5	Data 6	Data 7	Data 8	Data 9	Data 10	Data 11	Data 12	Data 13	Total
Subject	30.8	25.3	23.1	22.7	11.5	30.4	11.6	12.9	11.9	24.3	37.4	14.7	7.7	21.2
Complement	34.6	37.3	51.3	54.5	32.7	31.9	41.9	48.4	52.5	51.4	45.5	52.9	40.4	44.3
Object	30.8	24.1	15.4	18.2	32.7	21.7	34.9	25.8	15.3	8.1	8.1	16.7	28.8	20.2
Adverbial	0.0	0.0	2.6	0.0	1.9	0.0	4.7	0.0	6.8	2.7	1.0	7.8	7.7	3.0
Other	3.8	13.3	7.7	4.5	21.2	15.9	7.0	12.9	13.6	13.5	8.1	7.8	15.4	11.3
Total	100.0	100.0	100.0	100.0	100.0	100.0	100.0	100.0	100.0	100.0	100.0	100.0	100.0	100.0

data sets and reached its lowest figure of 7.7 in data 13. In contrast, *the* with Adverbial progressed from complete absence in data 1 and data 2 to its highest percentage of 7.8 and 7.7 respectively in data 12 and data 13. This might suggest that the use of *the* with Adverbial NPs was acquired later than the use of *the* with noun phrases playing other types of syntactic functions.

Correct Use of a/n with NP Types

Table 30 and table 31 report the frequency of correct use of *a* and *an* with different noun phrase types across different data sets. *A* and *an* are lumped into one category under the term of *a/n* because of the rare occurrence of the indefinite article *an* in the present data corpus.

As shown in tables 30 and 31, the correct use of *a/n* was largely linked with Singular Countable NPs, which occupied a percentage ranging from 87.8 to 100.0 across different data sets. Unlike *the*, *a/n* seemed far more restricted in its appearance in other types of noun phrases. No instance of the correct use of *a/n* could be found in the row of Plural Countable NPs. However, *a/n* was found used with Proper Noun Phrases, Uncountable NPs, and Pronoun Phrases. The acceptable occurrence of *a/n* with Proper Noun Phrases, Uncountable NPs, and Pronoun Phrases in the present data can be illustrated by the following examples:

> *To north and-and-and there is a Henderson.* [D12] (Proper Noun Phrase)
>
> *...because I haven't seen him for a long time.* [D13] (Uncountable NP)
>
> *I didn't get a big one.* [D2] (Pronoun Phrase)

The absence of the correct use of *a/n* with Proper Noun Phrases, Uncountable NPs, and Pronoun Phrases in data 1 might suggest that the correct use of *a/n* was later spread to these NP types. Based on the sequence of appearance in the data sets as well as on the percentage figures shown in the "total" column, it can be speculated that the correct use of *a/n* occurred first only with Singular Countable NPs and then spread to

TABLE 30. Correct use of *a/n* across different NP types in 13 data sets.

	Data 1	Data 2	Data 3	Data 4	Data 5	Data 6	Data 7	Data 8	Data 9	Data 10	Data 11	Data 12	Data 13	Total
Proper	0	0	0	0	0	1	0	0	0	0	0	3	0	4
Singular Coun	14	36	39	40	36	13	31	27	33	15	24	39	25	372
Plural Coun	0	0	0	0	0	0	0	0	0	0	0	0	0	0
Uncountable	0	0	0	0	0	0	0	0	0	0	1	0	2	3
Pronoun	0	5	1	1	0	0	0	0	1	1	0	1	0	10
Total	14	41	40	41	36	14	31	27	34	16	25	43	27	389

TABLE 31. Relative frequency of correct use of *a/n* across different NP types in 13 data sets.

	Data 1	Data 2	Data 3	Data 4	Data 5	Data 6	Data 7	Data 8	Data 9	Data10	Data11	Data12	Data13	Total
Proper	0.0	0.0	0.0	0.0	0.0	7.1	0.0	0.0	0.0	0.0	0.0	7.0	0.0	1.0
Singular Coun	100.0	87.8	97.5	97.6	100.0	92.9	100.0	100.0	97.1	93.8	96.0	90.7	92.6	95.6
Plural Coun	0.0	0.0	0.0	0.0	0.0	0.0	0.0	0.0	0.0	0.0	0.0	0.0	0.0	0.0
Uncountable	0.0	0.0	0.0	0.0	0.0	0.0	0.0	0.0	0.0	0.0	4.0	0.0	7.4	0.8
Pronoun	0.0	12.2	2.5	2.4	0.0	0.0	0.0	0.0	2.9	6.3	0.0	2.3	0.0	2.6
Total	100.0	100.0	100.0	100.0	100.0	100.0	100.0	100.0	100.0	100.0	100.0	100.0	100.0	100.0

Pronoun Phrases and then to Proper Noun Phrases and then to Uncountable NPs.

Correct Use of a/n with NP Functions

Table 32 and table 33 display various syntactic functions of noun phrases linked with the correct use of *a/n*.

As shown in table 32 and table 33, the correct use of *a/n* was mainly associated with complement noun phrases and object noun phrases, which occupied, respectively, a percentage of 45.8 and 37.0 among the total number of NP functions related to the correct use of *a/n*. While the highest percentage for noun phrases with other functions was 25.0 (data 5), the highest percentage for subject noun phrases and adverbial noun phrases was, respectively, 8.8 (data 9) and 5.9 (data 9). It can also be seen that the correct use of *a/n* appeared initially in data 1 only with complement noun phrases, object noun phrases, and subject noun phrases, then extended to noun phrases playing other functions in data 2, and finally made its first appearance with adverbial noun phrases in data 5.

Correct Use of zero article with NP Types

Table 34 and table 35 report the frequency of correct use of the zero article with different types of noun phrases across different data sets.

As expected with the present coding scheme (see chapter 3), the correct use of the zero article was confined to only two types of noun phrases, namely Plural Countable NPs and Uncountable NPs. Among these two types of noun phrases, Plural Countable NPs appeared, on the whole, more frequently than Uncountable NPs since the former category occupied a percentage of 51.1 among the total number of noun phrases linked with the correct use of the zero article, while the latter had a percentage of 48.9. As shown in table 35, the correct use of the zero article was at first more frequently related to Uncountable NPs from data 1 to data 8 and then more frequently related to Plural Countable NPs from data 9 to data 13. This changed pattern of frequency can be more clearly revealed and illustrated in the following figure, which shows the trend toward increased

TABLE 32. Correct use of *a/n* across different NP functions in 13 data sets.

	Data 1	Data 2	Data 3	Data 4	Data 5	Data 6	Data 7	Data 8	Data 9	Data 10	Data 11	Data 12	Data 13	Total
Subject	1	0	0	1	1	0	0	1	3	0	1	3	0	11
Complement	9	14	21	15	17	7	16	12	17	4	14	14	18	178
Object	4	22	13	24	8	7	8	10	10	9	6	16	7	144
Adverbial	0	0	0	0	1	0	0	1	2	0	1	2	1	8
Other	0	5	6	1	9	7	7	3	2	3	3	8	1	48
Total	14	41	40	41	36	14	31	27	34	16	25	43	27	389

TABLE 33. Relative frequency of correct use of *a/n* across different NP functions in 13 data sets.

	Data 1	Data 2	Data 3	Data 4	Data 5	Data 6	Data 7	Data 8	Data 9	Data 10	Data 11	Data 12	Data 13	Total
Subject	7.1	0.0	0.0	2.4	2.8	0.0	0.0	3.7	8.8	0.0	4.0	7.0	0.0	2.8
Complement	64.3	34.1	52.5	36.6	47.2	50.0	51.6	44.4	50.0	25.0	56.0	32.6	66.7	45.8
Object	28.6	53.7	32.5	58.5	22.2	50.0	25.8	37.0	29.4	56.3	24.0	37.2	25.9	37.0
Adverbial	0.0	0.0	0.0	0.0	2.8	0.0	0.0	3.7	5.9	0.0	4.0	4.7	3.7	2.1
Other	0.0	12.2	15.0	2.4	25.0	0.0	22.6	11.1	5.9	18.8	12.0	18.6	3.7	12.3
Total	100.0	100.0	100.0	100.0	100.0	100.0	100.0	100.0	100.0	100.0	100.0	100.0	100.0	100.0

Table 34. Correct use of *zero article* across different NP types in 13 data sets.

	Data 1	Data 2	Data 3	Data 4	Data 5	Data 6	Data 7	Data 8	Data 9	Data 10	Data 11	Data 12	Data 13	Total
Proper	0	0	0	0	0	0	0	0	0	0	0	0	0	0
Singular Coun	0	0	0	0	0	0	0	0	0	0	0	0	0	0
Plural Coun	1	7	5	3	5	3	2	9	4	15	15	13	31	113
Uncountable	5	8	11	17	7	3	5	13	2	6	15	3	13	108
Pronoun	0	0	0	0	0	0	0	0	0	0	0	0	0	0
Total	6	15	16	20	12	6	7	22	6	21	30	16	44	221

Table 35. Relative frequency of correct use of *zero article* across different NP types in 13 data sets.

	Data 1	Data 2	Data 3	Data 4	Data 5	Data 6	Data 7	Data 8	Data 9	Data 10	Data 11	Data 12	Data 13	Total
Proper	0.0	0.0	0.0	0.0	0.0	0.0	0.0	0.0	0.0	0.0	0.0	0.0	0.0	0.0
Singular Coun	0.0	0.0	0.0	0.0	0.0	0.0	0.0	0.0	0.0	0.0	0.0	0.0	0.0	0.0
Plural Coun	16.7	46.7	31.3	15.0	41.7	50.0	28.6	40.9	66.7	71.4	50.0	81.3	70.5	51.1
Uncountable	83.3	53.3	68.8	85.0	58.3	50.0	71.4	59.1	33.3	28.6	50.0	18.8	29.5	48.9
Pronoun	0.0	0.0	0.0	0.0	0.0	0.0	0.0	0.0	0.0	0.0	0.0	0.0	0.0	0.0
Total	100.0	100.0	100.0	100.0	100.0	100.0	100.0	100.0	100.0	100.0	100.0	100.0	100.0	100.0

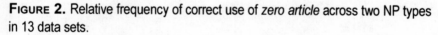

FIGURE 2. Relative frequency of correct use of *zero article* across two NP types in 13 data sets.

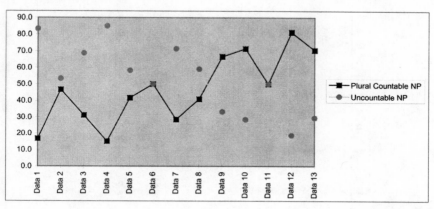

frequency of the correct use of the zero article with Plural Countable NPs and the decreased frequency of the correct use of the zero article with Uncountable NPs.

Correct Use of zero article with NP Functions
Table 36 and table 37 display the correlation between the correct use of the zero article and various syntactic functions of noun phrases.

As shown in table 37, the correct use of the zero article appeared most frequently with Object NPs and Complement NPs, while, in contrast, it appeared to absent in Adverbial NPs. It seems that the correct use of the zero article with Subject NPs and NPs playing other functions was acquired later by the informant. This is evident in data 1, where these two types of noun phrases showed a complete absence of the correct use of the zero article.

Table 36. Correct use of *zero article* across different NP functions in 13 data sets.

	Data 1	Data 2	Data 3	Data 4	Data 5	Data 6	Data 7	Data 8	Data 9	Data 10	Data 11	Data 12	Data 13	Total
Subject	0	3	0	1	0	1	0	0	1	2	9	0	5	22
Complement	4	4	5	6	4	2	3	8	1	9	7	5	16	74
Object	2	6	10	12	4	2	4	4	4	8	13	9	13	91
Adverbial	0	0	0	0	0	0	0	0	0	0	0	0	0	0
Other	0	2	1	1	4	1	0	10	0	2	1	2	10	34
Total	6	15	16	20	12	6	7	22	6	21	30	16	44	221

Table 37. Relative frequency of correct use of *zero article* across NP functions in 13 data sets.

	Data 1	Data 2	Data 3	Data 4	Data 5	Data 6	Data 7	Data 8	Data 9	Data 10	Data 11	Data 12	Data 13	Total
Subject	0.0	20.0	0.0	5.0	0.0	16.7	0.0	0.0	16.7	9.5	30.0	0.0	11.4	10.0
Complement	66.7	26.7	31.3	30.0	33.3	33.3	42.9	36.4	16.7	42.9	23.3	31.3	36.4	33.5
Object	33.3	40.0	62.5	60.0	33.3	33.3	57.1	18.2	66.7	38.1	43.3	56.3	29.5	41.2
Adverbial	0.0	0.0	0.0	0.0	0.0	0.0	0.0	0.0	0.0	0.0	0.0	0.0	0.0	0.0
Other	0.0	13.3	6.3	5.0	33.3	16.7	0.0	45.5	0.0	9.5	3.3	12.5	22.7	15.4
Total	100.0	100.0	100.0	100.0	100.0	100.0	100.0	100.0	100.0	100.0	100.0	100.0	100.0	100.0

Article Error by NP Types and Functions

This part of the section examines the noun phrase types and functions associated with the misuse of different types of articles across different data sets. It was assumed that the informant might make different article errors at different stages of the learning process. These errors might be related to specific syntactic categories or functions of noun phrases.

Error Types

As specified in chapter 3, 15 types of article errors were recognized and identified in the coding scheme, namely, Overuse of *the* to *a*, Overuse of *the* to *an*, Overuse of *the* to *zero article*, Overuse of *the* to non-use, Overuse of *a* to *the*, Overuse of *a* to *an*, Overuse of *a* to *zero article*, Overuse of *a* to non-use, Overuse of *an* to *the*, Overuse of *an* to *a*, Overuse of *an* to *zero article*, Overuse of *an* to non-use, Overuse of *zero article* to *the*, Overuse of *zero article* to *a*, and Overuse of *zero article* to *an*. Table 38 and table 39 report, respectively, the absolute frequency and the relative frequency of these types of article errors across different data sets. In the tables, the symbol "=>" stands for "overuse to."

The following findings can be obtained from table 38 and table 39:

1. No instance could be found of the four types of errors related to the indefinite article *an*. This means that the informant never committed an error in using *an* during the 13-month investigation.

2. Regarding the frequency of errors related to different types of articles, the ranking for percentage of errors made was in the order of the zero article, the definite article *the*, and the indefinite article *a*. In other words, errors appeared most frequently related with the zero article, and next with *the*, and lastly with *a*. This trend can be more clearly seen in figure 3.

3. *the* appeared most frequently overused in those contexts where no article was required. While there was a trend toward a decrease in overusing *the* in contexts where *a* was required, there was a tendency to increase overuse to *the* in contexts where the zero article was required.

TABLE 38. Error types across 13 data sets.

	Data 1	Data 2	Data 3	Data 4	Data 5	Data 6	Data 7	Data 8	Data 9	Data 10	Data 11	Data 12	Data13	Total
the => a	0	7	3	1	1	0	0	0	0	1	0	1	0	15
the => an	0	0	0	0	0	0	0	0	0	0	1	0	0	1
the => Ø	0	2	1	1	1	1	0	0	1	1	0	0	1	8
the => non-use	3	19	9	0	4	5	1	1	2	4	3	3	1	55
a => the	0	0	1	0	0	0	0	1	0	0	0	0	0	2
a => an	1	0	2	2	1	1	0	3	1	2	3	0	0	16
a => Ø	0	0	0	0	0	0	0	0	0	0	0	0	0	0
a => non-use	0	1	1	1	0	0	0	0	0	0	0	0	0	3
an => the	0	0	0	0	0	0	0	0	0	0	0	0	0	0
an => a	0	0	0	0	0	0	0	0	0	0	0	0	0	0
an => Ø	0	0	0	0	0	0	0	0	0	0	0	0	0	0
an => non-use	0	0	0	0	0	0	0	0	0	0	0	0	0	0
Ø => the	8	16	9	3	9	6	11	11	11	12	5	8	8	117
Ø => a	4	6	2	3	3	3	1	0	4	2	2	2	0	32
Ø => an	0	0	0	2	0	0	1	1	0	0	0	2	0	6
Total	16	51	28	13	19	16	14	17	19	22	14	16	10	255

TABLE 39. Relative frequency of error types across 13 data sets.

	Data 1	Data 2	Data 3	Data 4	Data 5	Data 6	Data 7	Data 8	Data 9	Data 10	Data 11	Data 12	Data 13	Total
the => a	0.0	13.7	10.7	7.7	5.3	6.3	0.0	0.0	0.0	4.5	0.0	6.3	0.0	5.9
the => an	0.0	0.0	0.0	0.0	0.0	0.0	0.0	0.0	0.0	0.0	7.1	0.0	0.0	0.4
the => Ø	0.0	3.9	3.6	7.7	0.0	6.3	0.0	0.0	5.3	4.5	0.0	0.0	10.0	3.1
the => non-use	18.8	37.3	32.1	0.0	26.3	25.0	7.1	5.9	10.5	18.2	21.4	18.8	10.0	21.6
a => the	0.0	0.0	3.6	0.0	0.0	0.0	0.0	5.9	0.0	0.0	0.0	0.0	0.0	0.8
a => an	6.3	0.0	7.1	15.4	5.3	6.3	0.0	17.6	5.3	9.1	21.4	0.0	0.0	6.3
a => Ø	0.0	0.0	0.0	0.0	0.0	0.0	0.0	0.0	0.0	0.0	0.0	0.0	0.0	0.0
a => non-use	0.0	2.0	3.6	7.7	0.0	0.0	0.0	0.0	0.0	0.0	0.0	0.0	0.0	1.2
an => the	0.0	0.0	0.0	0.0	0.0	0.0	0.0	0.0	0.0	0.0	0.0	0.0	0.0	0.0
an => a	0.0	0.0	0.0	0.0	0.0	0.0	0.0	0.0	0.0	0.0	0.0	0.0	0.0	0.0
an => Ø	0.0	0.0	0.0	0.0	0.0	0.0	0.0	0.0	0.0	0.0	0.0	0.0	0.0	0.0
an => non-use	0.0	0.0	0.0	0.0	0.0	0.0	0.0	0.0	0.0	0.0	0.0	0.0	0.0	0.0
Ø => the	50.0	31.4	32.1	23.1	47.4	37.5	78.6	64.7	57.9	54.5	35.7	50.0	80.0	45.9
Ø => a	25.0	11.8	7.1	23.1	15.8	18.8	7.1	0.0	21.1	9.1	14.3	12.5	0.0	12.5
Ø => an	0.0	0.0	0.0	15.4	0.0	0.0	7.1	5.9	0.0	0.0	0.0	12.5	0.0	2.4
Total	100.0	100.0	100.0	100.0	100.0	100.0	100.0	100.0	100.0	100.0	100.0	100.0	100.0	100.0

Figure 3. Relative frequency of article errors across 13 data sets.

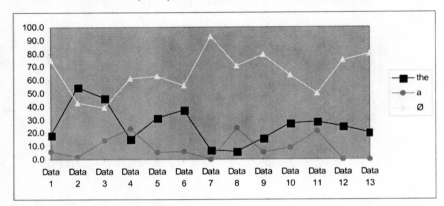

4. *a* appeared most frequently overused in those contexts where *an* was required. *a* was only found overused in non-use occasions in three data sets (data 2, data 3, and data 4) and overused to *the* in two data sets (data 3 and data 8). As reflected in those tables, *a* was never overused on those occasions where the zero article was required.

5. The zero article appeared most frequently overused in those contexts where *the* was required. This type of error occupied a percentage of 45.9 among the total number of article errors committed by the informant. Among the three types of zero article errors, the overuse to *a* appeared much more frequently than the overuse to *an*. The former had its highest percentage of 25.0 (data 1) and a percentage of 12.5 among the total number of errors, while the latter had the highest percentage of 7.1 (data 7) and a percentage of 2.4 among the total number of article errors.

Error the *with NP Types*

Table 40 and table 41 report different types of noun phrases related with the incorrect use of the definite article *the*.

TABLE 40. Incorrect use of *the* across different NP types in 13 data sets.

	Data 1	Data 2	Data 3	Data 4	Data 5	Data 6	Data 7	Data 8	Data 9	Data 10	Data 11	Data 12	Data 13	Total
Proper	0	3	0	0	4	0	1	0	2	3	2	2	1	18
Singular Coun	2	11	9	1	1	4	0	1	0	1	1	2	0	33
Plural Coun	1	4	2	1	1	1	0	0	0	0	1	0	0	11
Uncountable	0	1	2	0	0	0	0	0	1	1	0	0	1	6
Pronoun	0	9	0	0	0	1	0	0	0	1	0	0	0	11
Total	3	28	13	2	6	6	1	1	3	6	4	4	2	79

TABLE 41. Relative frequency of incorrect use of *the* across different NP types in 13 data sets.

	Data 1	Data 2	Data 3	Data 4	Data 5	Data 6	Data 7	Data 8	Data 9	Data 10	Data 11	Data 12	Data 13	Total
Proper	0.0	10.7	0.0	0.0	66.7	0.0	100.0	0.0	66.7	50.0	50.0	50.0	50.0	22.8
Singular Coun	66.7	39.3	69.2	50.0	16.7	66.7	0.0	100.0	0.0	16.7	25.0	50.0	0.0	41.8
Plural Coun	33.3	14.3	15.4	50.0	16.7	16.7	0.0	0.0	0.0	0.0	25.0	0.0	0.0	13.9
Uncountable	0.0	3.6	15.4	0.0	0.0	0.0	0.0	0.0	33.3	16.7	0.0	0.0	50.0	7.6
Pronoun	0.0	32.1	0.0	0.0	16.7	16.7	0.0	0.0	0.0	16.7	0.0	0.0	0.0	13.9
Total	100.0	100.0	100.0	100.0	100.0	100.0	100.0	100.0	100.0	100.0	100.0	100.0	100.0	100.0

As shown in table 41, errors with *the* were most frequently related to Singular Countable NPs, with a percentage of 41.8 among the total number of different types of noun phrases related with the incorrect use of *the*. The next most frequent category of noun phrases was Proper Noun Phrases, which had the highest percentage of 100.0 in data 7 and a percentage of 22.8 among the total number of different types of noun phrases related to the incorrect use of *the*. Errors with *the* appeared not very frequently related to the other three types of noun phrases.

Error the *with NP Functions*
Table 42 and table 43 display the NP functions related with the incorrect use of the definite article *the*.

As shown in the "total" column of table 43, errors with *the* were most frequently related to Complement NPs, which had a percentage of 40.5, while, in contrast, the errors were least frequently related to Adverbial NPs, which only had a percentage of 1.3. The next most frequent NP function was Object NPs, which had a percentage of 24.1 among the total number of NP functions related with the incorrect use of *the*. As reflected in the tables, errors with *the* were absent in the categories of Subject NP, Adverbial NP, and Other NP Functions in both data 1 and data 13. This might suggest that the informant stopped the misuse of *the* earlier in these syntactic contexts even though it was later spread to them.

Error a *with NP Types*
Table 44 and table 45 report the frequency of different types of noun phrases related with the incorrect use of the indefinite article *a*.

As shown in table 44 and table 45, errors with *a* were overwhelmingly related with Singular Countable NPs. Among the total number of 21 errors, 17 appeared with Singular Countable NPs. The absence of the error *a* in the row of Plural Countable NPs indicated that the informant did not commit any errors in this linguistic environment. The absence of errors with *a* in data 12 and data 13 might suggest that the informant had fully acquired the indefinite article *a* and used it correctly as amount of exposure to English increased.

TABLE 42. Incorrect use of *the* across different NP functions in 13 data sets.

	Data 1	Data 2	Data 3	Data 4	Data 5	Data 6	Data 7	Data 8	Data 9	Data 10	Data 11	Data 12	Data 13	Total
Subject	0	6	1	0	0	1	0	0	0	2	3	0	0	13
Complement	1	11	4	2	5	1	1	0	1	3	0	2	1	32
Object	2	6	6	0	1	0	0	0	1	1	0	1	1	19
Adverbial	0	1	0	0	0	0	0	0	0	0	0	0	0	1
Other	0	4	2	0	0	4	0	1	1	0	1	1	0	14
Total	3	28	13	2	6	6	1	1	3	6	4	4	2	79

TABLE 43. Relative frequency of incorrect use of *the* across different NP functions in 13 data sets.

	Data 1	Data 2	Data 3	Data 4	Data 5	Data 6	Data 7	Data 8	Data 9	Data 10	Data 11	Data 12	Data 13	Total
Subject	0.0	21.4	7.7	0.0	0.0	16.7	0.0	0.0	0.0	33.3	75.0	0.0	0.0	16.5
Complement	33.3	39.3	30.8	100.0	83.3	16.7	100.0	0.0	33.3	50.0	0.0	50.0	50.0	40.5
Object	66.7	21.4	46.2	0.0	16.7	0.0	0.0	0.0	33.3	16.7	0.0	25.0	50.0	24.1
Adverbial	0.0	3.6	0.0	0.0	0.0	0.0	0.0	0.0	0.0	0.0	0.0	0.0	0.0	1.3
Other	0.0	14.3	15.4	0.0	0.0	66.7	0.0	100.0	33.3	0.0	25.0	25.0	0.0	17.7
Total	100.0	100.0	100.0	100.0	100.0	100.0	100.0	100.0	100.0	100.0	100.0	100.0	100.0	100.0

Table 44. Incorrect use of *a* across different NP types in 13 data sets.

	Data 1	Data 2	Data 3	Data 4	Data 5	Data 6	Data 7	Data 8	Data 9	Data 10	Data 11	Data 12	Data 13	Total
Proper	0	0	0	0	0	0	0	1	0	0	0	0	0	1
Singular Coun	1	0	4	2	1	1	0	2	1	2	3	0	0	17
Plural Coun	0	0	0	0	0	0	0	0	0	0	0	0	0	0
Uncountable	0	0	0	0	0	0	0	1	0	0	0	0	0	1
Pronoun	0	1	0	1	0	0	0	0	0	0	0	0	0	2
Total	1	1	4	3	1	1	0	4	1	2	3	0	0	21

Table 45. Relative frequency of incorrect use of *a* across different NP types in 13 data sets.

	Data 1	Data 2	Data 3	Data 4	Data 5	Data 6	Data 7	Data 8	Data 9	Data 10	Data 11	Data 12	Data 13	Total
Proper	0.0	0.0	0.0	0.0	0.0	0.0	0.0	25.0	0.0	0.0	0.0	0.0	0.0	4.8
Singular Coun	100.0	0.0	100.0	66.7	100.0	100.0	0.0	50.0	100.0	100.0	100.0	0.0	0.0	81.0
Plural Coun	0.0	0.0	0.0	0.0	0.0	0.0	0.0	0.0	0.0	0.0	0.0	0.0	0.0	0.0
Uncountable	0.0	0.0	0.0	0.0	0.0	0.0	0.0	25.0	0.0	0.0	0.0	0.0	0.0	4.8
Pronoun	0.0	100.0	0.0	33.3	0.0	0.0	0.0	0.0	0.0	0.0	0.0	0.0	0.0	9.5
Total	100.0	100.0	100.0	100.0	100.0	100.0	0.0	100.0	100.0	100.0	100.0	0.0	0.0	100.0

Error a *with NP Functions*

Table 46 and table 47 display the correlation between different NP functions and the incorrect use of *a*.

Table 46 and table 47 show that errors with *a* were most frequently related with complement NPs, which occupied a percentage of 57.1 among the total number of 21 NP functions linked with the incorrect use of *a*. The second most frequent NP Function was Object, which occupied a percentage of 28.6 among the total number of NP functions associated with *a* errors. It can be seen that errors with *a* never appeared with Adverbial NPs. Nor did they appear in data 12 and data 13.

Error Ø *with NP Types*

Table 48 and table 49 report different types of noun phrases related with the incorrect use of the zero article.

As shown in the tables, the incorrect use of the zero article was most frequently associated with Singular Countable NPs, which occupied a percentage of 67.7 among the total number of the noun phrases related with the zero article errors. Proper Noun Phrases and Uncountable NPs, both occupying a percentage of 14.2 among the total number of the noun phrases related with the zero article errors, were the next two most frequent NP types in which the incorrect use of the zero article was found.

Error Ø *with NP Functions*

Table 50 and table 51 report different NP functions related with the incorrect use of the zero article.

As shown in the tables, the incorrect use of the zero article was most frequently related with Complement NPs, which occupied a percentage of 46.5 among the total number of NP functions related with zero article errors. NPs with other functions, occupying a percentage of 23.2 in the "total" column, represented the second most frequent function related with the incorrect use of the zero article. Object NPs, with a percentage of 18.7 in the "total" column, ranked third. It can be seen that the incorrect use of the zero article was not frequently associated with Subject NPs and Adverbial NPs.

TABLE 46. Incorrect use of *a* across different NP functions in 13 data sets.

	Data 1	Data 2	Data 3	Data 4	Data 5	Data 6	Data 7	Data 8	Data 9	Data 10	Data 11	Data 12	Data 13	Total
Subject	0	0	0	0	0	0	0	1	0	0	0	0	0	1
Complement	0	0	1	1	1	1	0	3	0	2	3	0	0	12
Object	1	1	2	1	0	0	0	0	1	0	0	0	0	6
Adverbial	0	0	0	0	0	0	0	0	0	0	0	0	0	0
Other	0	0	1	1	0	0	0	0	0	0	0	0	0	2
Total	1	1	4	3	1	1	0	4	1	2	3	0	0	21

TABLE 47. Relative frequency of incorrect use of *a* across different NP functions in 13 data sets.

	Data 1	Data 2	Data 3	Data 4	Data 5	Data 6	Data 7	Data 8	Data 9	Data 10	Data 11	Data 12	Data 13	Total
Subject	0.0	0.0	0.0	0.0	0.0	0.0	0.0	25.0	0.0	0.0	0.0	0.0	0.0	4.8
Complement	0.0	0.0	25.0	33.3	100.0	100.0	0.0	75.0	0.0	100.0	100.0	0.0	0.0	57.1
Object	100.0	100.0	50.0	33.3	0.0	0.0	0.0	0.0	100.0	0.0	0.0	0.0	0.0	28.6
Adverbial	0.0	0.0	0.0	0.0	0.0	0.0	0.0	0.0	0.0	0.0	0.0	0.0	0.0	0.0
Other	0.0	0.0	25.0	33.3	0.0	0.0	0.0	0.0	0.0	0.0	0.0	0.0	0.0	9.5
Total	100.0	100.0	100.0	100.0	100.0	100.0	0.0	100.0	100.0	100.0	100.0	0.0	0.0	100.0

TABLE 48. Incorrect use of *zero article* across different NP types in 13 data sets.

	Data 1	Data 2	Data 3	Data 4	Data 5	Data 6	Data 7	Data 8	Data 9	Data 10	Data 11	Data 12	Data 13	Total
Proper	4	5	3	0	2	2	2	2	0	0	1	1	0	22
Singular Coun	8	13	5	7	8	7	8	4	14	10	6	10	5	105
Plural Coun	0	1	1	0	0	0	0	0	0	0	0	0	0	2
Uncountable	0	2	2	1	2	0	3	6	0	2	0	1	3	22
Pronoun	0	1	0	0	0	0	0	0	1	2	0	0	0	4
Total	12	22	11	8	12	9	13	12	15	14	7	12	8	155

TABLE 49. Relative frequency of incorrect use of *zero article* across different NP types in 13 data sets.

	Data 1	Data 2	Data 3	Data 4	Data 5	Data 6	Data 7	Data 8	Data 9	Data 10	Data 11	Data 12	Data 13	Total
Proper	33.3	22.7	27.3	0.0	16.7	22.2	15.4	16.7	0.0	0.0	14.3	8.3	0.0	14.2
Singular Coun	66.7	59.1	45.5	87.5	66.7	77.8	61.5	33.3	93.3	71.4	85.7	83.3	62.5	67.7
Plural Coun	0.0	4.5	9.1	0.0	0.0	0.0	0.0	0.0	0.0	0.0	0.0	0.0	0.0	1.3
Uncountable	0.0	9.1	18.2	12.5	16.7	0.0	23.1	50.0	0.0	14.3	0.0	8.3	37.5	14.2
Pronoun	0.0	4.5	0.0	0.0	0.0	0.0	0.0	0.0	6.7	14.3	0.0	0.0	0.0	2.6
Total	100.0	100.0	100.0	100.0	100.0	100.0	100.0	100.0	100.0	100.0	100.0	100.0	100.0	100.0

TABLE 50. Incorrect use of *zero article* across different NP functions in 13 data sets.

	Data 1	Data 2	Data 3	Data 4	Data 5	Data 6	Data 7	Data 8	Data 9	Data 10	Data 11	Data 12	Data 13	Total
Subject	3	3	0	1	0	0	0	0	1	2	2	1	1	14
Complement	8	12	7	3	3	5	6	4	3	5	4	7	5	72
Object	1	4	2	3	2	2	0	4	4	2	1	2	2	29
Adverbial	0	0	0	0	0	0	0	0	3	1	0	0	0	4
Other	0	3	2	1	7	2	7	4	4	4	0	2	0	36
Total	12	22	11	8	12	9	13	12	15	14	7	12	8	155

TABLE 51. Relative frequency of incorrect use of *zero article* across NP functions in 13 data sets.

	Data 1	Data 2	Data 3	Data 4	Data 5	Data 6	Data 7	Data 8	Data 9	Data 10	Data 11	Data 12	Data 13	Total
Subject	25.0	13.6	0.0	12.5	0.0	0.0	0.0	0.0	6.7	14.3	28.6	8.3	12.5	9.0
Complement	66.7	54.5	63.6	37.5	25.0	55.6	46.2	33.3	20.0	35.7	57.1	58.3	62.5	46.5
Object	8.3	18.2	18.2	37.5	16.7	22.2	0.0	33.3	26.7	14.3	14.3	16.7	25.0	18.7
Adverbial	0.0	0.0	0.0	0.0	0.0	0.0	0.0	0.0	20.0	7.1	0.0	0.0	0.0	2.6
Other	0.0	13.6	18.2	12.5	58.3	22.2	53.8	33.3	26.7	28.6	0.0	16.7	0.0	23.2
Total	100.0	100.0	100.0	100.0	100.0	100.0	100.0	100.0	100.0	100.0	100.0	100.0	100.0	100.0

Semantic Functions of Articles

This part of the section presents the analysis of semantic functions of articles across the different data sets.

Types of Semantic Functions

As described in chapter 3, 10 types of semantic functions were recognized and identified in the present coding scheme. Among those ten types of semantic functions, six were related with the definite article *the*, two were related with the indefinite articles *a* and *an*, and two were related with the zero article. Table 52 and table 53 display the frequency of different types of semantic functions across different data sets.

As shown in the "total" columns of the tables 52 and 53, the ranking of different types of semantic functions by frequency was in the order of Individual *a/n* (389/28.9%), Setting *the* (277/20.6%), Parti Ø (202/15.0%), Specific Order *the* (168/12.5%), Unique *the* (91/6.8%), Earlier Mention *the* (90/6.7%), Postmodification *the* (73/5.4%), Generic *the* (37/2.7%), Toto Ø (19/1.4%), and Generic *a/n* (0/0.0%). This ranking order clearly indicates that the informant rarely used articles to express generic meaning. This is especially the case with the indefinite articles *a* and *an*, which were completely absent in this function across the whole data corpus.

Semantic Functions of the

Table 54 and table 55 report the frequency of different types of semantic functions of *the* across different data sets.

As shown in the "total" columns of table 54 and table 55, the ranking of different types of semantic functions by frequency was in the order of Setting (277/37.6%), Specific Order (168/22.8%), Unique (91/12.4%), Earlier Mention (90/12.2%), Postmodification (73/9.9%), and Generic (37/5.0%). Though the semantic type of Specific Order ranked second, it is interesting to note that it was the most frequently used semantic function in the initial data sets. This is especially evident in data 1, data 3, and data 5, in which it respectively occupied a percentage of 53.9,

TABLE **52.** Semantic functions across different data sets.

	Data 1	Data 2	Data 3	Data 4	Data 5	Data 6	Data 7	Data 8	Data 9	Data 10	Data 11	Data 12	Data 13	Total
Earlier Mention	2	31	4	5	1	2	6	4	2	9	9	10	5	90
Postmodification	0	2	0	2	2	2	6	3	12	6	12	16	10	73
Unique	2	8	8	6	15	12	9	5	4	2	4	5	11	91
Specific Order	14	11	14	8	16	12	11	9	21	3	10	29	10	168
Setting	5	27	12	21	15	35	10	7	19	16	62	38	10	277
Generic the	3	4	1	2	3	6	1	3	1	1	2	4	6	37
Individual	14	41	40	41	36	14	31	27	34	16	25	43	27	389
Generic a & an	0	0	0	0	0	0	0	0	0	0	0	0	0	0
Parti	6	12	16	18	10	5	7	22	6	20	28	15	37	202
Toto	0	3	0	2	2	1	0	0	0	1	2	1	7	19
Total	46	139	95	105	100	89	81	80	99	74	154	161	123	1346

TABLE 53. Relative frequency of semantic functions across different data sets.

	Data 1	Data 2	Data 3	Data 4	Data 5	Data 6	Data 7	Data 8	Data 9	Data 10	Data 11	Data 12	Data 13	Total
Earlier Mention	4.3	22.3	4.2	4.8	1.0	2.2	7.4	5.0	2.0	12.2	5.8	6.2	4.1	6.7
Postmodification	0.0	1.4	0.0	1.9	2.0	2.2	7.4	3.8	12.1	8.1	7.8	9.9	8.1	5.4
Unique	4.3	5.8	8.4	5.7	15.0	13.5	11.1	6.3	4.0	2.7	2.6	3.1	8.9	6.8
Specific Order	30.4	7.9	14.7	7.6	16.0	13.5	13.6	11.3	21.2	4.1	6.5	18.0	8.1	12.5
Setting	10.9	19.4	12.6	20.0	15.0	39.3	12.3	8.8	19.2	21.6	40.3	23.6	8.1	20.6
Generic the	6.5	2.9	1.1	1.9	3.0	6.7	1.2	3.8	1.0	1.4	1.3	2.5	4.9	2.7
Individual	30.4	29.5	42.1	39.0	36.0	15.7	38.3	33.8	34.3	21.6	16.2	26.7	22.0	28.9
Generic a & an	0.0	0.0	0.0	0.0	0.0	0.0	0.0	0.0	0.0	0.0	0.0	0.0	0.0	0.0
Parti	13.0	8.6	16.8	17.1	10.0	5.6	8.6	27.5	6.1	27.0	18.2	9.3	30.1	15.0
Toto	0.0	2.2	0.0	1.9	2.0	1.1	0.0	0.0	0.0	1.4	1.3	0.6	5.7	1.4
Total	100.0	100.0	100.0	100.0	100.0	100.0	100.0	100.0	100.0	100.0	100.0	100.0	100.0	100.0

TABLE 54. Semantic functions with *the* across different data sets.

	Data 1	Data 2	Data 3	Data 4	Data 5	Data 6	Data 7	Data 8	Data 9	Data 10	Data 11	Data 12	Data 13	Total
Earlier Mention	2	31	4	5	1	2	6	4	2	9	9	10	5	90
Postmodification	0	2	0	2	2	2	6	3	12	6	12	16	10	73
Unique	2	8	8	6	15	12	9	5	4	2	4	5	11	91
Specific Order	14	11	14	8	16	12	11	9	21	3	10	29	10	168
Setting	5	27	12	21	15	35	10	7	19	16	62	38	10	277
Generic the	3	4	1	2	3	6	1	3	1	1	2	4	6	37
Total	26	83	39	44	52	69	43	31	59	37	99	102	52	736

TABLE 55. Relative frequency of semantic functions with *the* across different data sets.

	Data 1	Data 2	Data 3	Data 4	Data 5	Data 6	Data 7	Data 8	Data 9	Data 10	Data 11	Data 12	Data 13	Total
Earlier Mention	7.7	37.3	10.3	11.4	1.9	2.9	14.0	12.9	3.4	24.3	9.1	9.8	9.6	12.2
Postmodification	0.0	2.4	0.0	4.5	3.8	2.9	14.0	9.7	20.3	16.2	12.1	15.7	19.2	9.9
Unique	7.7	9.6	20.5	13.6	28.8	17.4	20.9	16.1	6.8	5.4	4.0	4.9	21.2	12.4
Specific Order	53.8	13.3	35.9	18.2	30.8	17.4	25.6	29.0	35.6	8.1	10.1	28.4	19.2	22.8
Setting	19.2	32.5	30.8	47.7	28.8	50.7	23.3	22.6	32.2	43.2	62.6	37.3	19.2	37.6
Generic the	11.5	4.8	2.6	4.5	5.8	8.7	2.3	9.7	1.7	2.7	2.0	3.9	11.5	5.0
Total	100.0	100.0	100.0	100.0	100.0	100.0	100.0	100.0	100.0	100.0	100.0	100.0	100.0	100.0

35.9, and 30.8, which were the largest percentage figures in those data sets. This finding might suggest that the informant acquired this type of semantic function earlier than other types of semantic functions. It can also be seen that the row for Postmodification across different data sets reflected a tendency toward increased use ranging from total absence in data 1, to its highest percentage in data 9 (20.3), to its second highest percentage in data 13 (19.2). This might suggest that the informant used more postmodification functions of *the* as his level of the English language proficiency increased.

Semantic Functions of a/n

Table 56 and table 57 report the frequency of different types of the semantic functions of *a/n* across different data sets.

As shown in table 56 and table 57, the indefinite articles *a* and *an* were absent in the row for Generic in every data set. This suggests strongly that the informant had not acquired this semantic function of *a* and *an* during the entire investigation. In other words, the informant did not use this semantic function of *a* and *an* even after 21 months of exposure to English in the American context. It also suggests that the function of Individual was acquired by the informant far earlier than the function of Generic.

Semantic Functions of zero article

Table 58 and table 59 report the frequency of different types of the semantic functions of the zero article across different data sets.

As shown in the tables, the Parti function of the zero article was far more frequently used by the informant than its Toto function. While the former occupied a percentage of 91.4 in the "total" column, the latter had a percentage of only 8.6. The absence of the Toto function in data 1 and its rare use across different data sets suggests that this function of the zero article was acquired by the informant later than the Parti function.

TABLE 56. Semantic functions with *a/an* across different data sets.

	Data 1	Data 2	Data 3	Data 4	Data 5	Data 6	Data 7	Data 8	Data 9	Data 10	Data 11	Data 12	Data 13	Total
Individual	14	41	40	41	36	14	31	27	34	16	25	43	27	389
Generic a & an	0	0	0	0	0	0	0	0	0	0	0	0	0	0
Total	14	41	40	41	36	14	31	27	34	16	25	43	27	389

TABLE 57. Relative frequency of semantic functions with *a/an* across different data sets.

	Data 1	Data 2	Data 3	Data 4	Data 5	Data 6	Data 7	Data 8	Data 9	Data 10	Data 11	Data 12	Data 13	Total
Individual	100.0	100.0	100.0	100.0	100.0	100.0	100.0	100.0	100.0	100.0	100.0	100.0	100.0	100.0
Generic a & an	0.00	0.00	0.00	0.00	0.00	0.00	0.00	0.00	0.00	0.00	0.00	0.00	0.00	0.00
Total	100.0	100.0	100.0	100.0	100.0	100.0	100.0	100.0	100.0	100.0	100.0	100.0	100.0	100.0

TABLE 58. Semantic functions with *zero article* across different data sets.

	Data 1	Data 2	Data 3	Data 4	Data 5	Data 6	Data 7	Data 8	Data 9	Data 10	Data 11	Data 12	Data 13	Total
Parti	6	12	16	18	10	5	7	22	6	20	28	15	37	202
Toto	0	3	0	2	2	1	0	0	0	1	2	1	7	19
Total	6	15	16	20	12	6	7	22	6	21	30	16	44	221

TABLE 59. Relative frequency of semantic functions with *zero article* across different data sets.

	Data 1	Data 2	Data 3	Data 4	Data 5	Data 6	Data 7	Data 8	Data 9	Data 10	Data 11	Data 12	Data 13	Total
Parti	100.0	80.0	100.0	90.0	83.3	83.3	100.0	100.0	100.0	95.2	93.3	93.8	84.1	91.4
Toto	0.0	20.0	0.0	10.0	16.7	16.7	0.0	0.0	0.0	4.8	6.7	6.3	15.9	8.6
Total	100.0	100.0	100.0	100.0	100.0	100.0	100.0	100.0	100.0	100.0	100.0	100.0	100.0	100.0

Acquisition of Articles in Terms of the Learner's Usage

In this section, various tables display the analyses of the data from the perspective of the dynamic or usage paradigm, with the purpose of showing how the informant used articles within his IL system without the consideration of any native or target standard. This section is divided into three parts: articles, article-related determiners, and other determiners; article usage; and usage patterns of articles.

Articles, Article-related Determiners, and Other Determiners

This part of the section presents a general description of the article as a whole in relation to article-related determiners and other types of determiners. Their ratios to noun phrases were also investigated and reported. As reflected in the coding scheme specified in chapter 3, every determiner occurring before noun phrases in the present data corpus was recognized and classified. Three general categories were identified. They were Article, Article-related Determiner, and Other Determiner. The category of Article was further classified into the subcategories of *the*, *a*, *an*, and *zero article*. The category of Article-related Determiner was further classified into the subcategories of *this-those* (including *that* and *these*), *some*, and *one*. The category of Other Determiner was further classified into the subcategories of Quantifier, Possessive, and Wh-determiner.

Article, Article-related Determiners, and Other Determiners

Table 60 and table 61 report the frequency of the aggregate article, article-related determiners, and other determiners across different data sets.

As indicated in the "total" columns of table 60 and table 61, the ranking of different types of determiners by frequency is in the order of article (1603/57.9%), *quantifier* (385/13.9%), *possessive* (338/12.2%), *this* (277/10.0%), *some* (94/3.4%), *one* (69/2.5%), and *wh-determiner* (3/0.1%). It can be seen that there was a decreased trend in frequency for *quantifier*, which had its highest percentage of 30.2 in data 1 and lowest percentage of 9.3 and 9.4, respectively, in data 12 and in data 13. In contrast, there

TABLE 60. Articles, article-related determiners, and other determiners across different data sets.

	Data 1	Data 2	Data 3	Data 4	Data 5	Data 6	Data 7	Data 8	Data 9	Data 10	Data 11	Data 12	Data 13	Total
article	62	190	123	118	119	105	95	97	118	96	168	179	133	1603
this	8	18	27	28	28	17	24	15	16	13	32	25	26	277
some	10	25	25	10	5	0	3	6	0	0	2	3	5	94
one	1	16	12	6	7	5	3	0	2	2	9	3	3	69
qua	38	39	40	33	41	19	31	27	23	18	30	27	19	385
pos	7	31	26	39	51	10	29	23	11	18	23	54	16	338
wh	0	0	0	1	0	1	0	0	0	1	0	0	0	3
Total	126	319	253	235	251	157	185	168	170	148	264	291	202	2769

TABLE 61. Relative frequency of articles, article-related determiners, and other determiners across different data sets.

	Data 1	Data 2	Data 3	Data 4	Data 5	Data 6	Data 7	Data 8	Data 9	Data 10	Data 11	Data 12	Data 13	Total
article	49.2	59.6	48.6	50.2	47.4	66.9	51.4	57.7	69.4	64.9	63.6	61.5	65.8	57.9
this	6.3	5.6	10.7	11.9	11.2	10.8	13.0	8.9	9.4	8.8	12.1	8.6	12.9	10.0
some	7.9	7.8	9.9	4.3	2.0	0.0	1.6	3.6	0.0	0.0	0.8	1.0	2.5	3.4
one	0.8	5.0	4.7	2.6	2.8	3.2	1.6	0.0	1.2	1.4	3.4	1.0	1.5	2.5
qua	30.2	12.2	15.8	14.0	16.3	12.1	16.8	16.1	13.5	12.2	11.4	9.3	9.4	13.9
pos	5.6	9.7	10.3	16.6	20.3	6.4	15.7	13.7	6.5	12.2	8.7	18.6	7.9	12.2
wh	0.0	0.0	0.0	0.4	0.0	0.6	0.0	0.0	0.0	0.7	0.0	0.0	0.0	0.1
Total	100.0	100.0	100.0	100.0	100.0	100.0	100.0	100.0	100.0	100.0	100.0	100.0	100.0	100.0

was an increased trend in frequency for *article,* which progressed from the percentage of over 40 to over 50 to over 60 across different data sets.

Articles and Article-related Determiners

Table 62 and table 63 report the frequency of the aggregate article and the aggregate article-related determiner across different data sets. In the tables, "ARD" stands for article-related determiners.

As shown in table 62 and table 63, the category of Article was far more frequently used than the category of Article-related Determiner. The former occupied a percentage of 78.5 in the "total" column, while the latter occupied a much lower percentage of 21.5. It can also be seen that the category of Article exhibited a trend toward increasing frequency. This is reflected in the fact that figures in data sets before data 8 were generally lower than the percentage figure in the "total" column, and figures in data sets after data 7 were generally larger than the percentage figure in the "total" column. In contrast, the category of Article-related Determiner displayed a trend toward decreasing frequency. Evidence for this is seen in the fact that figures in data sets before data 8 were generally larger than the percentage figure in the "total" column, and figures in data sets after data 7 were generally lower than the percentage figure in the "total" column. These tendencies toward increase and decrease are revealed more clearly in the following figure.

FIGURE 4. Articles and article-related determiners across different data sets.

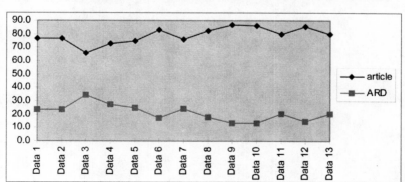

TABLE 62. Articles and article-related determiners across different data sets.

	Data 1	Data 2	Data 3	Data 4	Data 5	Data 6	Data 7	Data 8	Data 9	Data 10	Data 11	Data 12	Data 13	Total
article	62	190	123	118	119	105	95	97	118	96	168	179	133	1603
ARD	19	59	64	44	40	22	30	21	18	15	43	31	34	440
Total	81	249	187	162	159	127	125	118	136	111	211	210	167	2043

TABLE 63. Relative frequency of articles and article-related determiners across different data sets.

	Data 1	Data 2	Data 3	Data 4	Data 5	Data 6	Data 7	Data 8	Data 9	Data 10	Data 11	Data 12	Data 13	Total
article	76.5	76.3	65.8	72.8	74.8	82.7	76.0	82.2	86.8	86.5	79.6	85.2	79.6	78.5
ARD	23.5	23.7	34.2	27.2	25.2	17.3	24.0	17.8	13.2	13.5	20.4	14.8	20.4	21.5
Total	100.0	100.0	100.0	100.0	100.0	100.0	100.0	100.0	100.0	100.0	100.0	100.0	100.0	100.0

Articles and Determiners

Table 64 and table 65 report the frequency of the aggregate article and the aggregate other determiner, which includes all the determiners except articles, across different data sets.

As shown in table 64 and table 65, the category of Article was more frequently used than the category of Determiner. Among the total number of 2769, the former occupied a percentage of 57.9, while the latter occupied a percentage of 42.1. It can also be seen that the category of Determiner exhibited a higher frequency than the category of Article only in data 1, data 3, and data 5. This indicates that the informant used more determiners than articles in initial stages. However, as amount of exposure to English increased, the informant used more articles and relatively fewer other determiners.

Ratio of Articles, Article-related Determiners, and Other Determiners to NPs

Table 66 reports the ratio of the aggregate article, article-related determiners, and other types of determiners to noun phrases across different data sets.

As indicated in the total column, for 100 noun phrases, 21.1 articles, 5.1 quantifiers, 4.4 possessives, 3.6 *this*, 1.2 *some*, 0.9 *one*, and 0.04 *wh-determiner* were used in the whole corpus.

Ratio of Articles and Pronouns to NPs

Table 67 reports the ratio of the aggregate article and the aggregate pronoun to noun phrases across different data sets.

As indicated in the "total" column, Pronoun appeared far more frequently than Article. While the former occupied a percentage of 52.6 among the total number of noun phrases, the latter only occurred with 21.1% of noun phrases in the present data. It is interesting to note that Pronoun, with a ratio ranging from 47.2 to 60.1, showed no sign of decrease in frequency toward later data sets. In fact, it occupied a ratio of 56.7, the second highest ratio, in data 13. This finding suggests that the informant still frequently used pronouns even after 20 months of exposure to English in the American context.

TABLE 64. Articles and other determiners across different data sets.

	Data 1	Data 2	Data 3	Data 4	Data 5	Data 6	Data 7	Data 8	Data 9	Data 10	Data 11	Data 12	Data 13	Total
art	62	190	123	118	119	105	95	97	118	96	168	179	133	1603
det	64	129	130	117	132	52	90	71	52	52	96	112	69	1166
Total	126	319	253	235	251	157	185	168	170	148	264	291	202	2769

TABLE 65. Relative frequency of articles and other determiners across different data sets.

	Data 1	Data 2	Data 3	Data 4	Data 5	Data 6	Data 7	Data 8	Data 9	Data 10	Data 11	Data 12	Data 13	Total
art	49.2	59.6	48.6	50.2	47.4	66.9	51.4	57.7	69.4	64.9	63.6	61.5	65.8	57.9
det	50.8	40.4	51.4	49.8	52.6	33.1	48.6	42.3	30.6	35.1	36.4	38.5	34.2	42.1
Total	100.0	100.0	100.0	100.0	100.0	100.0	100.0	100.0	100.0	100.0	100.0	100.0	100.0	100.0

TABLE **66.** Ratio of articles, article-related determiners, and other determiners to NPs across different data sets.

	Data 1	Data 2	Data 3	Data 4	Data 5	Data 6	Data 7	Data 8	Data 9	Data 10	Data 11	Data 12	Data 13	Total
art	20.1	23.7	20.0	17.3	18.8	23.8	18.8	20.2	25.1	21.8	24.7	20.4	19.9	21.1
this	2.6	2.2	4.4	4.1	4.4	3.9	4.7	3.1	3.4	3.0	4.7	2.9	3.9	3.6
some	3.2	3.1	4.1	1.5	0.8	0.0	0.6	1.3	0.0	0.0	0.3	0.3	0.7	1.2
one	0.3	2.0	2.0	0.9	1.1	1.1	0.6	0.0	0.4	0.5	1.3	0.3	0.4	0.9
qua	12.3	4.9	6.5	4.8	6.5	4.3	6.1	5.6	4.9	4.1	4.4	3.1	2.8	5.1
pos	2.3	3.9	4.2	5.7	8.1	2.3	5.7	4.8	2.3	4.1	3.4	6.2	2.4	4.4
wh	0.0	0.0	0.0	0.1	0.0	0.2	0.0	0.0	0.0	0.2	0.0	0.0	0.0	0.0
Total	40.8	39.8	41.1	34.5	39.7	35.6	36.6	35.0	36.1	33.6	38.8	33.2	30.2	36.4

TABLE **67.** Ratio of articles and pronouns to NPs across different data sets.

	Data 1	Data 2	Data 3	Data 4	Data 5	Data 6	Data 7	Data 8	Data 9	Data 10	Data 11	Data 12	Data 13	Total
art	20.1	23.7	20.0	17.3	18.8	23.8	18.8	20.2	25.1	21.8	24.7	20.4	19.9	21.1
Pron	47.2	52.9	48.6	60.1	50.8	50.1	50.0	51.0	54.4	50.2	54.0	52.6	56.7	52.6

Article Usage
This section presents the analysis of the use of different types of articles, the ratio of different types of articles to noun phrases, as well as the correlation of different types of articles with their related determiners across different data sets.

Articles Across Different Data Sets
Table 68 and table 69 report the frequency of different types of articles across different data sets.

As shown in the "total" columns of the tables, the ranking of different types of articles by frequency is in the order of *the* (817/51.0%), *a* (408/25.5%), *zero article* (376/23.5%), and *an* (2/0.1%). In other words, *the* was the most frequently used type of article, *a* was the second most frequently used type of article, Ø was the third most frequently used type of article, while *an* was the least frequently used type of article. It can be seen that the percentage occupied by *the* was even higher than the combined percentage occupied by the other three types of articles. This indicates that *the* was far more frequently used by the informant than the other types of articles. In contrast, *an* was very rarely used by the informant, with an extremely low percentage of 0.1 among the total number of articles.

Ratio of Articles to Noun Phrases Across Different Data Sets
Table 70 reports the ratio of different types of articles to noun phrases across different data sets.

As shown in the "total" column, for every hundred noun phrases, 10.7 *the*, 5.4 *a*, 4.9 *zero article*, and less than one *an* were found to be used in the present data corpus. Across different data sets, the variation of the ratio was not great, even though some differences did exist. There was no indication of any progression patterns. In other words, the informant did not use a certain type of article more or less relative to increased proficiency level in English or increased exposure to English.

TABLE 68. Articles across different data sets.

	Data 1	Data 2	Data 3	Data 4	Data 5	Data 6	Data 7	Data 8	Data 9	Data 10	Data 11	Data 12	Data 13	Total
the	29	111	52	46	58	75	44	32	62	43	103	108	54	817
a	15	42	44	44	37	15	31	31	35	18	28	41	27	408
an	0	0	0	0	0	0	0	0	0	0	0	2	0	2
Ø	18	37	27	28	24	15	20	34	21	35	37	28	52	376
Total	62	190	123	118	119	105	95	97	118	96	168	179	133	1603

TABLE 69. Relative frequency of articles across different data sets.

	Data 1	Data 2	Data 3	Data 4	Data 5	Data 6	Data 7	Data 8	Data 9	Data 10	Data 11	Data 12	Data 13	Total
the	46.8	58.4	42.3	39.0	48.7	71.4	46.3	33.0	52.5	44.8	61.3	60.3	40.6	51.0
a	24.2	22.1	35.8	37.3	31.1	14.3	32.6	32.0	29.7	18.8	16.7	22.9	20.3	25.5
an	0.0	0.0	0.0	0.0	0.0	0.0	0.0	0.0	0.0	0.0	0.0	1.1	0.0	0.1
Ø	29.0	19.5	22.0	23.7	20.2	14.3	21.1	35.1	17.8	36.5	22.0	15.6	39.1	23.5
Total	100.0	100.0	100.0	100.0	100.0	100.0	100.0	100.0	100.0	100.0	100.0	100.0	100.0	100.0

TABLE 70. Ratio of articles to NPs across different data sets.

	Data 1	Data 2	Data 3	Data 4	Data 5	Data 6	Data 7	Data 8	Data 9	Data 10	Data 11	Data 12	Data 13	Total
the	9.4	13.8	8.5	6.8	9.2	17.0	8.7	6.7	13.2	9.8	15.1	12.3	8.1	10.7
a	4.9	5.2	7.2	6.5	5.9	3.4	6.1	6.5	7.4	4.1	4.1	4.7	4.0	5.4
an	0.0	0.0	0.0	0.0	0.0	0.0	0.0	0.0	0.0	0.0	0.0	0.2	0.0	0.0
Ø	5.8	4.6	4.4	4.1	3.8	3.4	4.0	7.1	4.5	8.0	5.4	3.2	7.8	4.9
Total	20.1	23.7	20.0	17.3	18.8	23.8	18.8	20.2	25.1	21.8	24.7	20.4	19.9	21.1

TABLE 71. *the* and *this* across different data sets.

	Data 1	Data 2	Data 3	Data 4	Data 5	Data 6	Data 7	Data 8	Data 9	Data 10	Data 11	Data 12	Data 13	Total
the	29	111	52	46	58	75	44	32	62	43	103	108	54	817
this	8	18	27	28	28	17	24	15	16	13	32	25	26	277
Total	37	129	79	74	86	92	68	47	78	56	135	133	80	1094

TABLE 72. Relative frequency of *the* and *this* across different data sets.

	Data 1	Data 2	Data 3	Data 4	Data 5	Data 6	Data 7	Data 8	Data 9	Data 10	Data 11	Data 12	Data 13	Total
the	78.4	86.0	65.8	62.2	67.4	81.5	64.7	68.1	79.5	76.8	76.3	81.2	67.5	74.7
this	21.6	14.0	34.2	37.8	32.6	18.5	35.3	31.9	20.5	23.2	23.7	18.8	32.5	25.3
Total	100.0	100.0	100.0	100.0	100.0	100.0	100.0	100.0	100.0	100.0	100.0	100.0	100.0	100.0

the *and Related Determiners Across Different Data Sets*

Table 71 and table 72 report the frequency of the definite article *the* and *this*, the cover term for *the*-related determiners including *this*, *that*, *these*, and *those*, across different data sets.

As shown in the tables, *the* was far more frequently used than *this*. While the former had its highest percentage of 86.0 in data 2 and its lowest percentage of 62.2 in data 4, the latter had its highest percentage of 37.8 in data 4 and its lowest percentage of 14.0 in data 2. It is interesting to note that the frequency or percentage figures for *this* were never higher than those for *the* in any data set. This finding suggests that the informant did not use *this* as a placeholder for *the* during the 13-month investigation.

a *and Related Determiner Across Different Data Sets*

Table 73 and table 74 report the frequency of the indefinite article *a* and its related determiner *one* across different data sets.

As shown in the tables, *a* was far more frequently used than *one*. While the former had its highest percentage of 100.0 in data 8 and its lowest percentage of 72.4 in data 2, the latter had its highest percentage of 27.6 in data 2 and its lowest percentage of 0.0 in data 8. It can be observed that the frequency or percentage figures for *one* were never higher than those for *a* in any data set. This finding can suggest that the informant did not use *one* as a placeholder for *a* during the 13-month investigation.

zero article *and Related Determiner Across Different Data Sets*

Table 75 and table 76 report the frequency of the zero article and its related determiner *some* across different data sets.

As shown in the tables, *zero article* was far more frequently used than *some*. While the former had its highest percentage of 100.0 in data 6, 9, 10, and its lowest percentage of 51.9 in data 3, the latter had its highest percentage of 48.1 in data 3 and its lowest percentage of 0.0 in data 6, 9, and 10. It can be seen that the frequency or percentage figures for *some* were never higher than those for Ø in any data set. This finding suggests that the informant did not use *some* as a placeholder for

TABLE 73. *a* and *one* across different data sets.

	Data 1	Data 2	Data 3	Data 4	Data 5	Data 6	Data 7	Data 8	Data 9	Data 10	Data 11	Data 12	Data 13	Total
a	15	42	44	44	37	15	31	31	35	18	28	41	27	408
one	1	16	12	6	7	5	3	0	2	2	9	3	3	69
Total	16	58	56	50	44	20	34	31	37	20	37	44	30	477

TABLE 74. Relative frequency of *a* and *one* across different data sets.

	Data 1	Data 2	Data 3	Data 4	Data 5	Data 6	Data 7	Data 8	Data 9	Data 10	Data 11	Data 12	Data 13	Total
a	93.8	72.4	78.6	88.0	84.1	75.0	91.2	100.0	94.6	90.0	75.7	93.2	90.0	85.5
one	6.3	27.6	21.4	12.0	15.9	25.0	8.8	0.0	5.4	10.0	24.3	6.8	10.0	14.5
Total	100.0	100.0	100.0	100.0	100.0	100.0	100.0	100.0	100.0	100.0	100.0	100.0	100.0	100.0

TABLE 75. *zero article* and *some* across different data sets.

	Data 1	Data 2	Data 3	Data 4	Data 5	Data 6	Data 7	Data 8	Data 9	Data 10	Data 11	Data 12	Data 13	Total
Ø	18	37	27	28	24	15	20	34	21	35	37	28	52	376
some	10	25	25	10	5	0	3	6	0	0	2	3	5	94
Total	28	62	52	38	29	15	23	40	21	35	39	31	57	470

TABLE 76. Relative frequency of *zero article* and *some* across different data sets.

	Data 1	Data 2	Data 3	Data 4	Data 5	Data 6	Data 7	Data 8	Data 9	Data 10	Data 11	Data 12	Data 13	Total
Ø	64.3	59.7	51.9	73.7	82.8	100.0	87.0	85.0	100.0	100.0	94.9	90.3	91.2	80.0
some	35.7	40.3	48.1	26.3	17.2	0.0	13.0	15.0	0.0	0.0	5.1	9.7	8.8	20.0
Total	100.0	100.0	100.0	100.0	100.0	100.0	100.0	100.0	100.0	100.0	100.0	100.0	100.0	100.0

the zero article during the 13-month investigation. It can also be seen in table 75 that there was a trend toward a decrease in frequency for use of *some*, which appeared more frequent in data sets 1–4 than in data sets 5–13.

Usage Patterns of Articles

In the section of article errors discussed previously, the findings suggest that in the obligatory context of one specific type of article, the use of other types of articles could also be found. In the accuracy paradigm, this kind of use is often called misuse, error, or overuse. In the dynamic or usage paradigm, this kind of use, however, can be regarded as part of the IL article system of the informant. Hence, it is not an error of any kind at all. In light of the variation analysis (Labov, 1973; Winford, 1990), the IL article system can be regarded as consisting of four variables, namely THE, A, AN, and ∅. Each variable is realized by two or more variants in the forms of *the*, *a*, *an*, and/or ∅. The following tables display the findings related to the informant's usage patterns of different types of articles.

Variants of THE Across Different Data Sets

Table 77 reports the frequency of different variants of THE across different data sets.

As shown in the table, THE was realized as *the*, *a*, and ∅. Among the three variants, *the* was used far more frequently than *a* and ∅. While *the* had a mean of 56.6, *a* and ∅ had respectively, a mean of 0.2 and 9.0 across different data sets. Considering the occurrence as well as the absence or disappearance of the variants, some usage patterns could be observed, as shown in table 78.

As indicated in the row for Pattern, two kinds of patterns were used by the informant. The first pattern consisted of the co-occurrence of *the* and ∅, while the second pattern consisted of the co-occurrence of *the*, *a*, and ∅. Across different data sets, Pattern 1 progressed to Pattern 2 and then back to Pattern 1. It can be seen that the reoccurrence of Pattern 1 was different in quantity in terms of the percentage ratio. This was

TABLE 77. Variants of *the* across different data sets.

	Data 1	Data 2	Data 3	Data 4	Data 5	Data 6	Data 7	Data 8	Data 9	Data 10	Data 11	Data 12	Data 13	Total	Mean	StdD
the	26	83	39	44	52	69	43	31	59	37	99	102	52	736	56.6	24.8
a	0	0	1	0	1	0	0	1	0	0	0	0	0	3	0.2	0.4
Ø	8	16	9	3	9	6	11	11	11	12	5	8	8	117	9.0	3.3
Total	38	99	49	47	62	75	54	43	70	49	104	110	60	856		

TABLE 78. Usage patterns related to variants of *the* across different data sets.

	Data 1	Data 2	Data 3	Data 4	Data 5	Data 6	Data 7	Data 8	Data 9	Data 10	Data 11	Data 12	Data 13
the	26	83	39	44	52	69	43	31	59	37	99	102	52
a	0	0	1	0	1	0	0	1	0	0	0	0	0
Ø	8	16	9	3	9	6	11	11	11	12	5	8	8
Pattern	1	2	2	1	2	1	1	2	1				

especially evident in the initial data sets and the final data sets. While *the* occupied a percentage of 76.5 and 83.8, respectively, in data 1 and data 2, and Ø occupied a percentage of 23.5 and 16.2, respectively, in data 1 and data 2, *the* occupied a percentage of 92.7 and 86.7, respectively, in data 12 and data 13, and Ø occupied a percentage of 7.3 and 13.3, respectively, in data 12 and data 13. It can be further speculated that Pattern 3, which consisted of only the variant *the*, would have been used if the informant had received more exposure to English. In this way, the complete usage patterns relating to THE in the informant's IL article system can be identified as the following sequence: Pattern 1 (*the* and Ø) → Pattern 2 (*the*, *a*, and Ø) → Pattern 1 (*the* and Ø) → Pattern 3 (*the*).

Variants of A across Different Data Sets

Table 79 reports the frequency of different variants of A across different data sets.

As shown in the table, A was realized as *a*, *the*, and ∅. Among the three variants, *a* was used far more frequently than *the* and ∅. While the former had a mean of 29.8, the latter two had, respectively, a mean of 1.2 and 2.5 across different data sets. Considering the occurrence as well as the absence or disappearance of the variants, some usage patterns could be discovered and identified. These are reported in table 80.

As reflected in the "Pattern" row, three patterns were used by the informant. The first pattern consisted of the co-occurrence of *a* and ∅, the second pattern consisted of the co-occurrence of *a*, *the*, and ∅, while the third pattern consisted of only *a*. Across different data sets, patterns varied from Pattern 1 (data 1) to Pattern 2 (data 2–6) to Pattern 1 (data 7) to Pattern 3 (data 8) to Pattern 1 (data 9) to Pattern 2 (data 10) to Pattern 1 (data 11) to Pattern 2 (data 12) and finally back to Pattern 3 (data 13). Though patterns varied, there were, however, only three patterns. Moreover, it can be observed that the reoccurrence of each pattern was generally accompanied by more use of *a* and/or less use of *the* or ∅. For instance, Pattern 1 occurred in both data 1 and data 7. However, *a* and ∅ had, respectively, the absolute frequencies of 14 and 4 in data 1, while

TABLE 79. Variants of *a* across different data sets.

	Data 1	Data 2	Data 3	Data 4	Data 5	Data 6	Data 7	Data 8	Data 9	Data 10	Data 11	Data 12	Data 13	Total	Mean	StdD
a	14	41	40	41	36	14	31	27	34	16	25	41	27	387	29.8	10.3
the	0	7	3	1	1	1	0	0	0	1	0	1	0	15	1.2	2.0
Ø	4	6	2	3	3	3	1	0	4	2	2	2	0	32	2.5	1.7
Total	18	54	45	45	40	18	32	27	38	19	27	44	27	434		

TABLE 80. Usage patterns related to variants of *a* across different data sets.

	Data 1	Data 2	Data 3	Data 4	Data 5	Data 6	Data 7	Data 8	Data 9	Data 10	Data 11	Data 12	Data 13
a	14	41	40	41	36	14	31	27	34	16	25	41	27
the	0	7	3	1	1	1	0	0	0	1	0	1	0
Ø	4	6	2	3	3	3	1	3	4	2	2	2	3
Pattern	1	2					1		1	2	1	2	3

their respective frequencies were 30 and 1 in data 7. Also, Pattern 2 first occurred in data 2 and last appeared in data 12. Even though *a* had the same frequency of 41 in both data sets, ∅ showed a decrease in frequency from 6 in data 2 to 2 in data 12. Ignoring the recurrence, the general usage patterns relating to *a* in the informant's IL article system could be identified as the following sequence: Pattern 1 (*a* and ∅) → Pattern 2 (*a*, *the*, and ∅) → Pattern 3 (*a*).

Variants of AN Across Different Data Sets

Table 81 reports the frequency of different variants of AN across different data sets.

As shown in table 81, AN has been realized as *a*, *the*, and ∅. Among the three variants, *a* appeared most frequently, with a total number of 15. ∅, *an*, and *the* had respective total numbers of 6, 2, and 1. The frequent use of *a* and rare use of *an* indicate clearly that the informant used *a* exclusively during certain stages in the acquisition process of *an*. Considering the occurrence as well as the absence or disappearance of the variants, some usage patterns related to the variable *AN* could be discovered and identified. Table 82 displays those findings.

As exhibited in the "Pattern" row, five patterns were used by the informant across different data sets. The first pattern consisted only of *a*, the second pattern consisted of the co-occurrence of *a* and ∅, the third pattern consisted only of ∅, the fourth pattern consisted of the co-occurrence of *a* and *the*, and the fifth pattern consisted of the co-occurrence of *an* and ∅. It can be seen that *a* can either occur by itself or co-occur with ∅ or *the*, but never co-occur with *an*. It can also be seen that *an* only occurs in data 12, the next to last data set. It is reasonable to speculate that the next possible pattern would only consist of *an* if the informant had been exposed to English for a longer period. Based on the previous findings, the general usage patterns relating to AN in the informant's IL article system can be classified into the following sequence: Pattern 1 (*a*) → Pattern 2 (*a* and ∅) → Pattern 3 (∅)→ Pattern 4 (*a* and *the*) → Pattern 5 (*an* and ∅) → Pattern 6 (*an*).

TABLE 81. Variants of *an* across different data sets.

	Data 1	Data 2	Data 3	Data 4	Data 5	Data 6	Data 7	Data 8	Data 9	Data 10	Data 11	Data 12	Data 13	Total	Mean	StdD
an	0	0	0	0	0	0	0	0	0	0	0	2	0	2	0.2	0.6
a	1	0	2	2	0	1	0	3	1	2	3	0	0	15	1.2	1.1
the	0	0	0	0	0	0	0	0	0	0	1	0	0	1	0.1	0.3
Ø	0	0	2	2	0	0	1	1	0	0	0	2	0	6	0.5	0.8
Total	1	0	4	4	0	1	1	4	1	2	4	4	0	24		

TABLE 82. Usage patterns related to variants of *an* across different data sets.

	Data 1	Data 2	Data 3	Data 4	Data 5	Data 6	Data 7	Data 8	Data 9	Data 10	Data 11	Data 12	Data 13
an	0	0	0	0	0	0	0	0	0	0	0	2	0
a	1	0	2	2	0	1	0	3	1	2	3	0	0
the	0	0	0	0	0	0	0	0	0	0	1	0	0
Ø	0	0	0	2	0	0	1	1	0	0	0	2	0
Pattern	1	1	1	2		1	3	2	1		4	5	

TABLE 83. Variants of ∅ across different data sets.

	Data 1	Data 2	Data 3	Data 4	Data 5	Data 6	Data 7	Data 8	Data 9	Data 10	Data 11	Data 12	Data 13	Total	Mean	StdD
∅	6	15	16	20	12	6	7	22	6	21	30	16	44	221	17.0	11.0
the	0	2	1	1	0	1	0	0	0	1	0	0	1	7	0.5	0.7
Total	6	17	17	21	12	7	7	22	6	22	30	16	45	228		

TABLE 84. Usage patterns related to variants of ∅ across different data sets.

	Data 1	Data 2	Data 3	Data 4	Data 5	Data 6	Data 7	Data 8	Data 9	Data 10	Data 11	Data 12	Data 13
∅	6	15	16	20	12	6	7	22	6	21	30	16	44
the	0	2	1	1	0	1	0	0	0	1	0	0	1
Pattern	1	2	2	1	1	2	1	1		2	1		2

Variants of Ø Across Different Data Sets

Table 83 reports the frequency of different variants of Ø across different data sets.

As shown in the table, Ø was realized as *Ø* and *the*. Among the two variants, Ø was used far more frequently than *the*. While the former had a mean of 17.0 across different data sets, the latter had a mean of only 0.5. Based on the occurrence as well as the absence or disappearance of the variants, some usage patterns could be discovered and recognized. Table 84 reports those discovered patterns.

As displayed in the "Pattern" row, two patterns were used by the informant across different data sets. The first pattern consists only of *Ø*, while the second pattern consists of the co-occurrence of *the* and *Ø*. It can be seen that the first pattern appeared in seven data sets (data sets 1, 5, 7, 8, 9, 11, and 12) while the second pattern appeared in six data sets (data sets 2, 3, 4, 6, 10, and 13). On the whole, the first pattern appeared more frequently in the late data sets. Based on these findings, the general usage patterns relating to Ø in the informant's IL article system can be categorized within the following sequence: Pattern 1 (*Ø*) → Pattern 2 (*Ø* and *the*) → Pattern 1 (*Ø*).

CHAPTER 5

SUMMARY, CONCLUSIONS, AND RECOMMENDATIONS FOR FUTURE RESEARCH

SUMMARY

This study combined qualitative and quantitative approaches in order to understand the acquisition sequence of English articles in the case of a Chinese, beginning English as a second language (ESL) learner in the American context. The longitudinal data collected during the 13-month investigation were, first, indexed by using the qualitatively-oriented computer software program NUD.IST and then statistically analyzed by using the quantitatively-oriented computer software program SPSS. An in-depth examination of different types of articles as well as their relation to noun phrases and other types of determiners was conducted in light of the perspectives derived from both the accuracy paradigm and the dynamic paradigm. The rationale behind the bi-paradigm approach was the belief that no single approach can provide a comprehensive description of the complexities involved in the acquisition process of English articles. Instead, a combined approach offers the advantage of viewing and investigating these complexities from different angles, hence one in which they complement each other.

A review of related literature concerning the acquisition of English articles showed (1) neglect in distinguishing *a* from *an*, in identifying the acquisition process related to the zero article, and in presenting a systematic description of noun phrases in conjunction with the use of articles; (2) a lack of an in-depth longitudinal study of Chinese ESL learners' acquisition process of the English article system; and (3) the necessity of testing the currently suggested acquisition sequences of the English article system with Chinese ESL learners. To test those suggested acquisition sequences as well as to explore those neglected areas, 15 research questions were posited to guide this longitudinal case study. A summary of the research questions as well as the answers to these questions follows.

First Research Question

What is the acquisition sequence of English articles as shown in the performance data of a Chinese ESL learner?

According to the findings derived from the revised scheme, the acquisition sequence of English articles for the present informant was in the order of *a*, *zero article*, *the*, and *an*.

Second Research Question

What are the acquisition stages for the definite article *the*?

Based on the analysis of the data, the acquisition stages for the definite article *the* could be described from two different perspectives. In terms of the higher degree of accuracy and the frequency of the semantic functions, the informant's acquisition stages for the definite article *the* were in the order of Setting/Specific Order, Unique, Earlier Mention, Postmodification, and Generic. In other words, the informant first acquired *the* to express its semantic functions of Setting and Specific Order, and lastly acquired *the* to express its semantic function of Generic.

In light of the variation analysis, the informant's acquisition stages for the definite article *the* could be classified into the following three progressive patterns: Pattern 1 (*the* and Ø) → Pattern 2 (*the*, *a*, and Ø) → Pattern 1 (*the* and Ø) → Pattern 3 (*the*). In other words, four stages for the acquisition of the definite article *the* could be recognized and identified. In the first stage, *the* and Ø were both used in the contexts where the definite article *the* was required. In the next stage, *a* was added as a co-variant. The third stage saw the disappearance of *a*. Though *the* and Ø were still used, there was some quantitative difference compared with Stage 1. Unlike in the first stage, *the* was used much more frequently while, in contrast, Ø was used much less frequently in the third stage. The fourth stage witnessed the disappearance of Ø. In this stage, only *the* was used.

Third Research Question
What are the acquisition stages for the indefinite article *a*?

Based on the analysis of the data, the acquisition stages for the indefinite article *a* could also be described from two different perspectives. In terms of the higher degree of accuracy and the frequency of the semantic functions, the informant's acquisition stages for the indefinite article *a* were in the order of Individual and Generic. In other words, the informant first acquired *a* to express its semantic function of Individual, and then acquired *a* to express its semantic function of Generic. The complete absence of generic *a* across different data sets indicated that the informant had not reached the second stage.

In light of the variation analysis, the informant's acquisition stages for the indefinite article *a* could be classified into the following three progressive patterns: Pattern 1 (*a* and Ø) → Pattern 2 (*a*, *the*, and Ø) → Pattern 3 (*a*). In other words, three stages for the acquisition of the indefinite article *a* could be recognized and identified. In the first stage, *a* and Ø were both used in the contexts where the indefinite article *a* was required. In the next stage, *the* was added as a co-variant. The third stage saw the disappearance of both *the* and Ø. In this stage, only *a* was used.

Fourth Research Question

What are the acquisition stages for the indefinite article *an*?

Based on the analysis of the data, the acquisition stages for the indefinite article *an* could be similarly described from two different perspectives. In terms of the higher degree of accuracy and the frequency of the semantic functions, the informant's acquisition stages for the indefinite article *an* were exactly the same as those for *a*. That is to say, the informant first acquired *an* to express its semantic function of Individual, and then acquired *an* to express its semantic function of Generic. The complete absence of generic *an* across different data sets indicated that the informant had not reached the second stage.

In light of the variation analysis, the informant's acquisition stages for the indefinite article *an* could be classified into the following six progressive patterns: Pattern 1 (*a*) → Pattern 2 (*a* and Ø) → Pattern 3 (Ø)→ Pattern 4 (*a* and *the*) → Pattern 5 (*an* and Ø) → Pattern 6 (*an*). In other words, six stages for the acquisition of the indefinite article *an* could be recognized and identified. In the first stage, *a* was the only variant in the contexts where the indefinite article *an* was required. In the next stage, Ø was added as a co-variant. In the third stage, Ø was the only variant in the contexts where the indefinite article *an* was required. In the fourth stage, both *a* and *the* were used. The fifth stage saw the first appearance of *an* co-varied by Ø. The sixth stage witnessed the disappearance of Ø. In this last stage, only *an* was used.

Fifth Research Question

What are the acquisition stages for the zero article?

Based on the analysis of the data, the acquisition stages for the zero article Ø could be presented from two different perspectives. In terms of the higher degree of accuracy and the frequency of the semantic functions, the informant's acquisition stages for the zero article Ø were in the order of Parti and Toto. In other words, the informant first acquired Ø to express its semantic function of Parti, and then acquired Ø to express its semantic function of Toto.

In light of the variation analysis, the informant's acquisition stages for the zero article Ø could be classified into the following three progressive stages with the use of two patterns: Pattern 1 (∅)→ Pattern 2 (∅ and *the*) → Pattern 1. In other words, three stages for the acquisition of the zero article ∅ could be recognized and identified. In the first stage, ∅ was the variant used. In the next stage, *the* was added as a co-variant. The third stage saw the disappearance of *the*. In this final stage, only ∅ was used. Though the first stage was similar to the third stage with ∅ as the only variant, one noticeable difference was that ∅ was greater in frequency in the third stage.

Sixth Research Question

What are the general features of noun phrases in the interlanguage (IL) of a Chinese ESL learner?

The analysis of the data showed the following two notable characteristics of noun phrases in the informant's IL:

1. At least half of the noun phrases did not require the use of any article or other determiners, since pronoun phrases alone occupied a percentage of 52.6 among the total number of noun phrases in the data corpus.
2. The informant tended to use more simple pronoun and countable noun phrases to play such grammatical functions as subject, direct object, and prepositional complement.

Seventh Research Question

What syntactic locations are associated with the correct use of different types of articles?

The analysis of the data showed that the correct use of *the* and *a/n* was most frequently related with singular countable noun phrases, while the correct use of ∅ was most frequently related to plural countable noun phrases. The most frequent NP functions related with the correct use of different types of articles were complement and object.

The findings also showed that, unlike the correct use of *the*, the correct use of *a/n* and ∅ was more restricted in occurrence with certain types of noun phrases. While the correct use of *a/n* never co-occurred with plural noun phrases and was rarely used with pronoun phrases, proper noun phrases, and uncountable noun phrases, the correct use of Ø was associated only with plural noun phrases and uncountable noun phrases.

Across different data sets, the following trends could be observed. The correct use of *the* showed an increase in frequency with plural noun phrases and uncountable noun phrases, while, in contrast, it exhibited a decrease in frequency with subject noun phrases. The correct use of *a/n* showed greater frequencies with different types of noun phrases and different types of noun phrase functions in the following order: singular countable noun phrases → pronoun phrases → proper noun phrases → uncountable noun phrases; complement/object/subject → other functions → adverbial. In regard to the correct use of Ø, there was a trend from less to more frequency with plural noun phrases and a trend from more to less frequency with uncountable noun phrases.

Eighth Research Question

What types of article errors are committed by a Chinese ESL learner?

The analysis of the data showed that the informant committed 10 types of article errors. Based on their frequency, these 10 types of article errors could be ranked in the order of overuse of *zero article* to *the*, overuse of *the* to non-use, overuse of *zero article* to *a*, overuse of *a* to *an*, overuse of *the* to *a*, overuse of *the* to *zero article*, overuse of *zero article* to *an*, overuse of *a* to *the*, overuse of *a* to non-use, and overuse of *the* to *an*.

Considering the frequency of errors related with different types of articles, the ranking was in the order of the zero article, the definite article *the*, and the indefinite article *a*. In other words, errors appeared most frequently related with the zero article, next with *the*, and lastly with *a*. As revealed in the data, the informant did not commit any errors with the indefinite article *an*.

Ninth Research Question

What syntactic locations are associated with the misuse of different types of articles?

The findings of this study revealed that the misuse of different types of articles was most frequently related with singular countable noun phrases. Moreover, it was also most frequently associated with complement noun phrases. In other words, the misuse of different types of articles had the same syntactic locations in terms of the highest frequency with noun phrase types and functions.

Tenth Research Question

What semantic functions of articles are used by a Chinese ESL learner?

The analysis of the data showed that the ranking of different types of semantic functions by frequency was in the order of Individual *a/n*, Setting *the*, Parti Ø, Specific Order *the*, Unique *the*, Earlier Mention *the*, Postmodification *the*, Generic *the*, Toto Ø, and Generic *a/n*. This ranking order indicated clearly that the informant rarely used articles to express generic meaning.

Eleventh Research Question

What is the general relation between articles, article-related determiners, and other types of determiners?

The analysis of the data showed that articles were used more frequently compared with other types of determiners. The ranking of different types of determiners by frequency was in the order of *article* (817/57.9%), *quantifier* (385/13.9%), *possessive* (338/12.2%), *this* (277/10.0%), *some* (94/3.4%), *one* (69/2.5%), and *wh-determiner* (3/0.1%). The analysis of the data also revealed that there was an increased trend in frequency for *article*, which progressed from the percentage of over 40 to over 50 to over 60 across different data sets. This indicates that the informant used more articles as his level of proficiency in English increased.

Twelfth Research Question

What is the ratio of articles to noun phrases?

The analysis of the data showed that for 100 noun phrases, 21.1 articles, 5 quantifiers, 4.4 possessives, 3.6 *this*, 1.2 *some*, 0.9 *one*, and 0.04 *wh-determiner* were used in the whole corpus. Among these

21.1 articles, 10.7 were *the*, 5.4 were *a*, 4.9 were *zero article*, and 0.03 were *an*.

The findings also suggested that pronoun phrases appeared used far more frequently than articles. While the former occupied a percentage of 52.6 among the total number of noun phrases, the latter only occurred with 21.1% of noun phrases.

Thirteenth Research Question
What is the specific relation between different types of articles and their respectively related determiners?

The analysis of the data showed that *the*, *a*, and *Ø* were used much more frequently than their respective, closely-related determiners *this*, *one*, and *some*. Across different data sets, *this*, *one*, and *some*, whether in absolute frequency or in percentage, were never respectively higher than *the*, *a*, and *Ø*. This suggests clearly that the informant did not use *this* as a placeholder for *the*, *one* as a placeholder for *a*, or *some* as a placeholder for *Ø* during the 13-month investigation. In other words, there was no indication that the informant would turn to use *this*, *one*, or *some* when he felt difficulty in using *the*, *a*, or *Ø* during the process of acquiring the English articles.

Fourteenth Research Question
What strategies might a Chinese ESL learner use in the acquisition of the English article system?

Two noticeable strategies could be observed in the informant's acquisition process of the English article system. One strategy used by the informant was that, whenever possible, he would use personal pronoun phrases or other pronoun phrases instead of articles. This was evident in the present data corpus where pronoun phrases were used the most frequently among the different types of noun phrases. Moreover, as mentioned previously, pronoun phrases were also more frequent in occurrence than articles. While the former occupied a percentage of 52.6 among the total number of noun phrases, the latter occurred with only 21.1% of noun phrases. Since pronoun phrases generally do not require the use of any type of article or determiner, the heavy use of pronoun phrases seemed to serve as a kind of strategy for replacing articles.

Another strategy used by the informant was that when he was not sure which article should be used, he would normally use the zero article. This was supported by the fact that article errors appeared most frequently related with the zero article. Among the total number of article errors, those errors related with the zero article occupied a percentage of 60.8.

Fifteenth Research Question
How might first language (L1) influence second language (L2) in the acquisition of articles?

The findings of this study revealed several ways in which the informant's Chinese L1 background influenced his acquisition of English articles. First, since there is no article system in Chinese, it might be the case that the informant simply ignored the use of any article or simply used the zero article on those occasions where the articles *the*, *a*, or *an* were required. This might explain why the overuse of the zero article was the informant's most frequent article error. Second, though there is no article system in Chinese, Chinese has a quantifier expression in the form of *yi* + (measure unit) that has the same semantic function of Individual as that of the English indefinite articles *a* and *an*. However, this Chinese quantifier expression can never be used to express a generic meaning. This might explain why the informant acquired *a* and *an* to express individual meaning long before their use in expressing generic meaning. Lastly, it can be observed that Chinese ESL learners tend to neglect the marked forms if there is only one equivalent form in Chinese. A well-known example is American professors' frustration with Chinese students' indiscriminate use of the personal pronoun *he* on those occasions where *she* or *it* should be used. However, from the perspective of L1 transfer, it is understandable why Chinese students commit such errors with the pronoun *he*, since in Chinese there is no distinction in spoken forms between *he*, *she*, and *it*. This might be the same case with *a* and *an*. Though there is a kind of partially equivalent expression in Chinese, as noted earlier, that expression has no varied form such as *an* for *a* in English. This might be the reason why the informant acquired *a* long before *an*, as shown in the analysis of the data.

CONCLUSIONS

This study was driven by a theoretical view that asserts that sequencing is fundamental in second language acquisition. The results of this study lend support to that theoretical stance by clearly identifying a number of acquisition sequences regarding the English article system as a whole, as well as each individual article in the case of a beginning Chinese ESL learner in the American context. In other words, the acquisition of the English article system, as well as each individual article, can be recognized and classified into distinctive sequences or stages.

One of the most important findings in this study is that the informant's acquisition of the English article system occurred in the following sequence: *a* → *zero article* → *the* → *an*. Considering the informant's L1 background, it is understandable why *an* was the last article to be acquired. As explained in the previous section, Chinese ESL learners often find it difficult to learn the marked forms when they can find a certain one-to-one "equivalent" expression in their native language. That might also be the main reason why the informant only used *a* on those occasions where *an* was required in the initial stages of the acquisition process. It can also be observed that this sequence reflects the difficult and complex levels embedded in different types of articles. In terms of syntactic and semantic functions, *the* is more difficult and complex than the zero article, while, in turn, the zero article is more difficult and complex than *a*.

This finding is, however, quite contrary to the proposed acquisition sequences documented in the current L2 research literature. The suggested sequences in the forms of *the* → *a(n)* (Chaudron & Parker, 1990; Thomas, 1989a) or *zero article* → *the* → *a(n)* (Gorokhova, 1990; Master, 1988) appear inapplicable in the case of a Chinese ESL learner. The difference in the order of different types of articles may partially result from the use of different methodologies. As shown in chapter 4, on the basis of this study's results, three different acquisition sequences could be presented by using three different schemes. Brown's scheme yielded the result of *zero article → a → the → an*, Pica's scheme produced the sequence of *a → the → zero article → an*, while the present investigator's revised scheme actualized the acquisition order in the form of *a → zero article → the → an*. Though different methodologies may produce different results, it seems clear that *the* was never acquired before *a* by the informant no matter what kind of scheme has been used. This also appears to explain why the position of the zero article can vary greatly in different schemes. As noted previously, the zero article was most frequently related to errors, especially overuse errors in non-obligatory contexts. Hence, in a scheme like Brown's, which does not count those errors, the zero article is likely to move to the front of the acquisition sequence.

Regarding the zero article, insight on another controversial issue may emerge from this study, where efforts have been made to clearly mark the linguistic environments in which the zero article is used. A common assumption in the current L2 acquisition research is that no use of an article is equivalent to the acquisition of the zero article. With such an assumption, it is not difficult to speculate an initial stage for Chinese beginning ESL learners where the so-called zero article is the first article to be fully acquired, since there is no article system in Chinese and Chinese beginning ESL learners are likely not to use any article at all. Using Brown's scheme worsens this situation because only the suppliance in the obligatory contexts is counted. However, based on the results of this study, it is the researcher's belief that using no article is not equal to the acquisition of the zero article. As the findings show, the informant had not fully acquired the use of the zero article even after 21 months of exposure to English in the American context, since he was still in the process of learning how to use the zero article to express the toto-generic meaning.

Another important finding in this study is that the term *acquisition* can only be understood in a relative sense. In other words, the criterion of over 90% or even 100% accuracy can only reflect a partial picture of the acquisition of certain linguistic forms. This is especially evident in the finding that though *a* can be identified as "acquired" based on the criterion of over 90% accuracy, it is clear that the informant was still far from full acquisition of the use of *a*, since no evidence could be found to show that he already knew how to use *a* to express generic meaning.

What follows is a list of other conclusions derived from analyses performed in this study. It is important to keep in mind that these conclusions are derived from the speech data of only one informant. As such, generalizing from this sample to a larger population should be done with utmost caution.

1. The acquisition of different types of articles could be classified into distinctive stages in terms of semantic functions and variation patterns.

2. *the* was the most frequently used type of article while Ø was the type of article most frequently related to article errors.

3. The indefinite article *an* was rarely used. However, when it was used, it appeared to be used correctly.

4. There was no evidence to show that the informant used article-related determiners as placeholders for articles during the process of English-article acquisition.

5. The correct use or misuse of different types of articles could be identified with specific types of noun phrases and specific syntactic functions played by noun phrases.

6. As the length of time the informant was exposed to English increased, there was a relative decrease in frequency with determiners, while, in contrast, there was an increased use of articles.

7. In the informant's IL, the ratio of different types of determiners to noun phrases was generally presented as follows: for 100 noun phrases, there were 10.7 *the*, 5.4 *a*, 4.9 Ø, 0.03 *an*, 5 quantifiers, 4.4 possessives, 3.6 *this*, 1.2 *some*, 0.9 *one*, and 0.04 *wh-determiner*.

8. It was at a much later stage that the informant acquired the use of different types of articles in expressing generic meaning compared with the use of different types of articles in expressing other types of semantic or discourse functions.

9. The informant's IL discourse was characterized by the frequent use of identified personal referents apart from two other general characteristics described by Larsen-Freeman and Long (1991) as "more oriented to the 'here and now'" (p. 122).

10. Noun phrases in the informant's IL were characterized by frequent use of personal pronouns and singular countable nouns; by frequent use of noun phrases playing such syntactic functions as subject, direct object, and prepositional complement; and by frequent use of noun phrases with simple structures.

11. L1 influence could be identified in the process of English-article acquisition.

PEDAGOGICAL IMPLICATIONS

As argued in chapter 1, successful learning of a second language can be best accomplished by following the natural developmental sequences rather than violating their orders. Hence, if it can be observed, as the present study showed, that there are natural orders for acquiring the article system and for acquiring each individual type of article, these discovered natural orders have to be followed in classroom instruction in order to achieve better teaching and learning results. It must be emphasized that caution has to be exerted when any generalization or implication is made based on the findings from one small sample. However, after a replication of the present study with a larger sample, the following general pedagogical implications may be derived.

1. Contrary to the suggestion of some researchers (e.g. Gorokhova, 1990), *a* should be introduced before *the*. If *the* is presented first in concordance with the suggestion of those researchers, learners are guided to focus their attention on a linguistic signal they should possess at a later stage, while, at the same time, to ignore the linguistic signal they are ready to acquire.

2. The indefinite article *an* should be introduced last among various articles rather than introducing it before *the* or together with *a*.

Few errors related with the use of *an*, as shown in this study, may suggest that not much teaching effort is required on the part of ESL instructors.

3. Using articles to express generic meanings should not be introduced to beginners. The current pedagogical practice of teaching and learning articles within one unit in two or three weeks should be reformed and reorganized. Otherwise, it is of little help for learners to master various uses of articles.

4. Since articles base their semantic values on discourse parameters, it is more efficient to teach and learn articles in discourse contexts than to teach and learn them in isolated sentences.

5. It might help Chinese ESL learners in learning articles if corresponding Chinese expressions can be introduced at the same time for the purpose of comparison and contrast. In this way, learners can get a clearer picture of what similarities and differences exist between the two languages regarding the article system. Their native knowledge can guide them to learn English articles in a more effective way.

6. The use of the zero article should be systematically introduced to learners rather than the present pedagogical strategy adopted and reflected in many ESL textbooks and reference books, where the use of the zero article is either not mentioned completely or described in a simplistic way.

These suggestions are only very general pedagogical implications for teaching and learning English articles. The specific teaching techniques that might be borne out of this study after the replication of a larger sample need further investigation and study.

RECOMMENDATIONS FOR FUTURE RESEARCH

Findings from this study challenge some important conclusions documented in the current L2 research literature regarding the acquisition of English articles. The established acquisition sequence of English articles, whether in the form of *the* → *a(n)* (Chaudron & Parker, 1990; Thomas, 1989a) or in the form of *zero article* → *the* → *a(n)* (Gorokhova, 1990; Master, 1988), appears inapplicable in the case of a beginning Chinese ESL learner. Furthermore, there is no evidence from this study to support Lee et al.'s (1994) conclusion that the developmental sequence of the English definite article *the* for a Chinese ESL learner can be displayed as a U-shaped pattern in the order of an unmarked phase (article-missing), a phase of sharp decrease of the unmarked occasions and the heavy use of *this/that* or *these/those*, a phase of sharp decrease of the use of *this/that* or *these/those* and the dominant use of *the*, a phase of the heavy use of *this/that* or *these/those* after the correct use of the definite article reaches its peak, and a final phase of the full acquisition of *the*. As indicated in the findings from this study, there is no such stage where *this/that* or *these/those* were used more heavily than the definite article *the*.

Findings from this study also provide some new ways to identify the acquisition sequence of the English article system and to mark the acquisition stages of each individual article. However, these findings have to be interpreted with caution as they are derived from the analysis of the longitudinal speech data of only one Chinese informant. Hence, what is needed in future research is the replication of the present study with a larger population of Chinese ESL learners or with a larger population of ESL learners with different language backgrounds to examine whether similar findings will occur.

It should be noted that some findings from this study are quite similar to those of L1 research. This is especially evident in the finding that *a* is acquired before *the*. However, further research can be carried out in this line of comparison and exploration. The relevant research questions may include the following: What is the similarity between L1 acquisition of English articles and L2 acquisition of English articles? What is the difference between L1 acquisition of English articles and L2 acquisition of English articles? What factors have caused such similarity and difference? What is the theoretical significance indicated by these similarities and differences?

The article system is only one component of the larger linguistic class referred to as determiners. Another possible research avenue could involve an investigation of the use of determiners and the use of noun phrases. Though the present study has touched upon some aspects of the use of other types of determiners as well as some aspects of the use of noun phrases, they have been examined mainly in connection with articles. So, the question "What are the acquisition sequences or stages of determiners?" and the question "What are the acquisition sequences or stages of noun phrases?" remain unanswered. Further research is needed in these areas.

By branching out into the broader area of the comparison of L1 and L2 acquisition processes, as well as the acquisition processes of the L2 determiner system and the L2 noun phrase system, the knowledge base underlying second language acquisition (SLA) theory can be expanded. Each new piece added to the SLA puzzle will allow it to fit together more snugly, thus shedding new light and insight into understanding the acquisition processes of ESL learners in a more comprehensive way.

APPENDIX A

OVERVIEW OF THE SOFTWARE PROGRAM OF NUD.IST

THE SOFTWARE PROGRAM OF NUD.IST

NUD.IST (Non-numerical Unstructured Data Indexing Searching and Theory-building) is one of the leading CAQDA (computer-aided qualitative data analysis) programs (QSR, 1998). This software program was developed out of research conducted by Lyn & Tom Richards at La Trobe University, Melbourne, Australia and is now produced by the Qualitative Solutions & Research Pty Ltd (Q.S.R.) and marketed by Scolari. The version of the software program used for this study is 3.0.4d. The information about the updated version is available at: http://www. qsrinternational.com/products_previous-products_n6.aspx.

As a software program, NUD.IST is designed to facilitate more efficient qualitative data management and analysis. It provides facilities for:

- managing, exploring and searching the text of documents
- developing a category system
- indexing qualitative data to categories
- exploring the relationships between categories
- testing theories about the data
- generating reports including statistical summaries
- combining qualitative and quantitative analysis
- exporting results to statistical and mapping software

The original concept of NUD.IST was as a package to aid a researcher in studying, indexing, and retrieving text stored in computer files such as unstructured interview transcripts. Its very powerful tree-structured indexing features, combined with the dozen or more analytical tools for studying and comparing indexing categories, have made it attractive for very large projects with hundreds of long documents. It has been reported that one large institute is putting over 50,000 interviews into NUD.IST for analysis (see Internet News for NUD.IST). At the same time its elegance and ease of use has gained it great popularity for small and simple qualitative analysis projects.

The pattern-based text search facility in NUD.IST plus the ability to index the findings of text search appear very attractive and useful in conducting a thorough linguistic analysis of any unstructured interview text. These facilities can be very helpful in an analysis of performance data for the purpose of identifying the acquisition sequences of some specific linguistic items because such an analysis often requires a careful coding and a thorough examination of the target linguistic items as well as their associated linguistic environment. The following is a list of all the nodes generated in NUD.IST for this study:

(1)	/appearance
(1 1)	/appearance/present
(1 1 1)	/appearance/present/the
(1 1 1 1)	/appearance/present/the/correct
(1 1 1 2)	/appearance/present/the/overuse
(1 1 1 2 1)	/appearance/present/the/overuse/to a
(1 1 1 2 2)	/appearance/present/the/overuse/to an
(1 1 1 2 3)	/appearance/present/the/overuse/to 0
(1 1 1 2 4)	/appearance/present/the/overuse/to non-use
(1 1 2)	/appearance/present/a
(1 1 2 1)	/appearance/present/a/correct
(1 1 2 2)	/appearance/present/a/overuse
(1 1 2 2 1)	/appearance/present/a/overuse/to the
(1 1 2 2 2)	/appearance/present/a/overuse/to an
(1 1 2 2 3)	/appearance/present/a/overuse/to 0
(1 1 2 2 4)	/appearance/present/a/overuse/to non-use

(1 1 3)	/appearance/present/an
(1 1 3 1)	/appearance/present/an/correct
(1 1 3 2)	/appearance/present/an/overuse
(1 1 3 2 1)	/appearance/present/an/overuse/to the
(1 1 3 2 2)	/appearance/present/an/overuse/to a
(1 1 3 2 3)	/appearance/present/an/overuse/to 0
(1 1 3 2 4)	/appearance/present/an/overuse/to non-use
(1 1 4)	/appearance/present/zero form
(1 1 4 1)	/appearance/present/zero form/correct
(1 1 4 2)	/appearance/present/zero form/overuse
(1 1 4 2 1)	/appearance/present/zero form/overuse/to the
(1 1 4 2 2)	/appearance/present/zero form/overuse/to a
(1 1 4 2 3)	/appearance/present/zero form/overuse/an
(1 2)	/appearance/absent
(1 2 1)	/appearance/absent/determiners
(1 2 1 1)	/appearance/absent/determiners/this-that/these-those
(1 2 1 2)	/appearance/absent/determiners/some
(1 2 1 3)	/appearance/absent/determiners/one
(1 2 2)	/appearance/absent/other determiners
(1 2 2 1)	/appearance/absent/other determiners/quantifier
(1 2 2 2)	/appearance/absent/other determiners/possessive
(1 2 2 3)	/appearance/absent/other determiners/wh-determiner
(2)	/np category
(2 1)	/np category/proper
(2 2)	/np category/common
(2 2 1)	/np category/common/countable
(2 2 1 1)	/np category/common/countable/singular
(2 2 1 2)	/np category/common/countable/plural
(2 2 2)	/np category/common/uncountable
(2 3)	/np category/pronoun
(2 3 1)	/np category/pronoun/personal
(2 3 2)	/np category/pronoun/other
(3)	/np function
(3 1)	/np function/S

(3 2)	/np function/DO
(3 3)	/np function/IO
(3 4)	/np function/PC
(3 5)	/np function/SC
(3 6)	/np function/OC
(3 7)	/np function/EC
(3 8)	/np function/ADV
(3 9)	/np function/CONJ
(3 10)	/np function/PREM
(3 11)	/np function/POSM
(3 12)	/np function/APPO
(3 13)	/np function/ABS
(3 14)	/np function/EXCL
(3 15)	/np function/VOC
(4)	/np structure
(4 1)	/np structure/Head
(4 2)	/np structure/DH
(4 3)	/np structure/(D)MH
(4 4)	/np structure/(D)HP
(4 5)	/np structure/(D)MHP
(5)	/semantic meaning
(5 1)	/semantic meaning/the
(5 1 1)	/semantic meaning/the/Earlier Mention
(5 1 2)	/semantic meaning/the/Postmodification
(5 1 3)	/semantic meaning/the/Unique Object
(5 1 4)	/semantic meaning/the/Specified Order
(5 1 5)	/semantic meaning/the/Given Setting
(5 1 6)	/semantic meaning/the/Generic
(5 2)	/semantic meaning/a(n)
(5 2 1)	/semantic meaning/a(n)/Individual
(5 2 2)	/semantic meaning/a(n)/Generic
(5 3)	/semantic meaning/Ø
(5 3 1)	/semantic meaning/Ø/Parti-generic
(5 3 2)	/semantic meaning/Ø/Toto-generic

Appendix B

Overview of the
Software Program of SPSS

The Software Program of SPSS

SPSS (the Statistical Package for the Social Sciences) is a powerful, comprehensive, and flexible statistical and information analysis system. It is regarded as the most widely used suite of programs for statistical analysis in the social sciences (Bryman & Cramer, 1990). This package was first developed in the late 1960s by SPSS Company Chairman of the Board Norman H. Nie, C. Hadlai (Tex) Hull and Dale Bent, three Stanford University graduate students, and was the first major attempt to provide software for the social scientist. It has since undergone numerous revisions and refinements. In 1992, SPSS became the first major statistical software which was compatible with Microsoft Windows. This software, known as SPSS for Windows, has also undergone a number of revisions. The latest version at the time of writing is Release 7.5., which was introduced in 1996. This version is a true Windows 95 product and takes full advantage of the latest computer technology. The following are some main features of this version (Norusis, 1997):

1. It is easy to install in a personal computer.
2. It contains the most popular statistical procedures for basic statistical analysis such as counts, crosstabs, descriptives, factor analysis, regression and cluster analysis. The complete statistical procedures as displayed in the tool bar in this version include:
   A. Summarize (Frequencies, Descriptives, Explore, Crosstabs, Case Summaries, Report Summaries in Rows, Report Summaries in Columns)

    B.   Compare Means (Means, One-Sample T Test, Independent-Samples T Test, Paired-Samples T Test, One-Way ANOVA)

    C.   General Linear Model (Simple Factorial, GLM-General Factorial, GLM-Multivariate, GLM-Repeated Measures, Variance Components)

    D.   Correlate (Bivariate, Partial, Distances)

    E.   Regression (Linear, Curve Estimation, Logistic, Probit, Nonlinear, Weight Estimation, 2-Stage Least Square)

    F.   Loglinear (General, Logit, Model Selection)

    G.   Classify (K-Means Cluster, Hierarchical Cluster, Discriminant)

    H.   Data Reduction (Factor)

    I.   Scale (Reliability Analysis, Multidimensional Scaling)

    J.   Nonparametric Tests (Chi-Square, Binomial, Runs, 1-Sample K-S, 2 Independent Samples, K Independent Samples, 2 Related Samples, K Related Samples)

    K.   Survival (Life Tables, Kaplan-Meier, Cox Regression, Cow w/ Time-Dep Cov)

    L.   Multiple Response (Define Sets)

3.   It is easy to present important information in the form of charts, tables or bars.

4.   The Output Navigator can quickly and easily review one's work, rearrange output, hide topics and print - all from one pane.

5.   It can present the results clearly in16 pre-formatted styles.

6.   It is convenient for selecting an appropriate statistical procedure with the help of On-Line Coach of Statistics.

As an illustration of this version, the following are the results obtained by performing some statistical procedures on one data set of the present study.

APPEARAN

		Frequency	Percent	Valid Percent	Cumulative Percent
Valid	12.00	224	72.5	72.5	72.5
	1111.00	24	7.8	7.8	80.3
	1121.00	15	4.9	4.9	85.1
	1141.00	10	3.2	3.2	88.3
	1211.00	8	2.6	2.6	90.9
	1212.00	4	1.3	1.3	92.2
	1221.00	7	2.3	2.3	94.5
	1223.00	10	3.2	3.2	97.7
	1224.00	1	.3	.3	98.1
	11123.00	1	.3	.3	98.4
	11124.00	4	1.3	1.3	99.7
	11222.00	1	.3	.3	100.0
	Total	309	100.0	100.0	
Total		309	100.0		

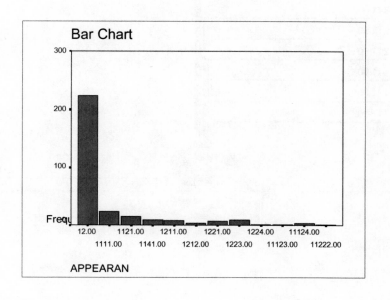

ANOVA

		Sum of Squares	df	Mean Square	F	Sig.
APPEARAN	Between Groups	4.4E+07	8	5453978	2.262	.023
	Within Groups	7.2E+08	300	2410600		
	Total	7.7E+08	308			

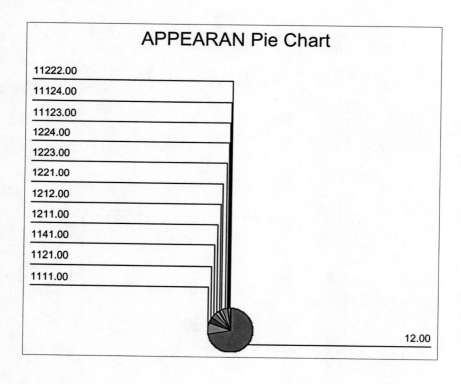

APPEARAN Pie Chart

11222.00
11124.00
11123.00
1224.00
1223.00
1221.00
1212.00
1211.00
1141.00
1121.00
1111.00

12.00

APPEARAN * STRUCTUR Crosstabulation

Count

		STRUCTUR				
		41.00	42.00	43.00	44.00	Total
APPEARAN	12.00	167	36	7	14	224
	1111.00		18	3	3	24
	1121.00		15			15
	1141.00	1	8		1	10
	1211.00	3		5		8
	1212.00	3	1			4
	1221.00		6		1	7
	1223.00		9		1	10
	1224.00			1		1
	11123.00		1			1
	11124.00			1	3	4
	11222.00			1		1
Total		174	94	18	23	309

APPEARAN

	Observed N	Expected N	Residual
12. 00	224	25.8	198.3
1111. 00	24	25.8	-1.8
1121. 00	15	25.8	-10.8
1141. 00	10	25.8	-15.8
1211. 00	8	25.8	-17.8
1212. 00	4	25.8	-21.8
1221. 00	7	25.8	-18.8
1223. 00	10	25.8	-15.8
1224. 00	1	25.8	-24.8
11123. 0 0	1	25.8	-24.8
11124. 0 0	4	25. 8	-21. 8
11222. 0 0	1	25. 8	-24. 8
Total	309		

Appendix C

Transcriptions of the Speech Interactions

The Transcriptions

K = the interviewer, a female native speaker of English

L = the informant, a boy coming from China

Y = the researcher

- = repetition of a word/sound or part of a word/sound as well as its normal function of connecting words

… = pause

xxx = an unintelligible utterance or portion of an utterance

____ = the abrupt stop when interrupted

/x/ = phonetic transcription of a word or sound

(x) = the missing part of a word or the correct form of a word

[x] = what contained in the square bracket is the situational context or explanation

word(s) italicized = foreign word(s)

Conversation 1: 9/28/1996

K: What you want to talk about today?

L: Um last week I change our classroom.

K: You did?

L: Yep.

K: Why?

L: Um I'm in Room 9, but now I'm in Room 12 because um we just start to this-this quarter um we just … there are many classroom we didn't like, we didn't use. Like um if there is something, then we use the room 12. Las-last year the room 12 is ESL.

K: Okay.

L: Um but this year um ESL is Room 5. Then we just go. There are many people going. There are many 5th grade going to Room 12. And there're 4th grade. There just a little bit 4th grade. But there are many like um 5th grade. So we just part two-two classroom.

K: Okay.

L: Then the 4th grade going to the other classroom. There just a little bit 5th grade. There are many 4th grade. But in 12, Room 12, there are just 5th grade.

K: Okay.

L: But in Roo-Room 9, there-there are 5th grade, there are 4th grade, there are two grade.

K: Okay.

L: And we have our other the three new teacher.

K: Yeah!?

L: Yeah. One is he just going to Cranbrook Monday. Then he'll go to high school.

K: Okay.

L: He just tell me to do something like-like um how to do the some puzzle like-like that. And the-the um second teacher is Mrs.-Mrs. Wall I think.

K: Okay.

L: The-the first one is Mrs. Norter. The second one is Mrs. Wall. She is good but she don't like this: some people like um they're not good like they are … um he she's talking then they're talking. And she don't like they. So there're one new teacher and they go to … they have some she don't like and go the room 12. But there're some she like go to Room 12 too. Yesterday we have our letter and the letter say I need to go Room 12 on Friday. We have our new desk and new teacher. Um um on Friday we just study like how, why you use the period.

K: Okay.

L: How use the comma um and how use the question marker and many thing. And she give me a paper. And we just on two o'clock, no I mean two or two fifteen. Um we not she, she tell you she tell me just do like um write the school rules.

K: Okay.

L: There are many school (rules) like no pushing, no-no making noising, no fight, um, and many things we just did.

K: Okay.

L: On the on the two-two I mean three o'clock, then I just going to ESL.

K: Okay.

L: Um ESL let me do a paper there. I'm not finished yet. This one here. It's for moon day.

K: Oh, wow!

L: It's a rabbit.

K: You made that?

L: Yeah.

K: Okay.

L: Then we just take this.

K: You used to take that?

L: Yeah. [showing how to make a paper rabbit for moon day]

K: Oh, and then you can hang it some where.

L: Yeah.

K: Fun. So this wasn't art class. This is regular class?

L: No, it's ESL.

K: E...?

L: ESL.

K: What's ESL?

L: Um English second language.

K: Ooooh, English second language. So any of your friends there with you

L: Yeah.

K: in Room 12?

L: Yeah. There're somebody go to like they're from Korea. They're from um Turkey.

K: Yeah!?

L: They're from Indian.

K: Okay.

L: Everywhere they're is.

K: They're from everywhere.

L: Yeah.

K: So you keep speaking English there?

L: Um ye.

K: Yeah.

L: We just speak English.

K: Okay. Wow, that's fun. So you just moved?

L: Yeah.

K: Just moved classrooms?

L: Yeah.

K: Ha, are you glad or no?

L: [nodding head]

K: It's fun?

L: Yeah, it's fun.

K: Then what you do with that?

L: This?

K: Yeah.

L: It's for Moon Day Moon Day so like m-o-n m-o-o-n.

K: I don't know what's that?

L: It's like … Friday. Yesterday is … um

K: It was a holiday?

L: Yeah, it's a holiday in China.

K: In China. Okay.

L: In China.

K: What you celebrate?

L: Like um um it's in many country like um Russia like many country with that holiday.

K: Okay. It's that your homework?

L: [shaking head] uh no.

K: No.

L: Like [showing a book] you know what's this?

K: What's that? Oh, the harvest moon. The moon festival. The play.

L: Yes.

K: Okay.

L: It's a holiday.

K: It's a holiday.

L: Yes, it's a holiday. xxx That's moon ruler. But yesterday we have some raining, so we can't see the moon.

K: Oooh, because of the eclipse?

L: Yeah.

K: Okay.

L: So I need to cut this, then try to found the moon is there.

K: Okay.

L: The big part is how much ____

K: How much the moon is?

L: Yeah.

K: Okay. Wow, that sounds fun. So this is new stuff you do in your classroom?

L: Yeah.

K: Classroom, is it 9? You used to be in?

L: No.

K: They don't do that?

L: This is ESL.

K: Oh, they do that too.

L: Yeah.

K: Okay.

L: Some class can get it are .... I don't know how to say that.

K: I see.

L: Like-like this. But I can draw that.

K: You can draw that?

L: Yeah. It's like this. Somebody some teacher give you like this.

K: Oh, pumpkin?

L: Yeah.

K: Yeah. And that's a good drawing.

L: Yeah, it's small.

K: You got a little pumpkin.

L: No, some-some the other classroom.

K: The other classroom?

L: Yeah. My friend cut this. But he's stupid. He cut that.

K: Oh [laughing]. Then what happened?

L: He want he want see how much seed in there.

K: Okay. But the little ones don't have many seeds, do they?

L: Yeah. xxx But it's good.

K: Yeah, that's fun. Oh what a neat idea! So you got a little pumpkin for your class.

L: Okay. Then I can get here.

K: Yeah. Do you have to pick it back to school or no?

L: Um I don't think so.

K: No. xxx Wow, did you know you're going to switch the classroom?

L: No but I get a letter.

K: You got a letter.

L: Yeah.

K: So you just switched on Thursday?

L: Yeah.

K: Some of your friends in your class?

L: Yeah.

K: That's good. Will you will you still see other people in your class?

L: Yeah.

K: You still have gym?

L: Yeah. There are many-many room like people in my class.

K: Yeah.

L: This Saturday five girl there. There are fifteen boys.

K: Five girls?

L: Yeah.

K: Poor girls.

L: It's just the five people in the room 9. They're just five people in the 5th grade. Other people in the 4th grade.

K: Okay. Everybody in your class the 5th grade, right?

L: Yeah.

K: Wow, that sounds fun. That sounds you like it.

L: Yeah.

K: Do you?

L: Yeah, I like it.

K: You do.

L: Um the room 9 there're just five boy, there're many girls.

K: Hmm. What you do when it rains? Do you still go outside to recess?

L: No.

K: What you do?

L: We just in the classroom watch TV.

K: You watch TV?

L: Yeah.

K: What you watch?

L: Um like American's funniest um funniest home video.

K: You watch American's funniest home video?

L: Yeah. Sometimes we watch that; sometimes we watch video; sometimes we watch the other culture, some ... um like um a pig. There's many sheets in there. Pig like a dog wan wan. Then sheet is go away. That-that's very fun. Sometimes we can't understand this.

K: Yeah.

L: Like a sheet, like a pig ____

K: Um-hmm.

L: He wants like a dog. She says wan-wan-wan and that pig ha-ha-ha. And we don't know what he say with sheet. She is /gou/-/gou/-/gou/ like some dogs /gou/. And sheet is going somewhere.

K: Okay, that's funny.

L: Yep.

K: You just watch TV? Do you play game?

L: [shaking head] un-un.

K: No, only watch TV.

L: Sometimes we can play some games like cheese.

K: Cheese?

L: No no no I mean like ... I don't know how to say that.

K: Is that a board game?

L: Yeah. But some girls know how to play this game too.

K: Yeah.

L: Like um there're many games like Monopoly

K: Yeah.

L: and many game.

K: Okay. Do you ever what you like better: to stay inside watch TV or go outside and have recess?

L: Go outside to have recess.

K: Yeah.

L: You can play football.

K: You play football?

L: Yeah.

K: But what you do in winter when it's cold when it snows?

L: We can play.

K: You can still play.

L: Sometimes um there're some raining we can't play. If it snow, we can.

K: You can't play.

L: Yes, we can.

K: Oh, you can but other than raining.

L: Yeah.

K: Wow. What time you get up to school?

L: Um eight o'clock.

K: Eight o'clock?

L: Yeah.

K: The bus comes at …?

L: Eight forty-five.

K: Eight forty-five.

L: Sometimes it's late.

K: The bus is late?

L: Yeah.

K: Then what you do? Just wait?

L: Yeah, just wait.

K: Wow, where they pick you up? Right here?

L: Um no [showing the place from the window].

K: Oh, on the main road. Okay.

L: Yeah, just in the road of Colony Square. We go there. And there is xxx

K: Then what time you get home from school?

L: Um sometimes go home four o'clock. Sometimes just um two o'clock three o'clock.·

K: Okay. What you're going to do today? You have no school.

L: Yeah, I need working.

K: What you're working at?

L: Working this. It's a test for six o'clock, no I mean for 6th grade.

K: It's a test?

L: Yeah.

K: Are you studying?

L: Yeah. I just can do math. xxx

K: Is your writing? You write them?

L: Yeah.

K: That's nice writing. Nice hand signature.

L: There are many things here like that …

K: Citizenship?

L: Yeah. And here's reading.

K: You have to read it?

L: Yeah. Here's writing.

K: What's the hardest part, reading or writing?

L: The reading.

K: What do you practice?

L: Practice?

K: Yeah. Practice your reading, what you do?

L: Like read a-a story and answer the question.

K: Oh, make sure that you understand xxx

L: Yeah.

K: Okay. Did you ever read that one?

L: [shaking head] un-un. I just want to do math. There're many thing need a answer booklet. But I don't get it.

K: Oh, you don't get an answer booklet.

L: Yeah.

K: That makes it hard, do they?

L: Yeah.

K: Hmm. You're going to work on it all day?

L: Um not all day. Just um maybe four hours.

K: Okay.

L: Just um in-in Friday I didn't read my homework. So on Saturday and Sunday I have to do that.

K: Oh, your dad came back!

Y: Yeah, so you can stop.

---End of Conversation---

CONVERSATION 2: 10/5/1996

K: Tell me something.

L: Um well I mean in Room 12 I have a new teacher. This teacher um she is um …

K: You have a new teacher in Cranbrook?

L: Yeah.

K: Oh!

L: He is I mean she is um she did not give many work, but the work is very difficult for me. We need to write journal. We need seven lines.

K: Oh.

L: Hmm.

K: Today I was walking home and I saw some kids get off the bus. They cut through the woods to get here. Do you do that?

L: Yeah.

K: There is a little path?

L: Yeah.

K: Yes. Are those your friends?

L: Yeah.

K: Yeah, okay. What you talk about today?

L: Um ...

K: Tell me about art class. What you've done in art class lately?

L: Oh, art. Now art we need do the three D, some Columbus building.

K: What is that?

L: There are some building like um a building like this. I don't know its name.

K: Okay.

L: It's just in Columbus downtown.

K: Oooh.

L: Five-five or six building you need draw and (in) three D.

K: You need to draw it in three D?

L: Yeah.

K: Is that hard?

L: No, not for me.

K: No. You are a good artist. Hmm.

L: Yeah.

K: Okay, what about October? Are you are you studying Halloween stuff yet?

L: No.

K: What are you doing now? What you are doing every day in school?

L: We work on um on um um two um one um one o'clock. Then we just recess. Then we finish our recess and teacher will reading some books

K: Okay.

L: for we. Um...

K: She reads to you?

L: No, to everybody. Then we just write handwriting one page.

K: Okay.

L: Then she's read-read-read on um tow-two one thirty then we can drink some water.

K: Water? Why?

L: Yeah, drink water.

K: Oh.

L: We go to recess on

K: Okay.

L: on um twelve, twelve thirty to one o'clock.

K: Okay.

L: Then we have to drink water. Um on-on two thirty we go back to-to the classroom and then we read um the some spelling-spelling work. Sometimes we have some sheets. Sometimes we need copy some word. Sometimes we need do something. Sometimes we have spelling test.

K: You do?

L: Yeah.

K: Do you like that?

L: Um a little bit.

K: Okay. Do you like your new room?

L: Yeah.

K: You told me last week you got a new room.

L: Yeah.

K: A lot of fun?

L: Yeah.

K: Hmm.

L: There are many game in there.

K: Many games?

L: On Friday, Friday afternoon then we can play.

K: You play game?

L: Yeah.

K: What game you play?

L: Um like Sorry like Trouble

K: [laughing]

L: like some toy um some puzzle. We just play every game you can.

K: Okay, what's your favorite one?

L: I just play one. I just play Sorry.

K: You like Sorry?

L: Yeah.

K: I like that game too. It's fun to knock the other people off the board

L: Yeah.

K: and let them go back to start it. Hmm. When it's your birthday?

L: Birthday?

K: Um-hmm.

L: Um August twenty three.

K: Oh you just had birthday!

L: Yeah.

K: What did you do for your birthday?

L: My grandmom and granddad buy a puzzle three D puzzle.

K: Um-ha.

L: It's a um US capitol.

K: Okay I saw it

L: Yeah.

K: in your house. Did you put it together?

L: Yeah.

K: Okay.

L: Um and my dad and my aunt um she-she is in the um Ja-Japan and she give me one um one hundred one hundred dollar and I buy um a video game.

K: You did! What video game?

L: Ahh Sega.

K: Sega.

L: Yeah.

K: Okay. Do you do that a lot?

L: Not a lot now.

K: Are you gonna do something outside?

L: Yeah.

K: Play sports?

L: Yeah.

K: I saw you and your friends playing and kicking the ball and stuff.

L: Yeah.

K: Interesting. You like Christmas?

L: Yeah.

K: Yeah. What you want to do for Christmas?

L: We have many big party.

K: A big party?

L: Yeah. My friends one of my friends his birthday is in Christmas.
K: No way.
L: Yeah.
K: So does he get Christmas presents and birthday presents?
L: Yeah. Then he just have a party for his birthday and for Christmas.
K: Okay, just one party.
L: Yeah.
K: What did you do in China for Christmas?
L: We don't know Christmas. We don't know. We just …
K: You don't have Christmas?
L: We don't have that.
K: You don't!?
L: Yeah.
K: Um there's no Santa Claus?
L: Un-un [shaking head]. Nothing.
K: Is there any kind of holiday?
L: No.
K: No! There's no holiday in China?
L: No.
K: Oh! Do you ever have party?
L: No.
K: No! Do you like Christmas?
L: Yeah, yeah.
K: Yeah. Do you hope you keep doing it when you go back to China?
L: Yeah.
K: You like it.
L: My mom let me go America is August tenth because she wants I see the American's Christmas.
K: Okay.
L: Like the Chinese happy New Year.
K: Okay.
L: Yeah.
K: Okay, all right. Do you have a fireworks?
L: Yeah.
K: In Chinese New Year?
L: Yeah.
K: What you do for Chinese New Year?

L: We have some-some money.

K: Some money?

L: But-but in America um we have um Chinese New Year. My mom give me one dollar. My-my grandfather give me one dollar.

K: Okay.

L: Only one dollar!

K: [laughing]

L: But in um in China I can get one hundred dollar and everybody give me one hundred. I can get um I mean five hundred dollar.

K: Wow, that's lot of money.

L: Yeah.

K: Hmm. Do you have Halloween? In China?

L: Halloween?

K: Yeah.

L: Um it's not it's not ten it's not on October seven, fifth. It's on July fifteenth.

K: Really?

L: Yeah. I think so.

K: Do you dress up? In costumes?

L: Um sometimes we are not. Sometimes we do.

K: Yeah. Are you going to do it here? On October?

L: No.

K: You are not going to dress up?

L: I don't know what's the date.

K: It's October thirty first.

L: Thirty first?

K: Um-hmm, the last day of October. Are you going to dress up for anything?

L: Um I don't know.

K: Are you going to go Trick or Treating?

L: Um I don't know.

K: Okay. Did you do it last year?

L: No.

K: No! Were you here last year in October?

L: No.

K: When did you come?

L: What?

K: When did you come to America?

L: Um on December tenth.

K: December tenth. Oh, you got just in time for Christmas!

L: Yeah.

K: Yes, okay. Wow, do you know what they do for Halloween? The-the kids are all dress up.

L: Yeah.

K: They go to people's house and get candy.

L: Like a witch.

K: Yeah, some people are witches. If you could dress up, what would you be?

L: I don't know.

K: You don't know? Okay. Will you have a Halloween party at school?

L: No.

K: No!

L: I don't know. I think so.

K: You think so. Hmm.

L: What's this for? [pointing to a small pumpkin on the window sill] It's for ...?

K: It's for Halloween.

L: It's for Halloween. I think we can get a this for Halloween.

K: Yeah.

L: Because I see my teacher have a big box this. Many this in the box.

K: Those are pumpkins.

L: Yeah, pumpkin.

K: Pumpkin. Are you going to carve one?

L: No.

K: Have you seen that where you take the knife and you take out the insides and you make a face?

L: Make a face?

K: Yep, make a face out of it and then you put a candle in it. And you put it outside your door and it glows. It's a kind of fun. Are you going to do that?

L: I didn't get a big one.

K: No.

L: If I get a big one then I want.

K: Yes, it's fun to do. I did one when I was little. I think I still might do it. It's fun. Do you have those at school then?

L: I think so.

K: Hmm.

L: A small one.

K: A little one. Just like that little ones?

L: Yeah, Room 12.

K: Room 12 and the old one was ...? 9? No? Yeah?

L: Yeah.

K: Yeah.

L: I think so. I don't know because I didn't go to Room 9.

K: What are you gonna do today? Today is Saturday, free day.

L: Um watch the movie.

K: What movie?

L: Batman.

K: Batman Returns or The First Batman?

L: Yeah, Batman the Movie, Batman the Cartoon, Batman um Forever.

K: Yeah.

L: And many Batman.

K: You like Batman?

L: Yeah.

K: How come?

L: Because Batman is good.

K: He's good?

L: I can watch Batman the Cartoon every day.

K: You can?

L: Yeah.

K: You like it? The Cartoon um I don't think I've seen that.

L: The Cartoon is xxx

K: Do they have the things where the words on the screen and says: Ka Pow, Bang? Do they have those? No?

L: Yeah.

K: Like when Batman gets in a fight and he's beating someone up and it says Pow or something on the screen?

L: Yeah.

K: Yeah, that is a fun one.

L: Yeah.

K: I have seen that. That's good. After you watch the movie, what will you do?

L: Um watch the football.

K: What football?

L: Today we have our football.

K: You're going to watch Ohio State?

L: Yeah.

K: Yeah. Do you like Ohio State?

L: Yeah.

K: You do.

L: They play a good.

K: Yeah. You want them to win?

L: Yeah.

K: What you can do if they win?

L: I ... don't know.

K: [laughing] I guess we have to stop now.

L: Okay.

K: Your dad said it's time. No more pressure.

L: Okay.

---End of Conversation---

CONVERSATION 3: 10/13/1996

L: [pointing to the video tapes] Yesterday I borrow that in the Upper Arlington library.

K: Oh.

L: His name is Willy.

K: Willy, okay.

L: And this-this small children he-he like that. A big whale.

K: Um-hmm.

L: So there're somebody take him in a pool

K: Um-hmm.

L: like a swimming pool.

K: Yes.

L: So his family in the in the water the other water.

K: Okay.

L: They dive (are divided), okay? Then he-he need do something for the every body like Sea World.

K: Um-hmm.

L: You need going there. You need some money, then you can watch the he do something.

K: Okay.

L: As he like him so he everyday he going to there help him. He want him like do something. If he say um "up", then he do something. He say something then he do something. But one day there're many people are coming want see what he do. But there're-there're many people don't know why he can't-can't do anything. He ask him "Come on, Willy! Let's-let's do". But he say he say like this [shaking head]. Because um there're somebody in the down the um like basement

K: Um-hmm.

L: basement down the pool.

K: Um-hmm.

L: Then we can see the-the whale in the um glasses.

K: Okay.

L: We can see in there. They all do like this [knocking the table]. Then he-he were scared. He don't know what they want they will do for him. So he don't want to be [give a performance]. He want go-go to his house.

K: Okay.

L: So the-the Willy's boss's Willy. So the-the boss say he can do nothing. So he want to take him. He want sale-sale him

K: Um-hmm.

L: or kill him.

K: Okay.

L: So one day they do um they take the basement.

K: Hmm.

L: They take the glasses broken. Then the water is go out.

K: Hmm.

L: Then if-if you-you're not quick, then he will die, right?

K: Um-hmm.

L: Then the three good people one is he one is the his mom and his dad to take a car. Go to the um car wash and he can get some water because if you going to pool you don't have water, then he will die.

K: Okay.

L: And he get some water.

K: From the car wash?

L: Yeah.

K: Okay.

L: His dad in the car wash doing something. He's the boss in the car wash.

K: Okay.

L: Then they take some water. Take him, then they go to the beach.

K: Um-hmm.

L: But the boss see the um the whale is not in the pool.

K: Um-hmm.

L: Then he will go to beach quickly because they got go to car wash.

K: Okay.

L: So they going to stop they because the boss want sale this whale this-this um one hundred million dollars.

K: Okay.

L: Then he don't want they sale that because or-or kill him

K: Okay.

L: because he like him.

K: Right.

L: So he want he want him go to the with his family.

K: Um-hmm.

L: Then the his dad and mom take him on the car go to the beach. But the boss in the beach-beach enter. They want stop them stop. They just um stand in the enter. They don't care him. Then they just going-go-going to enter, then take him down when the um then he's go away. But some boss's people take a-a bag (net) like a bag. Then the him going to there and he need to back to there to again. So he just tell him: "You have to go the other way. Then you need jump-jump over this [showing the picture on the video-tape]".

K: Yes.

L: "Over this. If you're not, you can't go-going there. If you going there, then they-they will they will take you in the bag".

K: Okay.

L: So he want him jump-jump high in there. So he-he going there, then he with his family. He was happy.

K: Oh.

L: Yeah. But the boss is not happy.

K: Oh, I bet not.

L: Yeah.

K: He was probably mad. Um... was that the end?

L: The end is like this [showing the picture on the video-tape].

K: The end is to jump over.

L: Yeah.

K: Okay. Was it a good movie, did you like it?

L: Yeah.

K: Yeah, oh good. You said you got it at the library?

L: Yeah.

K: How did you do that?

L: Borrow.

K: Oh, you just you can borrow videos too?

L: Yeah.

K: Oh.

L: I borrow five on three day.

K: Five for three days.

L: Yeah.

K: What other videos did you borrow?

L: Um there [going to another desk to get the videos]. And this [showing one]. I like this [showing one] and this [showing one].

K: Oh, Jurassic Park!

L: You watch that before?

K: We watched it last night. Jos [Kelly's husband] and I watched it last night.

L: The video?

K: Um-hmm, the video. At my mom and dad's house, we watched it. What was your favorite part?

L: It's the-the they say they saw the-the somebody the-the dinosaur.

K: Um-hmm.

L: And one people going to restroom.

K: Um-hmm.

L: You saw that?

K: Yeah.

L: It's funny.

K: Yeah.

L: Then the restroom is broken. Just him stay on a toilet.

K: Um-hmm.

L: And the dinosaur eat him, then just go away.

K: Right. Jos likes that part too.

L: Yeah, it's funny.

K: It's so funny, yeah.

L: And the they-they three they three

K: Um-hmm.

L: going to the like um we just because the big dinosaur like this.

K: Um-hmm.

L: They're coming and they go down the tree.

K: Um-hmm.

L: Then they go up the tree.

K: Oh right, yeah.

L: Then they-they say (see) some high dinosaur like this [showing the picture].

K: Okay.

L: Then they get the them some um trees.

K: Yeah.

L: Yeah.

K: They fed the dinosaurs.

L: Yeah.

K: And then it sneezed on the girl.

L: Yeah.

K: Remember that? It was funny.

L: Remember the a bad man?

K: Um-hmm.

L: A bat …

K: Um-hmm.

L: Um he's fat.

K: Okay.

L: Somebody give him um a million dollars. And he do he did some-something in the a-a can.

K: Um-hmm.

L: In a can.

K: Oh, yeah.

L: That's bad, right?

K: A can like this?

L: Um like this. Um yeah, just a can.

K: A big can?

L: No, just like that big.

K: This is big.

L: Yeah. Then he going to a-a special place.

K: Um-hmm.

L: But he see a small dinosaur. You saw that? He the dinosaur do /buuun/.

K: [laughing]

L: You saw that?

K: Um I didn't watch didn't watch Batman.

L: Not Batman.

K: Oh, it's in Jurassic Park?

L: Yeah. It's um …

K: Ah, it was the scary part? I didn't watch the scary parts.

L: I don't know.

K: Was the-the Raptors? You know the one that ah the little fast ones? The really fast ones?

L: Yeah.

K: It was a part like that?

L: Ah, a-a-a man, a fat _____

K: Oh, yes, the fat man.

L: Yeah, the fat man, right. He going he going he is scare.

K: Right.

L: And he go. He see a small dinosaur.

K: Oh yeah, the one that spit in his face.

L: Yeah.

K: Oh, yeah. I didn't like that part either. Did you like the part where the Raptors chased the two kids in the kitchen?

L: Yeah.

K: Yeah. Um I didn't like that part. I was scared.

L: The dinosaur he see the mirror.

K: Um-hmm.

L: He going there, but the children is in the other side.

K: Okay.

L: The dinosaur is in there.

K: Yeah it's in the cupboard.

L: And he think the children is in there. He going there /buuuun/, then he is dead.

K: Yeah, it was yucky.

L: Then the big dinosaurs is change to good.

K: Yeah. And they ate the little dinosaurs.

L: Yeah.

K: Then they got away. It was the end. I watched that part. That-that was good.

L: Yeah.

K: What else did you watch?

L: These three.

K: Jurassic Park?

L: And this. I watch that before.

K: Yeah.

L: This Batman Cartoon.

K: Um-ha.

L: I don't know I watch it. So I borrow it. I watch that before. And that's my mom borrow that.

K: Your mom borrow that one.

L: Read English Today.

K: Hmm. You're already reading English so you don't need to watch, right?

L: Um I watch or not watch it's okay.

K: Yeah. Oh well, that one fast, isn't it? [showing the time is up] Push this one? [pointing to the buttons on the tape-recorder]

L: Yeah.

---End of Conversation---

CONVERSATION 4: 10/23/1996

K: Okay. So what's been happening?

L: Um …

K: I haven't seen you in a long time.

L: I think this Sunday I got go to the um a garden.

K: Um-hmm.

L: There is many apple tree in there.

K: Okay.

L: And we can get some apple

K: Yeah.

L: in there. If um my mom say it's very funny. You need go long-long way, then you can go in there.

K: Okay.

L: I think it's very big because it like the um … like the what
    … like you go in the garden, then you just found apples, then
    you get it
K: Okay.
L: in one bag. Then how much for one bag, then …
K: Okay. So you're gonna apple orchards?
L: Yeah.
K: Is that called?
L: Yeah.
K: Okay.
L: I think this Sunday.
K: This Sunday you're going.
L: Yeah.
K: Okay.
L: My mom say this-this is the this Sunday is the last day of um
    the garden sale.
K: Okay. Ye(s), it might be.
L: Yeah.
K: Hmm. How's school?
L: School?
K: Um-hmm.
L: Um today I have a test, two test.
K: Oh, yuck.
L: Health and Social Study.
K: Okay. What-what was your health test on?
L: Um like-like you complete the sentence
K: Okay.
L: with the word. Um they've like thousand of what make your
    make your body. Like thousand of the cells
K: Okay.
L: make human's body. This me study this-this unit?
K: Hmm.
L: This restudy the um bone
K: Okay.
L: muscle and the cell.
K: Okay.
L: And we study um why you are tall, are short.
K: Okay. Why?

L: Because um some-some your mother, your father are short, then you will get some, you will like not be very tall.

K: Okay.

L: And um if you're a girl you are girls um like um one or two um year you-you growth up are quick.

K: Okay.

L: And girls are um it's seven um to eleven old years old then you grow up very quick.

K: Okay.

L: Some boy-boy is like um eleven to thirteen years old grow quick.

K: Okay.

L: So in fifth grade classroom there is like girls eleven old um twelve old and boys ten old ten years old. So there are many different size of the fifth grade.

K: Okay.

L: Because they're all in the eleven-eleven years old. That means girls are really finish his um grow-up's time.

K: Okay.

L: But boys growth up quick in eleven old to thirteen years old.

K: Okay. And how old are you?

L: Me? Um I'm ten years old.

K: Oh, so next year you're gonna grow quick.

L: Yeah.

K: Wow.

L: And the next Wednesday we have a Halloween party.

K: Really!?

L: Yeah.

K: Do you have to dress up?

L: Um I don't know.

K: Are you going to?

L: I don't know.

K: Are-are you going to do Trick or Treating?

L: I don't know.

K: Yeah. In the neighborhood here

L: Yeah.

K: you will costume and go knock on doors.

L: Yeah.

K: You're gonna do that?

L: I think so.

K: You think so.

L: We have a party in the Mike's office, you know?

K: No. Oh, yeah.

L: Room Two.

K: Right. Are you gonna go?

L: Yeah.

K: Me too.

L: It's tomorrow.

K: Starts tomorrow?

L: Yeah. I think tomorrow is twenty four.

K: It is, isn't it? I'm gonna on Friday.

L: Friday?

K: The twenty fifth.

L: Okay.

K: Yeah. Did you get a pumpkin yet?

L: No.

K: No! You can have that one.

L: That one?

K: Um-hmm.

L: Sure. That one is too big.

K: It's too big? We have smaller ones in the bathroom. And you want a smaller one?

L: It's okay.

K: Or you want a big one?

L: It's okay.

K: Either one you can have.

L: I want small one.

K: I think the small one is inside the bathroom. I'll go get it.

L: You get three pumpkin?

K: And I got by my mom and dad's house.

L: Oh.

K: Ou-oh, we're not talking into the tape. Your dad can be mad. [laughing] We'd better set that down.

L: It's not like same. This one is small a little bit.

K: You want the big one?

L: It's okay.

K: Whatever, you can have any one you want.

L: There.

K: Yeah. Ah, let's say, did you see any movies lately?

L: Movie?

K: Um-hmm.

L: I borrow the movie.

K: What movie?

L: Um one is um the like told you how to be how to do the magic.

K: Um-hmm.

L: Be a magic game [How to be a magician].

K: Oh.

L: There are something you do not know how do how do they do like they get some a paper in the there, then-then they open it _____

K: It's gone?

L: It's gone. So there're many thing you don't know how do they do that.

K: Oh. Can you do it?

L: I can do some like I use a-a um something to go up your hand.

K: Okay.

L: Then you do like this [showing]. Then it's out. It's-it's not in there.

K: Yeah!

L: It's gone.

K: How do they do it?

L: Um you need a like-like this …

K: A cord for this work? [showing a tape measure]

L: No, it's too big.

K: Too big.

L: Small is better.

K: Oh you need a thin something.

L: Then you need do like this.

K: You need to wrap it around your hand?

L: Then you /buuuuun/, then it's gone. My grandma told me how to do that.

K: Yeah.

L: Yeah.

K: Ha.

L: But I-I maybe-maybe seven to eight years old, I can do magic on the neck.

K: Um-hmm.

L: Then you do like this. [showing a cord around the neck] It's gone too.

K: Oh, that's scary.

L: I-I use the Chinese the um box of-of the matches.

K: Um-hmm.

L: Then I cut the half. Then I-I take the other side. This match is in the other side. You don't see that.

K: Okay.

L: Like you have a box, then I give I give you see one half, then-then it's this match. But the other the other half you see, there's no matches.

K: Hmm!

L: Because I cut it there.

K: Oh.

L: Then the half matches in the other side.

K: Okay.

L: Then you can see it.

K: So it's a big trick.

L: Yeah.

K: I don't know about that.

L: It's fun.

K: Yeah. Were you watching TV just now?

L: Yeah.

K: Yeah. So you had to come over here to talk. You want to watch TV, right?

L: Yeah.

K: Yeah. Sorry.

L: No problem.

K: Well, what about your social study test?

L: Social study?

K: Um-hmm, how to go?

L: Um we study the land form.

K: Oh, really!

L: Yeah. And we study um like United States is-is called what.

K: Okay.

L: There are some um some rock.

K: Um-hmm.

L: It's just um … there're some mountain, there're many mountain. And there is the just the like um there is just like nobody can living there. There is just um like um like this over there.

K: This plant?

L: Yeah, like plant. Like all plants you can't living there.

K: Um-ha.

L: There're some place. And they tell me the-the plant like this the big place is mountain

K: Um-hmm.

L: in the map. You can-can call that a country, right?

K: Right.

L: Because if this is United States

K: Um-hmm.

L: then there is Canada.

K: Um-hmm.

L: And there is big is mountain

K: Um-hmm.

L: all the mountain. Then you can call the this mountain are divide country.

K: Right.

L: And United States is-is this. This half mountain is United States. This half is Canada.

K: Okay.

L: And um …

K: Did you do good on the test?

L: Um because me and the um the other Korean girl our English not good, so we can look the book.

K: Oh.

L: But there're something you can't found in the book.

K: Right.

L: We need we need write some notes every day you study.

K: I think your English is good.

L: But I need go to ESL.

K: Oh, the English only class.

L: Yeah.

K: Is it English second language class?

L: Yeah.

K: Is that what it is? Oh. Well, but you like school?

L: Yeah.

K: You do. That's good. Tell me more about you Halloween party.

L: Oh, we can take some we can take some cookie
K: Um-hmm.
L: and the um some fruit.
K: Um-hmm.
L: The teacher give you-you a paper. Write the letter. What do
     you what do you can help-help the Halloween party.
K: Um-hmm.
L: Because it is for the school.
K: Oh, the whole school?
L: Yeah.
K: Okay.
L: So on next Wednesday in the afternoon we have Halloween
     party.
K: Okay, in the afternoon.
L: Yeah.
K: All afternoon?
L: Yeah.
K: Okay. [laughing when see the researcher entering] No more
     talking.
---End of Conversation---

CONVERSATION 5: 11/2/1996

K: What did you do today?
L: Um today I with my friends go to the Magic Mountain.
K: Yeah!
L: Today is his birthday.
K: Okay.
L: No, um next Tuesday is his birthday. But he got school in the
     next Tuesday, so he want to change his birthday to today.
K: Okay.
L: He take me and some his friends six-six children go to the
     Magic Mountain.
K: Okay.
L: We playing there. Um we play um um golf
K: Okay.
L: um and the … with some coin to play some game. Then get
     some ticket to change some toy or pencil
K: Okay.

L: or something. Um we play the my-my friend he going to there. Then he saw the that games with the coin to play that games. He-he saw there are many games in there so he want playing there. But his dad say we got go to play the golf first. But he don't want to because he saw that game is a fun. In the morning it's a little bit warm. But in the afternoon it's very cold. So we just go play the-the golf a little bit because it's very cold. There is we have six people. There is two people don't want to play that. There is one is a girl. One is a um first-grade. They don't know how to play that.

K: [laughing]

L: And he is very cold. Then we play the that games first. And there're many games in there like um video game, that big video game.

K: Um-hmm.

L: You can get some point or some game you like there is a there is some number in there. There is a ball like this. Then you put one cent. The ball must stop and is going there. You get that four ticket when you're going to that four number, number four. If you going to five, you get five tickets by there. One coin you can play one. But some game you need two coin to playing.

K: Okay.

L: Um there is many thing you can do change. Like you have ah you have um one hundred fifteen point, you can change a ball like this.

K: Oh, yeah.

L: Yeah. There're some good thing like some puzzle you need maybe one thousand.

K: Is that what you got this?

L: No.

K: No.

L: I got this. [going to get it, but hitting something and almost falling down from the chair]

K: Whoops! [laughing] Are you okay?

L: xxx The ticket.

K: Oh, the ticket.

L: Like this.

K: Oh, yeah.

L: I get this.
K: You got this there?
L: Yeah, this from the fifteen ticket.
K: Fifteen tickets?
L: Yeah.
K: What's this?
L: This is a sticker.
K: Oh.
L: This is three ticket. This is um twenty five ticket.
K: That's nice, though.
L: Yes. xxx
K: How many tickets?
L: It's fifty.
K: Fifty?
L: Yeah.
K: How many tickets did you have?
L: I don't know. A lot. [showing and counting] Fifteen. It is twenty
     five. It's fifty. It's three. It's this fourteen. And is thirty, thirty
     three,
K: A hundred thirty three?
L: thirty four, thirty five. Yeah, one hundred and thirty five.
K: And the candy is from?
L: From the Meijer.
K: Oh, not from Magic Mountain.
L: Yeah.
K: Um-hmm. Did you eat at the Magic Mountain?
L: Yeah.
K: What did you eat?
L: I eat a birthday cake.
K: Okay.
L: Yeah, a little half and three piece pizza.
K: [laughing] What kind of pizza?
L: Pepperonian pizza.
K: Pepperonian pizza.
L: Yeah.
K: And what did you drink?
L: Ah we drink um Pepsi
K: Pepsi.
L: and the orange juice.

K: Orange juice.

L: Yeah.

K: That's healthy. So it's a fun party.

L: Yeah.

K: Hmm.

L: He get many gift.

K: Oh, yeah. What did he get?

L: He get a /qita/.

K: /qita/?

L: Um like um for the …

K: Is that an animal?

L: No.

K: Oh.

L: It's a … um like …

K: Can you draw it?

L: Yeah, I can draw it. [drawing] Like somebody hold it like this, then this, this. Here is a hole. The other end is this.

K: Oh, guitar!

L: Yeah.

K: Oh, wow!

L: He get a small one like that big.

K: Okay, what else?

L: And he get two video games.

K: Two video games?

L: Yeah.

K: Okay. It's like Sega game?

L: Yeah.

K: Okay.

L: And Four Square Ball.

K: Four square?

L: Yeah.

K: Four …?

L: Ball, a ball.

K: Ah, a ball.

L: Yeah.

K: Yes.

L: Maybe a toy, a Axman toy.

K: Okay.

L: Yeah, it's all.

K: That's a lot.

L: Yeah.

K: Wow! So he take the four square ball to school and you play the four square?

L: No, we can't.

K: Why not?

L: Because we-we have ball(s) in the in the school.

K: Oh.

L: Um some teacher say you get the ball. Then they say it's the school.

K: Okay.

L: We can play that ball in the some place. We can't play ball in the-the Colony Square.

K: You can't?

L: We can't.

K: Why?

L: Because Mike say you can't play on the parking space and the-the some the garden.

K: You can't play in the garden?

L: We can't.

K: Oh.

L: Because he say if we play ball, somebody will be there broke some window.

K: Oh.

L: Or in the parking you will broke some car's window.

K: Okay.

L: Yeah. And the other place somebody will going there, then you playing ball, then they don't like you.

K: Oh.

L: So we got play in the other apartment because the other apartment is very close.

K: Okay.

L: So we can playing ball there.

K: The one by the bus stop?

L: Yeah.

K: Okay.

L: These two apartment close.

K: Okay. And your friends live there?

L: No, he just live in here, in Colony Square. And we just going to there. It's too close.

K: Okay.

L: Yeah.

K: Hmm. Did you play Four Square today?

L: Yeah.

K: At the Magic Mountain?

L: No.

K: No.

L: Because there is no square in there.

K: Oh, there is no square?

L: Yeah.

K: Oh.

L: There's no place for Four Square.

K: Oh. Was this part of the whistle?

L: Yeah, but it's broken. I don't know why.

K: Ah.

L: See, like this.

K: Oh, yeah, that must be got cold and broke.

L: Yeah.

K: Hmm.

L: And I use-use my hands in there and /ba/ [indicating the sound of breaking].

K: Oh, it's broken.

L: Yeah.

K: How about take it back?

L: Yeah.

K: You can do that?

L: Yeah.

K: Do you want to take this to school and use that in school?

L: Yeah.

K: That's a nice one.

L: Yeah. There're some regular (ruler) like that, ruler.

K: Hmm.

L: Just change the color.

K: Oh, yeah.

L: But this, it is around.

K: It goes around in circle. Also it looks like that, right?

L: Yeah.

K: It's an optical illusion. What's on the back?

L: It's a xxx

K: Oooh, Multiplication Table.

L: I can remember all of that.

K: Yeah, okay. What is six times five?

L: Thirty.

K: What's seven times seven?

L: It's forty-nine.

K: What's nine times seven?

L: It's sixty-three.

K: Oh, you're good. What's three times nine?

L: Twenty-seven.

K: You're good.

L: I can remember it in the second grade.

K: You can remember all of it?

L: Yeah, in second grade in China.

K: In China you do?

L: Yeah.

K: So you already knew that before you came here.

L: Yeah.

K: Wow. How do you count to ten in-in Chinese?

L: Ten?

K: Um-hmm.

L: We don't we don't … Ten is, eleven times ten is just eleven add a zero.

K: Add a zero. Okay. And how do you say one, two, three, four, five in Chinese?

L: In Chinese?

K: Um-ha.

L: *Yi er san si wu.*

K: [laughing] Oh. Hmm, so you know all those?

L: Yeah.

K: So what you do in math now?

L: It's too easy.

K: Here is too easy?

L: Yeah.

K: Because you've already done it.

L: Yeah.

K: Did you take art class in China? You're very good artist.

L: Yeah.

K: That's good, very good drawing. Um so Magic Mountain is fun.

L: Yeah.

K: You want to go there for your birthday?

L: Yeah. Then there're some place are room(s) just for party.

K: Really.

L: Are-are birthday party (ies). There're many people just for birthday going there.

K: Okay. And you have the pizza and cake?

L: Yeah.

K: In that room?

L: Yeah.

K: And all the presents too?

L: Yeah.

K: Ah, where is Magic Mountain?

L: It's in the … I think … you know the Best Buy?

K: Um-hmm.

L: It's … if you going to Best Buy, there's a … like a like a like this [drawing a picture]. Here there's a house looking like this. And there we play we play the golf there.

K: Okay.

L: We got going there and we got going there, then go with the other one. There is a room there. We can go further there.

K: Oh, okay. So it's putt-putt golf? Miniature golf?

L: Yeah. There's a big hole in there, a big hole. There's water in there.

K: Okay.

L: We can going all room there.

K: Oh. Do your balls fall in the water?

L: No, because no water is there.

K: Where's the water?

L: It's a hole.

K: Just a hole, no water?

L: Yeah, no water in there. And we can from there going to there.

K: Hmm. Did you get a hole in one?

L: Yeah.

K: You did! How many times?

L: Um three.

K: Three times!?
L: Yeah.
K: That's good, really good.
---End of Conversation---

CONVERSATION 6: 11/30/1996

K: So what's been the happening?
L: Um yesterday ... um do you know that we're in 113, right?
K: Um-hmm.
L: Then Room 110 she there is a there is a um ... how to say it? [thinking] They are my friends.
K: Um-hmm.
L: And they-they yesterday they give me that football. Um it's for my Christmas gift.
K: Oh, fun!
L: Yeah.
K: Christmas already.
L: Un-un [shaking head]. Oh, yeah, they already give me Christmas gift.
K: Did you do anything for Thanksgiving in your class?
L: Yeah, we have a ice-cream party.
K: An ice-cream party?
L: And we can watch TV um watch video. We watch The Witches. It's a nice it's a nice a nice video.
K: Yeah.
L: Um do you watch that before?
K: The Witches?
L: Yeah.
K: I don't think so. What's it about?
L: It's a very-very bad a witches. Like um one day there is a grand-grandmother and a young children. Um he is about um eight years old or ... But his grandma boughts he him to some vacation.
K: Um-hmm.
L: They are live in the hotel. Um their Thanksgiving his-his-his grandma give him a xxx like um a um like a house for some birds. So that but it's-it's not good in there, there are some mouse. You know the mouse?

K: Um-hmm.

L: So he-he likes that mouse. So he take that to the hotel.

K: Ou-oh.

L: One day he-he open that-that door. Then one mouse is coming. Then he want he just like to playing with them, give
them some water or eat something. Then he forget to take that
back. So then one day the house-house-housekeeper come-
come in there. He see he see a he saw a mouse.

K: Um-hmm.

L: /aaaaaa/ he-he crying.

K: [laughing]

L: Then the manager was coming. The house-housekeeper say
he saw a mouse. But that young that young children say he
didn't-didn't take that mouse out. So one day one day he-he
take that mouse in a church in that hotel. There is a church in
that hotel.

K: Hmm.

L: And in there he take three mouse three mice in there. Um
then took a corner to do some fun things or some else with
that mouse. Then when he do that, the-the witches are coming for a um for like a party.

K: Um-hmm.

L: Every witches are coming in that hotel. The-the grand witches
is the badest one so they-they can take the-the face out

K: Hmm.

L: change to witches.

K: Nmm.

L: They can take their fingers out. I don't like that part. And there
are many there are every kind of witches. They don't have hairs.
They have a big nose, a big ear, or a long finger, or something.

K: Scary.

L: Yeah.

K: Why did you watch it?

L: Nmm?

K: Why did you watch it?

L: Because um my-my teacher every day we have some reading
time. So he read that book. So us we want to watch that TV.

K: Oh, I see.

L: It's hard to borrow that.

K: Yeah.

L: Yeah.

K: Hmm.

L: Um and um we didn't finish that-that video. We didn't finish.

K: No. Did you watch it on Monday?

L: I don't know.

K: Did you have two days off school? Thursday and Friday no school?

L: No school. We have um Thursday, Friday, um Saturday and Sunday

K: No school.

L: no school.

K: Four days, wow. Did you do something fun?

L: Um … oh, today I will go to somebody's house because we got a turkey

K: Oh.

L: Because we don't know how to do that. My mom my mom's working hotel

K: Hmm.

L: we got a free turkey.

K: Oh, yeah!

L: We don't know how to do it. We don't know how to cook.

K: Okay.

L: We took that turkey to some friend's house.

K: Um-hmm.

L: Then today we'll go to his house and some our the other friends go to his house to eat that turkey.

K: Did you eat turkey on Thursday?

L: Um Thursday let me see it [thinking] I eat turkey on … yes Thursday.

K: On Thursday you ate turkey.

L: Yeah, on somebody's house.

K: Was it good?

L: Yeah.

K: Yeah. Did you eat pumpkin pie?

L: Un-un [shaking head].

K: No.

L: We didn't got a pumpkin pie. We did have turkey. We didn't eat rice. We didn't eat noodle.

K: I see.

L: Just pumpkin, just um turkey.

K: Hmm. Did you sell um a lot of staff for school?

L: Un-un [shaking head].

K: No.

L: Just the two.

K: Just two.

L: Yeah.

K: What did you win?

L: I don't know. He didn't tell me. He didn't give me that things back.

K: Do you get your prize soon?

L: What?

K: Do you get your prize soon?

L: Yeah.

K: In December?

L: Yeah.

K: Yeah.

L: I think so.

K: Oh, fun.

L: Last time my school give us a book.

K: Um-hmm.

L: They call it um Children DC I think. I don't know. There is a it's like a coupon book. It is all coupon in there. If you can use all the coupon, then you can get some money.

K: Oh!

L: It's just for twelve dollar.

K: For twelve dollars you selling the coupon book?

L: Yeah, but I didn't sell. And I didn't buy one.

K: You didn't.

L: I didn't. If I-I sell one, I will get some more gifts.

K: You will.

L: Yeah.

K: It's-it's an entertain book? Is that what it's called?

L: Un-un [shaking head].

K: No.

L: It's just like a book. Like this.

K: Um-hmm.

L: And it write children's … I don't know. Children's DC I think. Children's C Book.

K: Hmm, I don't know I've heard of that.

L: Like a month we just see on TV. We have there and there.

K: Yeah. Is only with Cranbrook-Cranbrook?

L: No.

K: No, all schools.

L: All schools

K: Hmm.

L: in Columbus.

K: I don't know that.

L: Is there many coupon in there.

K: Hmm. Did you make that on the wall?

L: Yeah.

K: That's pretty. How did you do that?

L: Um it's I'm in fourth grade I did this.

K: Oh, you made that last year.

L: Yeah.

K: It's pretty. Oh, it's yarn.

L: Yeah. We did that. No, we-we did this first. You know how to do this?

K: So it's a piece of cardboard that you cut up? Is that what it was?

L: Yeah. It's same thing with this. We got two of this.

K: Okay.

L: So I cut one. Cut … no this one suppose be like this, just like this.

K: Okay.

L: Like a-a square. I cut that. So I-I need do this first. I need do like this. I need write one two three four on every one.

K: Okay.

L: And this one two three four one two three four one two three four [showing]. There is seven in there. So I draw one to this one. Then two then go back. Then on the back go back two-two three-three four-four. So I get that.

K: Okay.

L: This one is I did. The first part is difficult to did. I didn't-didn't do that.

K: You didn't. Who did that?

L: My teacher.

K: Oh.

L: Mr. A.

K: Mr. A. And the rest you did yourself.

L: Yeah.

K: It's nice.

L: He did that.

K: It's pretty.

L: There're many pictures in my school.

K: What-what do you color it?

L: Color?

K: Um-hmm.

L: This, this is just the color. There's no color in there.

K: Oh, just color that.

L: Yeah, a little bit.

K: I see.

L: There is no more place for me. There is no place either. So no more.

K: Oh, so you have to stop.

L: Yeah.

K: But it's pretty like that. Did you color this first or this first?

L: What do you mean?

K: Did you ____

L: No, I-I do that first then color it.

K: Then you color it. It's so pretty.

L: Mine in my class is the biggest one.

K: There is a bigger one? The whole class put together?

L: No, it's the biggest one like you cannot do any more. There are many people just-just do like this.

K: Oh, you did it until this completely full.

L: Yeah.

K: Wow.

L: It's hard to do. I did I did that four days.

K: Really?

L: Yeah.

K: Shoo, it's pretty though.

L: Not all day. Like four hours.

K: Four hours.

L: Because our-our art class just have one hour in one week.

K: I see. So it took four weeks. It's nice though. So ... three eight ninety six. So that was the last Spring.
L: Yeah.
K: Did you write this?
L: Yeah.
K: You did. It's nice handwriting. Hmm.
L: Anybody wants mine.
K: Everybody wants yours?
L: Yeah. My grandma say don't give to anybody. Just give it to me.
K: It's pretty.
---End of Conversation---

CONVERSATION 7: 12/8/1996

K: Ah what're you doing? Doing homework?
L: Yes. This is my D.A.R.E. book.
K: What's a D.A.R.E. book?
L: D-A-R-E.
K: What's it mean?
L: This.
K: [reading] Drug Abuse Resistance Education, ah. What do you have to do in D.A.R.E?
L: Um I did this already. [showing] I need like ... We already finish all that book. We need like this: How do you feel about the D.A.R.E. program? Now I can write
K: What did you write?
L: like this seventeen-week we can get what just this seventeen week in D.A.R.E.. Like learning. We can do that. It's just the seventeen week.
K: Okay.
L: Okay. Um to what D.A.R.E is.
K: Okay.
L: D.A.R.E. is very exciting and good. It has helped me to like um not use drug.
K: Okay.
L: And this second thing is: you can use what do you have learned in D.A.R.E that tells you ...? I didn't copy it there and there. I've learned like what's-what's drug. And how do you like um somebody give you some drug how-how do you tell him like

I-I say tomorrow let's have some drug, then what you say?
What you're going to do? You have some ways to say ways
to say no. Say "no, thanks". Give a um someone um excuse.
Repeat it. Or-or keep saying no just like our say no. Walking
away. Change the subject. What's this? What's this?

K: Oh, oh, avoiding the situation?

L: Yeah.

K: Okay, what is it?

L: Yeah, what is it?

K: Um it's just said there if you know something like certain
people in school using drugs, you just stay away from those
people.

L: Cold shoulder?

K: Um just ignore them.

L: Yeah.

K: Hmm that's neat. So this is you did _____

L: What's this?

K: Oh, strength in numbers?

L: Yeah, what does it mean?

K: Um that means hanging around with people that don't use
drugs. And so that you're not by yourself. That's neat.

L: Yeah.

K: So you did this every year in school? Or … I don't know.

L: No, it's just for this year.

K: Okay.

L: I already did that. So I don't need do that in the middle
school.

K: Okay. Are you in the middle school now?

L: No.

K: No, next year?

L: Yep.

K: Okay, wow that's neat. So you just have to finish it up and
take it back to school tomorrow?

L: No, just this.

K: Just that.

L: Sometimes we do this in the school.

K: Um-hmm.

L: Like this work every time teacher give the D.A.R.E. officer
um a paper put that on the on wall um a wall

K: Um-hmm.

L: then we just copy that. xxx We just copy.

K: Okay, wow. Where did you get these-these ah definitions?

L: Copy from the-the like a paper.

K: Hmm.

L: She just write a big paper. She just write on there.

K: Okay, your teacher did it.

L: Yeah, then we just copy that.

K: Neat. And then you wrote it in Chinese too?

L: [shaking head]

K: Oh, no.

L: And I write many things in there. This is you like Wendy. She's eight grade. She always study good. But one day she did no good. She got a F on her science.

K: Oh, no.

L: So she is just use drug. So tell you the drug was no good.

K: Okay, she use drug because she got F on her paper?

L: No because she use drug so she got F.

K: Oh, she use drug then she got F. Oh, I see, I see.

L: This is what happen if you use drug xxx This is just come on come on let's drink some beer, then what they are going to say? They just going to say this:

K: Okay.

L: "I don't want this". Like "No, thanks".

K: Okay.

L: "I didn't do this". Like this is just like-like some of your friends

K: Um-hmm.

L: in your classroom

K: Um-hmm.

L: you have a grade like this. Like um you don't use drug.

K: Okay.

L: If-if somebody saw you use drug, they-they will write like that.

K: I see.

L: Yeah. And this is three-three-three ideas to like um out of drugs somebody give you drug you say no.

K: Okay.

L: Okay this-this is take a test. This is like last-last month.

K: Um-hmm.

L: If you do if you do that thing you write yes. If you no, you write no. I have six things. That means you need like very be careful.

K: Um-hmm.

L: Um like you are very scared.

K: Okay, yep.

L: Like you have many things to do.

K: Okay, then the numbers are higher?

L: Yeah. So I have six. So I am writing on there. So I am six to ten.

K: You said here that you had something exciting happened to you. What happened to you that was exciting?

L: Um oh I write this on November. ... [thinking] Oh, my grandma go back to China.

K: Oh, yeah. Hmm that was a good thing to check then, huh?.

L: Yeah, take a test.

K: You took a test?

L: Yeah.

K: Um what else did you say? You have too many things to do?

L: Like-like this you just how do you re-reduce like how do you _____

K: Okay, how do you reduce your stress?

L: Yeah. So it's like he just like taking a test. Study be-be prepared.

K: Okay.

L: I just write I have too many things to do. Do anything fast.

K: [laughing] It's a good way to do it.

L: I have trouble with school. Study hard and be patient.

K: Okay.

L: And this is like a story.

K: Yeah.

L: This-this tell you like I'm the coach

K: Um-hmm.

L: you playing. This last one was the baseball.

K: Um-hmm.

L: We just play.

K: Um-hmm.

L: You lose the ball.

K: Um-hmm.

L: So I am the coach. I am saying you are you are not playing good. Then he just playing the ball. He just ask that coach. Say why-why you not blame the people before me. Because he is the last one people to playing that. It's the last round. So he ask him why you do not blame the people lost before me. Why you don't say that to them.

K: Right, okay.

L: But-but the coach say you are the last one. If you got this one, then we will win. If you are not, we will lose. This story tell you how to how do you like um _____

K: Oh, I know. Like how you get off this situation.

L: Yeah.

K: How you make it okay.

L: Yeah, there is something like you think it's not his fault. Then we say it's his fault. Then-then this page I didn't xxx like me I have some trouble.

K: Okay. So you wrote it about yourself.

L: Yeah.

K: That's good idea.

L: I didn't like this. We don't do this. We do this. Like this she just moved to the other city.

K: Um-hmm.

L: To have a new neighbor. She doesn't have any friend.

K: Okay.

L: Um so-so one of the-the girl who live across the street invite her to a party. She say it's a good way to-to get her some friends.

K: Okay.

L: Because in the party there is many people in there.

K: Um-hmm.

L: She can get to know many. The girl tell-tell her to take some beer.

K: Oh, no.

L: So what is the risk? So I write this and there. If you go, you'll get drunk.

K: Okay.

L: What-what are the possible choices? Um don't go to that party or don't take what's that

K: Oh, the liquor?

L: Yep, the liquor. Okay. What is the good happen? Good happen could has some new friends.

K: Um-hmm.

L: Bad happen could be liquor.

K: Right. Okay.

L: Which choice may have better result? It's just still go to that party but don't bring that liquor.

K: Oh, yeah.

L: She need talking with-with she's some like teacher, she's mom, she's parents.

K: Okay.

L: She need talk with she's parents because she is taking she's-she's parent's beer.

K: Right.

L: Okay this is like the same thing. Oh there is a coupon in there.

K: Oh, what's it for?

L: I don't know.

K: Um I don't know what that's for.

L: Let me do this.

K: Oh, you make something.

L: Yes, makes like this. I know how to make this. It 's very easy. So you just need get a square.

K: Um-hmm. You just fold it?

L: I can do it

K: You're artistic. You can do anything, can't you?

L: Not anything.

K: [laughing] You do this in school too?

L: No.

K: No, how do you know how to do it then?

L: Because

K: Oh, you just read the book?

L: Yeah, I just read the book.

K: Oh, it tells you how to do it.

L: You have that paper

K: Um-hmm.

L: You can't take that out.

K: You can't. How come?

L: Because sometimes the teacher tell everybody how to do it. You need have a paper. You don't have it ____

K: Oh, yeah. Then you get trouble, don't you?

L: Yeah, I get trouble, big trouble.

K: You'd say ou-oh.

L: You need do like this.

K: Okay, you fold it and make a triangle.

---End of Conversation---

CONVERSATION 8: 12/16/1996

L: What are we going to do?

K: [laughing] Well what you want to talk about?

L: Um ...

K: [pointing to the sewing kit Langtian sent her as a Christmas gift] Did you bring this from China when you when you were there a year ago?

L: No.

K: No.

L: Somebody bring that.

K: It's nice. I like it. Thanks.

L: [laughing]

K: So how many more days for school?

L: Um today is [going to look at a calendar and counting]

K: Done.

L: One, two, three, four.

K: Four more days.

L: Yes.

K: Then what you're going to do?

L: We have long-long-long [counting] one two three four five six seven eight nine ten eleven twelve thirteen fourteen fifteen sixteen ... we have sixteen.

K: Sixteen days, wow! Are you gonna do something fun?

L: Yes, my mom will take me to a party.

K: Yep. What kind of party?

L: For Christmas. Because her like her when he in the high school

K: Um-hmm.

L: he have many many classmate in America.

K: Okay.

L: So they want meeting. They have a party. But everybody from like from California, Ohio, every place going to one people's house.

K: Wow!

L: So he going to bring me to for Christmas.

K: Okay.

L: We-we going to Virginia and Washington, D.C..

K: Wow! How long will you go?

L: Um twenty-three to twenty-seven.

K: Shoo, that's long time! Five days! Are you excited?

L: Yes.

K: Um-hmm. What you doing in school this week?

L: School? This week we just have like we just study something fun.

K: Um-hmm.

L: We study math. Like we study um like every body have any kind of like … do you know everybody every finger you have every line in there?

K: Oh, yep, everybody has his own finger print?

L: Yes. Then we just use like a color print.

K: Um-hmm.

L: We just use a finger put in there, then put a paper.

K: Okay. For all your fingers or just one?

L: A one.

K: Just one.

L: Everybody get one. Then if you are this kind of like-like your just like this kind of

K: Um-hmm.

L: then you going to this group.

K: Okay.

L: If you like this kind of if you like this [drawing]

K: Oh, yep. I wonder what I am. Oh, I'm like this kind.

L: Yes.

K: Yep. What are you?

L: I'm this kind.

K: This kind, round? Let me see let me see.

L: I have many is that.

K: That's really neat.

L: And one more kind of is like this [drawing]

K: Oh, little lines.

L: Like no lines.

K: Okay. And when you went to separate groups, what happened?

L: Um we just in groups. And this group we have we have eight peoples.

K: Um-hmm.

L: This we have one people.

K: Really?

L: Yep.

K: How many in this group?

L: I think this ... no I think this is more. This is six.

K: Okay.

L: So we have sixteen peoples. This is fourteen and this is just two.

K: Just two?

L: We have sixteen we have nineteen people in-in our classroom. But there is one two there is three people in ESL, so they didn't like their English their English is not good. They just come for many by three month.

K: Okay.

L: So they need go to ESL

K: Okay.

L: many times.

K: I see.

L: So they didn't-didn't not they are not in my classroom when we-we do-doing that.

K: Okay.

L: So we didn't have these three people.

K: I see. Are a lot of the students in your school sick?

L: Yes.

K: Yep. I saw the news that a lot of people had the flu.

L: Yes.

K: Did you have it?

L: No.

K: No, you are not going to get it, ah?

L: Oh, yesterday oh today

K: Um-hmm.

L: my friend my mom's friend um she say he got she got a friend he got like he got sick.

K: Um-hmm.

L: Um like our regular we are having like right there, right? [pointing to a thermometer on the wall] It's one hundred.

K: Like ninety-eight?

L: Yes, it's ninety-eight.

K: Um-hmm.

L: In China, it's thirty-thirty seven.

K: Oh, it's Celsius. Oh, yep.

L: Oh, yep, thirty-seven is ninety-eight.

K: Um-hmm.

L: But he has a hundred and more.

K: Oh, no. So he has a fever.

L: Yep. So he got go to hospital.

K: Really?

L: But today some body call us he-he give us a message. He say tomorrow like maybe he gave him a give the hospital a call.

K: Hmm.

L: Say tomorrow they will come to his house. But the hospital give me give us a call. Say tomorrow she will coming to there.

K: Hmm.

L: She got a wrong number.

K: Yes, I guess. So he is really sick?

L: Yes.

K: But you're not gonna get it.

L: Yep. I didn't sick three and four years.

K: You got sick three times in four years?

L: No, I didn't sick every time.

K: No.

L: No time

K: No time. Oh, wow!

L: In three or four years.

K: What's your secret?

L: I don't know.

K: No, you don't know. Do you get a flu shot?

L: No.

K: No. I didn't either.

L: I got in China. It's all for free.

K: Is it? To go to the doctor?

L: Some is for free. But no not go to the doctor.

K: Hmm.

L: Every-every year we have a like a test. Test your eyes,

K: Oh, yep.

L: your ears, your nose, your mouth, your this [pointing to his pulse].

K: Your pulse?

L: Yeah. And your heart.

K: Okay.

L: And if you are okay, it's just okay. If you are not okay like your teeth,

K: Um-hmm.

L: the school will give you a paper. It write your teeth are not good. Your parents need to bring you to the hospital.

K: I see. So you've to go to the dentist's.

L: Yep. If you didn't go to and you didn't take that paper back, you will get in trouble.

K: Really! So the doctor comes to your school to do that?

L: No. We go to the-the doctor.

K: Oh, you go to the doctor. So who checks you at school? Like who checks your nose, your mouth and your teeth at school?

L: No. In-in the hospital.

K: Oh, in the hospital.

L: We're all going to the hospital.

K: I see.

L: Some day all for the elementary schools.

K: Um-hmm.

L: Because in I live in a university, so there is just one there is just one elementary school.

K: Okay.

L: So every-every year we just do this in elementary school.

K: Okay, wow. Do you like all the Christmas lights?

L: Yes.

K: Are they pretty?

L: Do you know yesterday we have a fire in here?

K: Yes. Did you see it?

L: Yes xxx

K:　Did you see it on the news?

L:　Yes.

K:　I did it too. It's scary.

L:　It's it's a little boy. He playing with that Christmas tree. And there is a light in there and he put some water in there.

K:　Hmm.

L:　And there's just him in his house. And it's just [imitating the sound of fire] And it's fire. He just call 911. He just go.

K:　Oh, he called 911?

L:　Yeah.

K:　The little boy did!?

L:　Yeah.

K:　Oh, I didn't know that. That was good. He knew how to do that.

L:　Yep. He's smart.

K:　The building looks terrible, doesn't it?

L:　Yeah.

K:　No roofing, yuck. All those people no place to live. It's kind of scary.

L:　My friend say he got (saw) a bus was coming and it just bring them to the other place to live.

K:　Oh, yep, the Fawcett Center I think.

L:　Yeah.

K:　You knew some people that lived there?

L:　Un-un [shaking head]

K:　No, you didn't. None of your school friends. [pointing to the sewing kit] What you call this in China?

L:　You mean in Chinese?

K:　Yeah.

L:　*Zhenxianbao.*

K:　[laughing] Say it again.

L:　*Zhenxianbao.*

K:　Hmm.

L:　Like *bao* means it just like a box.

K:　Okay. Oh, box.

L:　Yep. *Zhenxian zhen* is this is this.

K:　It's the thread or the pin?

L:　The pin, yes. *Xian* means this.

K:　The thread?

L: Yep.

K: Oh, so it's the pin-thread box.

L: Yep.

K: Oh, that's neat.

L: We have every kind of this.

K: I like it. It's fun. I can put these pins in there now instead of wearing them on my shirt. Good idea?

L: Yeah.

K: Put holes on my shirt.

L: You can put them there. There is a place in this. Or you can put back of this.

K: Yep, that's a good idea. Oh, thanks.

L: Wow!

K: Oh, yes.

L: How much you got?

K: Oh, well I was making a big project. So I have a lot of pins. I put them together. That help? So you've been to Magic Mountain lately?

L: No.

K: No.

L: Just once.

K: Just once. What happened to all your Magic Mountain stuff? Looks like maybe you've been to McDonald's lately?

L: Yes.

K: When did you go to McDonald's?

L: Yesterday.

K: Yesterday! And did you get happy meal?

L: Yes.

K: Hey, look! This is made in China too.

L: Um-hmm.

K: That's neat.

L: I have two more.

K: You have been there a lot.

L: I've been there every week.

K: Yeah. Which one is your favorite?

L: This one.

K: This one.

L: This one looks good. See.

K: Yeah, it's cute. What are their names?

L: I don't know. I just think they don't even got a name.
K: Do you ever got to the McDonald's here? The one close?
L: Yes.
K: Yes.
L: I'm not I'm not going to far away. My dad don't want to bring me to do that.
K: Not too far away.
L: Yes.
K: That's a good idea. We have a close one. Why should we go far away?
L: Yeah.
K: Yeah. Did you see any good movie lately?
L: No.
K: Nothing?
L: I didn't see that movie.
K: Have you seen um How the Grinch Stole Christmas?
L: No.
K: That's a good one, Christmas classic. Have to be sure to see it. Do you like Christmas?
L: Yes.
K: Um-hmm. That's your favorite?
L: Yes.
K: Is it? Why? You don't have school?
L: Yes.
K: [laughing] Oh! Are you doing homework?
L: I'm finished.
K: What're you doing?
L: Um my reading.
K: Reading.
L: Oh, um what I'm going to say um I think I forgot.
K: Ou-oh. Who is Paul Bunyon?
L: It's a people.
K: It's a person?
L: It's a big people.
K: Oh, big guy. What did he do?
L: Maybe he got his knees this-this high … was six feet ten inches.
K: Just from his foot to his knees?
L: Yeah, yeah.

K: No.

L: The book say that.

K: Yeah. It's a true story?

L: I don't think so.

K: I don't think so either. Did he have a big blue ox?

L: Yes.

K: Name Blue?

L: He got a blue axe.

K: No, that ox like a big animal.

L: Oh.

K: You know like a big cow.

L: Oh, yeah.

K: Yeah, he does?

L: He does [showing the book]

K: I guess I bet ... oh, yeah. Okay.

L: See this-this story was funny. Yes, he does. That's his second.

K: Oh, it was a tall tale. That means not true.

L: See some say he wasn't much taller the house. Others say he must be taller. He says he did like six feet into his pocket blowing birds out the air when he sleeps.

K: Oh, no. That must not be true.

L: Yeah. See this picture.

K: That's your reading book?

L: Yes, no.

K: No.

L: It's just a little reading book.

K: A little reading book.

L: See you can ...

K: Oh!

L: So we don't want like reading this. We don't need that.

K: You don't-don't have very long, ha?

L: Yeah.

K: Do you have another reading book go with that?

L: Yes.

K: Hmm.

L: A big one.

K: A big, thick one?

L: It not go with that. There're many-many stories from there.

K: Did you have to write sentences about what you've read?

L: No.

K: No.

L: I have our reading sheet. You need do this.

K: Hmm, I see.

L: Oh, this is my mom's friend

K: Um-hmm.

L: when he is in high school. See he got a restaurant.

K: Um-hmm.

L: He got ____

K: Here in-in ____

L: No, it's not this. He-he just take this.

K: Oh, he just make it.

L: Here.

K: But this is in America, right?

L: Yes.

K: Yeah.

L: She got her she got her like um own restaurant.

K: Okay, her friend does.

L: Yes.

K: Is that the picture of the restaurant?

L: Yes.

K: Wow! Looks like a good place, yep.

L: I think he got two.

K: Looks like a good place to eat.

L: There are many pictures in there.

K: Yeah.

L: She will go to the party too.

K: Yeah. Ou-oh, your dad back.

---End of Conversation---

CONVERSATION 9: 1/12/1997

K: Tell me about Washington, D.C..

L: Washington, D.C.?

K: Um-hmm.

L: Um last time in the summer August we go to Washington, D.C. too, you know. I with my grandmom and my grandpa, my dad and my mom go to Washington, D.C.. There is many-many peoples.

K: Hmm.

L: You can see everywheres so many peoples.

K: Wow.

L: But this time we go to this ... like Columbus, you can't you can't see many people walk on the hall(road)way or their out driver or in their house or walking.

K: Okay.

L: This time we go to ... we're very amazing because Washington, D.C. is a-a capital

K: Okay.

L: so it-it su-suppose to be have many peoples, right?

K: Hmm.

L: But-but we don't know why there is just a little bit people walking. I think it's because it's Christmas.

K: Oh.

L: It is Christmas that day we go to Washington.

K: Oh, like December 25th you went?

L: Yes.

K: Okay. Was it cold?

L: Not very cold.

K: No.

L: We just can no we need a-a T-shirt and a coat, it's okay.

K: Okay.

L: It's not very cold.

K: Okay. What's your favorite thing there?

L: There? Um ... you know yesterday I told you where I go in Washington, D.C., you still remember?

K: Um-hmm.

L: The place is?

K: Ah, the place you went is ... um did you just go to the Capitol?

L: No, not the Capitol.

K: Something wrong?

L: No. It's a-a thing like-like this, five side.

K: You mean it has five sides?

L: Yes, it is five side. Oh ... [trying hard to think of the name] It is ...

K: It is really tall?

L: No, not very tall. It's ...

K: No.

L: Okay, I can tell you that. It's like this [drawing] A house very-very high.

K: Okay.

L: Do you know what that is?

K: Um it's the Washington Monument?

L: Yes.

K: Okay, did you like that?

L: Yes, we like that and the Lincoln what-what-what-what …?

K: Oh, the Lincoln Memorial?

L: Yeah.

K: Yeah.

L: And we got we not got in there because last time we get in there. Walk a long way and just see a Lincoln is like a thing.

K: Yep, like a statue of him.

L: I saw there are many thing about Lincoln like Lincoln-Lincoln's T-shirt or something

K: Okay.

L: Glasses, yeah.

K: Did you see the Vietnam Memory? That big-big really long black thing with all the names on it?

L: Oh, yeah.

K: Yep. Did you like that?

L: Many-many names from little to big to little.

K: Yeah, many-many names, hmm.

L: And we-we take picture on the walk side

K: Okay.

L: to the to the Lincoln …

K: Okay.

L: We take many pictures on there. And from there just this is the Capitol Hill.

K: Um-hmm.

L: And you need to get up and you can see. This side you can see the Capitol, this side you see the White House.

K: Yes. You saw the White House?

L: Yes.

K: Did you see the president?

L: No.

K: No, just his house.

L: Yeah.

K: So it was fun. How many days were you there?

L: Twenty-three to twenty-seven, four days.

K: Twenty-three to twenty-seven. Where did you stay?

L: In my mom's younger friend's house.

K: Oh.

L: She when he she is thirteen or fourteen

K: Um-hmm.

L: there're-there're many good friends.

K: Okay. So you stayed in someone's house?

L: Yes.

K: Oh, that's fun.

L: It's fun.

K: Did you go to McDonald's?

L: No.

K: No.

L: See one day I go to ... she have many friends. One is from-from Atlanta [pointing at the map] from there.

K: Okay, from Atlanta?

L: Yeah. Um we-we we're-we're going to Pittsburgh like that.

K: Yeah.

L: My dad take me and my mom to Pittsburgh. Then this she just one his friends is in Pittsburgh.

K: Okay.

L: So we're going to his house. Then he just bring us to like the go to the Virginia.

K: Okay.

L: Then-then go to there Virginia. Then we just everybody from ... one is from there, Atlanta-Atlanta.

K: Hmm.

L: So Atlanta to the Virginia, and from Pittsburgh to Virginia, these two place because there is many there is almost seven or five people seven or six people.

K: Um-hmm.

L: One is from there and-and the other people is from Detroit

K: Um-hmm.

L: going to our house.

K: Okay.

L: We bring her to the Pittsburgh and Pittsburgh bring her to Virginia.

K: Okay.

L: So she is the like the best one because she go to many place.

K: Yes, she does. Wow!

L: And we all going to Virginia. This-this people from Atlanta just stay on maybe six hour or ten hour because he just the airplane.

K: Okay.

L: And we just stay in the Virginia.

K: The big plan.

L: Where's the map. If I have a map, I can show you.

K: The map on the wall doesn't work?

L: No, because we're going place like the places like five side. It's called …?

K: Is it a state?

L: No.

K: No.

L: It's a it's a big house.

K: With five sides?

L: Yes, with five sides. You know that.

K: It-it's in Washington?

L: Yes, the side beside-beside the side of Washington.

K: So the side of Washington?

L: Yes, it's very close to Washington.

K: It's famous?

L: Yes, it is.

K: So the five sides?

L: Ah, very-very important place.

K: Um important to the government? No.

L: Army or …

K: Oh, the Pentagon.

L: Yes.

K: Yeah. That was your favorite?

L: Yes.

K: What did you do there?

L: I got a picture.

K: Yeah?

L: Yes. It's a airplane. And we watch the video.

K: Um-hmm.

L: And there is a people who is tell you what's that picture what's that. That people is very funny. And our stay on the front because he is one people. Then there is many people in there.

K: Right.

L: So we need money to get a card. Money then we write down our names. He just read our names then you go get a card

K: Okay.

L: on your on your um clothe.

K: Okay.

L: So-so he knows you are in this group. We are go together.

K: Okay.

L: This is very funny. We just write our names ... all five-five, yes, it's five people. Two-two child and one man and two ladies. So we just write down our names. Then you need write down you are lady, children or man.

K: Um-hmm.

L: Then he just saw we're together.

K: Um-hmm.

L: He don't know how to say our names.

K: Oh!

L: So he just give he-he say two-two child um two-two ladies and a man is the same thing. So he-he don't know names, just give us.

K: [laughing] Okay.

L: My mom asking him, "Are you sure?" He say, "Yes, because I don't know how to say your name."

K: Oh.

L: So he just give me a card.

K: Okay. What's this? Is this from Washington?

L: No.

K: Where is it from?

L: From my mom. My dad give it to me.

K: Yeah. What does it mean?

L: A flag.

K: Are they American flags or what other kind?

L: I don't know.

K: It's nice. You wore out last night too, didn't you?

L: Last night?

K: Yeah.

L: Yes, to a party. [telling K to take it off his clothe] Get it out, get it out!

K: [reading the words on the badge] United States Marine Corps.

L: Marine Corps.

K: Oh, it's the Maine Corps flags and the United States flags.

L: Yes.

K: That's neat. Was that the Christmas present?

L: No.

K: No.

L: Oh ... [going to get a book] State Flag.

K: Oh, wow! Where did you get that?

L: From my school's library.

K: Oh, wow!

L: Columbus elementary.

K: Yep. Can you-you get to like tear out the stickers?

L: No, you can't.

K: No. You're not allowed.

L: This is our flag.

K: This is whose flag?

L: I mean the um ...

K: Oh, the Ohio flag?

L: Yes.

K: Is it?

L: It is.

K: Oh!

L: Let me see page three.

K: I even don't know.

L: Yes, this one, Ohio.

K: I should know that shouldn't I live here. I know Michigan though. Let me find Michigan for you. You properly know.

L: No.

K: Yes, this one.

L: This one?

K: Michigan.

L: Michigan.

K: See Michigan?

L: No.

K: We'll look it up to make sure it's right.
L: Illinois.
K: Illinois, yes.
L: Iowa.
K: I wonder who's that is?
L: I don't know.
K: This is a funny looking flag, isn't it?
L: Yeah.
K: It's not straight. It's kind of crooked.
L: Yeah, every-every ____
K: Whose is that? Oh this one's funny?
L: Yeah.
K: With stars on it.
L: This one looks like American flag.
K: Yep. But looks like kind of Britain too.
L: Yeah.
K: Like the British flag. What does China's flag look like?
L: Um maybe you know that.
K: Do you think I've seen it before?
L: Yes, this is a flag just a big page.
K: Okay.
L: It's one big star and some little stars. It is all that. This is yellow.
K: It's a square and star is yellow and flag is all red.
L: Yes.
K: Hmm.
L: And every these little-little ____
K: So there're five stars total?
L: Yeah, five star.
K: Okay, neat.
L: Neat.
K: Yeah.
---End of Conversation---

CONVERSATION 10: 1/19/1997

K: Ou-oh I'm shy today.
L: [laughing]
K: What shall we talking about?
L: Um um you know the Ohio State?

K: Um-hmm.

L: They play the Rose Bowel.

K: Yep.

L: They win.

K: Did you watch it today?

L: No, not today.

K: No.

L: Football.

K: Yep, it was on TV today.

L: Today?

K: Yep, they play it and watch, show it again

L: Oh.

K: on TV, yeah. Ah, it's on now, Channel Four. Um it started at two thirty.

L: Oh, no. It's-it's Bull's game.

K: Oh.

L: It's a game, NBA.

K: Oh, is that Channel Four?

L: Yes.

K: Yeah, hmm. I saw it on the paper that it was on again today, the Rose Bowl.

L: The last nineteen minutes they got a touchdown.

K: Yeah. So you watched it?

L: Yep.

K: You liked it?

L: All game.

K: Yeah. Hmm.

L: The NBA I-I just ... the football I just like-like to watch the last quarter.

K: Um-hmm.

L: Yeah, and the NBA and the-the like playing balls

K: Um-hmm.

L: um basketball, football I always like to ... and my dad always like to watch the last quarter.

K: Yeah, only the last quarter? Hmm, well I guess that's when they win, ha?

L: Yeah.

K: Yeah.

L: So if-if the at the first quarter it's they're playing football they're it's it is twenty-five to nothing, so we don't want to watch it any more.

K: Hmm.

L: They going to win.

K: Right.

L: Yeah, one hundred ninety per cent. Ninety per cent it's going to win.

K: They're going to win.

L: Yeah.

K: Hmm. Did you go shopping today too?

L: Yes, I go with them.

K: Yep.

L: Um they shopping just-just buy any clothe or pants.

K: [laughing]

L: They go to Lazarus

K: Um-hmm.

L: the City Center.

K: Um-hmm. And you didn't like it?

L: I like some.

K: Yeah, too long, ha?

L: Yeah. I'm just watching the game.

K: Hmm.

L: And they just like … I just go to the that-that place. It's sold the sold the TV

K: Okay.

L: and that place sold the sofa.

K: Hmm.

L: I'm just sit down the sofa to watch the TV

K: Oh.

L: the game.

K: [laughing]

L: So they're just going to buy some clothe.

K: Yeah.

L: They want me to see the clothe nobody will take them.

K: Okay.

L: So they'll not put our clothe on the hand or something.

K: Ha, well that was good of you to go. Hmm, what's new in school?

L: New?

K: Okay.

L: Oh [going to get something]

K: What is this?

L: This, Drug Abuse Resistance Education.

K: Oh, yes, you told me about this. Why did you get this?

L: Because my essay is the best.

K: The best?

L: No, not the best. There is eight people in my school got that.

K: But you're one?

L: Yeah.

K: Wow!

L: Here, this is my essay. It's just that page. It's tear from that you know that D.A.R.E. book.

K: Oh, ya, this is what you wrote and they really liked it.

L: So the back it's right there.

K: Okay, that's great.

L: Yeah.

K: So did you wear this to school?

L: Yes.

K: What's that?

L: This is my-my writing test.

K: Oh.

L: We need write the our collections.

K: Um-hmm.

L: You know I collect many coins [going to get his box of coins].

K: Oh.

L: These are my coins.

K: You collect coins?

L: Yes.

K: Oh, wow! Look at all of those!

L: This is my best one.

K: Yeah, what is that one?

L: The United States this is a dollar.

K: One dollar.

L: Yes. This is hard to get …

K: Um-hmm.

L: And I thought the new one just maybe yes this one. This is a dollar____

K: From where?

L: from Mexico.

K: Mexico.

L: Yeah.

K: Hmm.

L: And look, these are some coins. See this is our dollar from Canada.

K: Okay, yep.

L: They're not same. See the-the people.

K: Yeah. Oh, the queens changed on them.

L: Yeah, so the new kind.

K: Yeah.

L: This is nineteen ninety four. And this is nineteen eighty eight.

K: Okay.

L: And this is a dog. This is ... What is that?

K: Looks like a statue or something.

L: Yeah.

K: Yeah. So you've from Canada, Mexico, America

L: Australia.

K: Australia?

L: Yeah.

K: Who went to Australia?

L: Oh, this is Canada. I thought it is Australia. About many like my mom ____

K: Where is this one come?

L: Oh, this is Hong Kong.

K: Oh, yeah.

L: Because my mom ____

K: How about this one?

L: [laughing]

K: What's this?

L: This is a coin ____

K: [laughing] from Subway.

L: And my mom he work in hotel.

K: Um-hmm.

L: Sometimes the-the guest give-give just give some-some no like you give me um take a Pepsi for you

K: Hmm.

L: from the …

K: All right.

L: So you-you just give me a little bit money.

K: Right.

L: Yeah.

K: Sometimes they give foreign money?

L: Yes, sometimes.

K: What's this one?

L: There is many they're come from many countries. So they're-they're leave some special coin to us. Their-their countries just regular coins but in America _____

K: They're special.

L: Yeah, special.

K: I bet Jos has some Dutch money he'd give you.

L: Okay. I'm looking for another one. This one, this one.

K: What's that?

L: This is a ten dollar you can I can use in Atlantic City.

K: Oh. So that's a _____

L: Ten dollar.

K: That's used to play those _____

L: Yeah.

K: Yeah. What's the two color one?

L: Yeah. Oh, the Mexican.

K: The Mexican.

L: This is from Mexico?

K: Yeah.

L: I don't know where that from. Oh, yeah, this is Mexico. This is my other one. I have the other one like this.

K: You've two like that?

L: See this.

K: You mean this one?

L: I don't know what's that. Oh, there is the other one, there.

K: Italy.

L: Italy. I don't know what's what is that from. Oh, Italy.

K: Oh, yeah. Okay.

L: This one is big.

K: Yeah.

L: It is hard to found.

K: That is hard to find. How did you find it?

L: My dad give it to me.

K: Yep. So many _____

L: But you can you can change some-some of like this. This is a dollar, this.

K: Oh, yeah. I-I think I have some dollars like this.

L: Yeah.

K: But never big one like this.

L: Yeah.

K: What year this is from?

L: Oh, this is were-were like Independent Free ...

K: Oh, so the special one.

L: Two hundred, yeah the special.

K: Special.

L: This one is the same.

K: A half dollar.

L: Yeah, a half dollar.

K: Is this what this one is? No, that's a one dollar.

L: Yeah. Um see this is ... I don't know who is this. See this say two hundred years of

K: Freedom.

L: freedom. Freedom two hundred years.

K: Yeah.

L: Who is that?

K: Um ...

L: I know this is John F. Kennedy.

K: Yeah.

L: This one is ...?

K: That one is Kennedy?

L: Yeah.

K: Oh, yeah, that's him. Um I don't know who that is.

L: Oh, I know this. This one can be a quarter.

K: Oh, yeah.

L: When you maybe you can't get in the call phone. But you can get when-when it's-it's a box. Then you put some money for-for candy.

K: Um-hmm.

L:　You can use that, too.

K:　You can?

L:　Yeah.

K:　In the America?

L:　Yeah, this is Canada a quarter.

K:　Hmm.

L:　A Canada quarter.

K:　Hmm.

L:　Um I have Chinese coins too.

K:　You do?

L:　It's hard to find one cent in Chinese.

K:　Yeah?

L:　This is all my Chinese coins. This is our cents.

K:　Okay, one …

L:　This is one. This is two. Five is hard to found right now.

K:　Then how come?

L:　Because we-we are not using five any more like we are have the new kind.

K:　Oh yes.

L:　A dollar and ten cents. This is our new kind from nineteen ninety one I think.

K:　Okay.

L:　Or nineteen ninety two. So this is our new kind of. We use that just a little bit.

K:　Okay.

L:　So this is hard to found.

K:　Because they are too small.

L:　Yeah, too small. So we use this and this. Regular we just use this coin.

K:　Yeah.

L:　A little bit use that.

K:　Hmm, that's neat. Yeah, I think I do have a little Dutch money. They have really tiny money.

L:　Hmm.

K:　I'll bring it to you next time. What's this one?

L:　This is …

K:　Saudi Arabia.

L:　Yes, Saudi Arabia.

K:　One …

L: One dollar. Yeah, it's a dollar.

K: Who is that?

L: I don't know. I think their king.

K: Their king?

L: Their's king.

K: Yeah, that's neat. What a neat collection? So you wrote a story about what you collected?

L: Yeah, it's just that like why you collect, what is my favorite one, um what I going to do is if-if I I'm older or what I'm going to do with my coin.

K: Okay.

L: This one is mine. I'm going to save that coin forever and forever.

K: [laughing] Because that's the biggest you said.

L: Yeah. And my oldest one.

K: Yeah. When you're older, what you're going to do with them. [reading the essay] "I'll give all my collection to them." Who is them?

L: Oh …

K: "And tell them to save them forever and forever."

L: Oh, who is them? I don't know.

K: Oh!

L: I'm writing wrong.

K: You will give it to some one?

L: Yeah, I already write my best one.

K: Okay, this is only a copy.

L: Yeah, I still got many copies. I don't know where is the other copies. So this one is.

K: Okay. Do you have to turn this in tomorrow?

L: No.

K: No.

L: We already do it in Friday. So …

K: Hmm, so you've turned it in already.

L: Yeah.

K: Okay.

L: Stop now.

K: [laughing]

---End of Conversation---

CONVERSATION 11: 2/2/1997

K: So what's this mean?

L: This is this we can look at this book. I think there is English right there.

K: Oh!

L: Um see this is the story of the Chinese …

K: Zodiac?

L: zodiac like um in China um people had ways to keep track of the years so they um they-they want the they want a Chinese zodiac system. They-they use twelve-twelve-twelve animals to-to-to count the years.

K: Right. So there is only twelve years?

L: No-no, there is twelve animals, twelve kind of years.

K: Okay, twelve kind of years. Hmm.

L: So I am born in-in nineteen eighty six so that year the tiger is like the best animal in that year.

K: Okay. But this year is the ox?

L: Yes.

K: The last year was the rat?

L: Yes.

K: There is always the same order?

L: Yeah, it always the same order. This is a story just tell you why the little mouse ____

K: So the next year is the tiger.

L: Yeah.

K: And then the rabbit.

L: Yeah.

K: And then the dragon.

L: Yeah, dragon, snake, then horse,

K: snake, then horse.

L: sheep, monkey, cock, dog and the /bou/ (boar).

K: The boar.

L: The boar, yeah.

K: That is the wild pig. Is it that is? A boar?

L: Yeah.

K: Ha, weird. That's a neat looking book, though.

L: Yep.

K: Where did you get it? Written in Chinese and ____

L: No, um from the …

K: From the library.

L: Yeah, the library.

K: Hmm. And you said your friend is coming over today. What time does he come? Your friend? Today? The puzzle?

L: Oh, yep. And they just coming. We just take she to the to McDonald's when we eat.

K: Um-hmm.

L: She is eating very-very slow.

K: Oh, you already went there.

L: Um …

K: You went this morning?

L: You mean McDonald's?

K: Yeah.

L: Yeah, we-we went to there for lunch.

K: Oh, for lunch. I see.

L: Then she got go to Chinese school.

K: Okay.

L: Um so she need she had to be quick. If she is not, she got waste his time.

K: Right.

L: Because she got go to Chinese school one o'clock.

K: Oh.

L: When we done then take she to back to his house, it is already twelve fifty six.

K: Ah, so she was late.

L: Yep.

K: Oh, no. Did she get in trouble?

L: Um it's okay.

K: It's all right.

L: See um long time ago, the-the cat and the-the little um mouse

K: Is it rat?

L: Yep, are the are the friends, the best friends.

K: Um-hmm.

L: Okay. One day um the god say um we need get um we need have a um um like a … oh, yeah, we should found a way to keep track of time. Otherwise we'll get very inconvenient. I plan to hold a race. The first twelve animal cross the river will be the-the …

K: Oh!

L: the zo ...

K: Yeah, the zodiac

L: the zodiac

K: calendar.

L: Yeah, candidates.

K: Okay.

L: So the-the mouse and the cat they don't can't swim, right?

K: Right.

L: So the no the-the ...

K: The ox?

L: the ox, yep, the ox can is very-very tall you know. So he so he could swim.

K: Okay.

L: But he is very-very old, he can't see very well. So they just want sit on the ox. Then they help the ox to go the way.

K: Okay. All right, so they can help each other.

L: Yeah.

K: The ox can swim. They're going to tell him where to go because he can't see.

L: Yeah, he is very-very old.

K: Okay.

L: Then when it's-it's not maybe it's three o'clock, then they just go, go swim. The-the they're on the ox. The mouse just put the ... when they-they almost get on get over the river, the mouse just push the-the cat in the river.

K: Um-ha.

L: And the so the cat the mouse say this the idea is mine, so just I can just I can be the first one.

K: Okay.

L: So they just go they go to the-the ... then they just go. They get in there. You know the little mouse is very fast.

K: Um-hmm.

L: They just get in there. Um so he just go very-very fast. Because the ox is very-very old,

K: Okay.

L: he can't go very fast.

K: Right.

L: So he the mouse just go very-very fast and get the first one.

K: So he's the first.

L: Yeah. The ox is second. Then ____

K: The cat is not in there at all because the cat is in the water.

L: Yeah. The now everybody is from every place then coming, yeah. Then everybody is found its xxx The ...

K: Wow!

L: So the cat when the cat see the mouse, they just try to eat him.

K: Right.

L: You know that after that ____

K: So what happened to the cat? The cat drowned? Where is the cat?

L: The cat no this is the-the monkey. The cat the cat didn't get anything.

K: You're kidding?

L: There is no cat in there.

K: Is there a giraffe in there? What's the top one?

L: This, horse.

K: Oh, horse.

L: Mouse, ox, tiger, rabbit, dragon, snake, horse, um sheep, monkey, um cock, dog and ...

K: The boar.

L: the boar, yeah. This the last part is very-very funny. Look at this.

K: Ou-oh.

L: When every time, look at this, when the cat see the mouse, they just trying to eat him.

K: Oh, so the cat and the rat used to be friends. And because of this, the cat and the mouse are enemies now.

L: Yeah.

K: Oh, wow!

L: So the every get every one get one. See look at this, the Heavenly God came down ... rat, ox, tiger, um rabbit, dragon, snake, horse, goat, monkey, rooster, and dog. And there is just only eleven. One-one more ... And at the very moment the pig is with a no "I'm-I'm starved".

K: [laughing] So when he wants to win, he is usually hungry.

L: Yeah.

K: Oh.

L: He get the last one.

K: That's funny.

L: Yeah.

K: Ha.

L: So this year we're the we're ox.

K: Okay. And you got this at the Whetstone library.

L: Yeah.

K: Is this the one you go to more often or do you go to the one downtown?

L: No, I go to the Upper Arlinton library.

K: Upper Arlinton.

L: Yeah.

K: Okay.

L: This is because this is my friend you know you know last time you go to she's house to the party.

K: Um-hmm.

L: You know just ____

K: Yep, Ping.

L: Yeah, Ping.

K: Yep.

L: He is tiger too. He born in tiger too.

K: Okay.

L: And his mom too.

K: Ping is or Daxin is?

L: Um Ping. He she is born in the tiger too.

K: Okay. When was she born then? In um sixty two?

L: Maybe.

K: Yep?

L: Yeah.

K: Hmm. So we're the three here, sixty two, seventy four, eighty six. Jos is seventy three. Which one is he?

L: This one, ox.

K: He is the ox.

L: My dad is horse.

K: Um-hmm.

L: My mom is dog.

K: Dog, ha, neat. That's really neat. Where did you get this? At a restaurant?

L: Yeah.

K: Which one?

L: Um /future/ (Fortune), you know. Just in the university village.

K: Oh, the one right here?

L: Yeah.

K: You eat there?

L: Yeah.

K: Is it good?

L: Yeah.

K: Hmm.

L: You know Ping's mom?

K: Hmm.

L: Every week they have um a group of Chinese

K: Um-hmm.

L: Chinese um like she very-very old from China they can't speak English.

K: Okay.

L: So they just get-get a group.

K: Um-hmm.

L: They just go to the go to …

K: I think they go to the restaurant.

L: go to the restaurant every week.

K: Okay, and they chat together.

L: Yep.

---End of Conversation---

CONVERSATION 12: 2/16/1997

K: Okay, you're doing the trick?

L: Yes.

K: Okay, let's see it.

L: [putting down the cards] One two three four, one two three four. You need re-remember the card you found it. Don't tell me.

K: I can pick any card on one of those four rows?

L: Yeah.

K: But don't tell you which one?

L: Yeah.

K: Okay.

L: And you got remember. It's that on this row?

K: I don't want to tell.

L: Yep, you have to.

K: No, it's not on that row.

L: How about this?

K: Um no.

L: This?

K: Yep.

L: [gathering the cards and laying them down again] Okay, did you see your card?

K: Um-hmm.

L: Is it in this row?

K: Um no.

L: This row?

K: No.

L: This row?

K: Yes.

L: [gathering the cards and laying them down a third time] Oops. Okay, this is a house. There're four houses. Okay, pick one, two houses.

K: Two houses?

L: You just pick, okay? I do what I'm doing.

K: Okay, I got my two houses.

L: Say to me. Tell me.

K: Oh, tell you which two? This one and this one.

L: Okay, pick one house.

K: One more house?

L: Pick two rooms. This is a room. Pick two. This?

K: This one and this one.

L: Okay, pick one room.

K: This one.

L: Okay, good. [showing the card]

K: [surprise] How did you do that?

L: [laughing]

K: How did you do that?

L: Um ___

K: Do it again.

L: Okay.

K: How did you do that? Oh, forget it. I know what you did.

L: What?

K: Do it again. I'm watching this time.

L: What I do? What I do? Tell me.

K: I know. I'll know when you do it this time. Okay, I got mine.

L: This?

K: No.

L: This?

K: Yep. Are you thinking? Did you do it wrong?

L: I don't know. Maybe. I don't see it. Is that in this row?

K: Yes. Oh, I know what you do. No, maybe I don't.

L: Pick two house.

K: This one, this one.

L: Pick one house.

K: This one.

L: Pick two room.

K: This one and this one.

L: Take one room.

K: This one.

L: [showing the card]

K: That's not my card. [laughing] This was my card.

L: Oh, yes.

K: Oh, yep. I think when you stacked them up the first time. What's wrong?

L: I don't know.

K: Ha-ha. It was a good trick. What you doing in school these days?

L: Study.

K: Study, what're you studying?

L: Um you mean what?

K: Um re-remember the time you told me you were studying was about how-how different boys and girls grow?

L: Oh.

K: Are you still studying that?

L: No.

K: What's that? Social Study?

L: No, Health.

K: Oh, Health. What're you studying in Health?

L: Right now?

K: Um-hmm.

L: No, we not study so much in Health right now.

K: Um-hmm, how come?

L: Because this quarter we just study we just finish the American colonies.

K: Oh, yes.

L: [giving her one small packet of haw flakes]

K: Hey, thanks.

L: The colonies, the American colonies. You know the Boston Tea Party?

K: Oh, yep, you study that? What do you think about that? Good idea or bad idea?

L: Good.

K: It was good?

L: And we study the-the colonies and the American independence.

K: Oh, yep. Did you study about Paul Revere?

L: [showing the facial expression of not understanding]

K: Paul Revere, did you study him? The guy that told them that the red coats were coming with the lantern in the top of the church?

L: [shaking head]

K: Oh, okay. Well, what else do you study?

L: Math.

K: Is that in Social Study? The colonies?

L: Yes.

K: What you study in Math? Fractions?

L: Math, I can't remember all these stuffs in Math. Oh, we just finish the-the graph.

K: Oh, yes.

L: The circle graph,

K: Um-hmm.

L: bar graph, and the line graph.

K: Oh, wow. Did you like it?

L: Yeah, that's easy.

K: You like Math, don't you? It's easy for you. What about Art? You're such a good artist. What you're doing in Art?

L: No, we not-not do Art any more.

K: Why not?

L: Yeah, this is the first two quarter we finish all Art.

K: Hmm. So what you're doing now when it's Art time?

L: We don't have Art time.

K: You have Music?

L: Yeah.

K: What you ___

L: Look, recorder.

K: Oh, you're still doing the recorder. You did that a couple of weeks ago.

L: [going to get the recorder]

K: Can you play a song now?

L: The song?

K: Yeah.

L: I don't think so. I can play a part of this song.

K: Okay, let me hear it. You have a test on this?

L: Yeah, every week we need have like last week this week we need do the-the third one.

K: Okay.

L: Last week we do the first two lines.

K: Oh, this is a good song too.

L: What is it?

K: It's from the that play um about the ballerina play at Christmas time they do all the time.

L: Oh.

K: You know what I mean. I think it's also the same song from the old Smurf's show.

L: Okay.

K: I think.

L: Oh, gosh.

K: Ha, all ready. So you know the first two lines?

L: I think so.

K: All right, let's hear it.

L: I don't know if I know this week. How long you're how long in that-that space?

K: How long?

L: Yeah.

K: Um one. And this get two beats.

L: No.

K: Oh!

L: How long you will these two beats? Like /nnnn/ or /nnn/?

K: However you do it normally is fine.

L: I don't know what is it.
K: I think it's two like in each-each measure there is three.
L: Like this [playing the recorder]
K: Yep, so it will be one two three, rest for three then ___
L: No, I think it's two.
K: Oh, you're right. That ___
L: That's not one.
K: It's not. What's that?
L: This is just tell you … I don't know what is it.
K: Oh.
L: My teacher will tell me later.
K: So I guess it's cut time, isn't it? So there're just two beats for measure?
L: Yeah.
K: Okay, so then just hold that for one.
L: [playing] Oops, it's G.
K: Oh, it's okay. I didn't know.
L: [playing] What's wrong with this?
K: It sounds okay.
L: I don't think so.
K: So is there a frog in there or something?
L: Sounds like there're running water in there.
K: Oh, some spit.
L: [playing]
K: Good job.
L: What's this?
K: That's the same note as this.
L: Which one?
K: This.
L: I need color this. I can't read this. I have to color it so I know what is it.
K: I see.
L: This is a A.
K: A, and this is B. And this is A?
L: Yeah.
K: This is ___
L: Yeah, stop from there.
K: D? From here?
L: Yeah.

K: Okay.

L: [playing] No, I don't know this is a B. Sorry.

K: [laughing] It's okay.

L: [playing] B?

K: G.

L: Here is G?

K: G.

L: Oh, no.

K: A, B. And between these two, there is no rest.

L: What is this? This is …?

K: A

L: A

K: B

L: B

K: A

L: A

K: Rest

L: Rest

K: G

L: G

K: A

L: A

K: B

L: Oh B. Okay. How about this? GG

K: GG AA

L: AA

K: Ou-oh, that's funny rhythm, isn't it? It's like one and two. So there is only half a beat.

L: Yeah, this is hard.

K: Hard one.

L: How do you how do you say that?

K: What? How do you count it?

L: Yep.

K: You say um rest and two. Because it is like you break down the one and two and it will be rest and two.

L: Oh. Oh, no, that's hard.

K: Yeah, it is hard. You can do it though.

L: [playing] Oh, man! What I ___

K: Are you doing this one?

L: Yeah.

K: You can take a break between ___

L: Yeah. [playing] Oh, man. What ___

K: That was great.

L: I'm keep looking at the break. [playing] Oh, I don't know I'm getting too fast. So how do you say that? [singing]

K: Yep, that's right.

L: You need say together or not like this [showing]

K: Yes.

L: [playing]

K: Yes, that's right.

L: Or like this or like this [playing]

K: Um no. It's not slurred, it's like it was the first time.

L: [playing]

K: Yep. [counting the measure] One two one two one two rest rest one two one two GG.

L: Oh, I think I get there too-too long.

K: Yep, those are shorter.

L: [playing]

K: [counting the measure] One two one ___

L: Like this [playing]

K: Yeah. [counting the measure] one two one two. Yep, that's perfect. You're good.

L: [playing] Oops, I forget ___

K: What?

L: Oh, yep, I thought it's D. If it's D, I need take-take this.

K: Oh, if it's a D? Oh, the back one.

L: I thought it's a D.

K: Great.

L: It's a G.

K: You don't have any D's yet.

L: [playing]

K: [counting the measure] One two rest rest one two one two.

L: Oh, it's like [playing]

K: Oh.

L: Yeah.

K: Good.

L: [playing] Oh, no, I need to get this faster. [playing] So I need start over.

K: Okay.

L: [playing] What's wrong with this?

K: Ou-oh. I think your fingers don't cover the holes completely when it does that.

L: This one, you need a whole ___

K: Oh, yep, make a whole new finger.

L: If it's not, this is bad.

K: Yep.

L: [playing] Oh, no, faster again. [playing]

K: [counting the measure] One two and one.

L: GG, AA.

K: Yep, that's exact the rhythm. Good.

L: [playing]

K: Good. That's perfect.

---End of Conversation---

CONVERSATION 13: 3/2/1997

K: Did you sell any candies yet?

L: Un-un. [shaking head]

K: No.

L: I got too much homework these days.

K: You've no time to sell.

L: Yeah. Every day right now we have you know we have our extra reading book.

K: Why?

L: You have to read every chapters. Every day you have to read that chapter and you need you got a vocabulary sheet and-and a question sheet and answer. That is very hard for me.

K: Okay.

L: You got you got to know to read this books.

K: Hmm.

L: Very hard to me so my dad can help me some. And today like Friday we have homework it's two chapters four and five together thirty pages.

K: [whistling to show surprise]

L: Oh, my god. I don't know how to read those. So I can't even read. Just-just do it.

K: Right.

L: Just see the question like a few how old like just ask you how old is she. I just found how old is she in the book. Answer it. So I don't read it.

K: Oh, you don't read it.

L: I don't read it.

K: What if your teacher hear this tape?

L: Ou-oh.

K: You're in trouble. So what-what's the book about? Are they fun books?

L: It's about a boy and a girl. They out of the home and they go to the museum

K: I see.

L: in the New York. You know the Art Museum?

K: In New York? Is that a big one?

L: Yeah. It's mon-montria? Metrolia?

K: Oh, the metropolitan.

L: Yeah.

K: Yeah, okay.

L: It's a big art museum.

K: Okay.

L: Yeah. So they study Michelangelo.

K: Okay.

L: You know what's that guy's name? Um it's-it's another turtle.

K: Leonardo [da Vinci]?

L: Yeah.

K: Yeah.

L: You know what is the picture of a girl? What's that name? Monsaliya (Mona Lisa)?

K: Yeah, yeah, his painting.

L: Yeah.

K: [someone coming in] Jos lost his key. Well, just a second.

L: So those boys and they is talking about how they leave like they use a violin case

K: Um-hmm.

L: and put all the stuffs in there. Everybody the boys got out. That boy got a violin case and the girl got a violin case. So they could put their things in there.

K: Oh, I think I think I saw the movie. Is there a movie too?

L: Yeah, this is Mrs. Bathel.

K: Yeah.

L: Mrs. Bathel E. and Claudia and Jamie.

K: Yeah. And they go to the museum and take a bath in the fountain

L: Yeah.

K: and they take all the money out.

L: Yeah.

K: Yeah. Actually I saw that movie. It was funny.

L: Yeah, I just read the Chapter 5. That's just talking about they got money for free in the fountain.

K: From the fountain. Funny. Ha, I bet it's a good book.

L: Yeah, I know. It's talking you know I-I think the last the last chapter maybe they will go home because they-they the girl get out because-because she think like I'm the biggest one. She is the biggest one then everybody she need like-like these three cake: these are little boy, a little brother, another brother and a little sister. And these three cake then all his brother and sister got it. He can get nothing.

K: I see.

L: So he is the biggest one. So she don't like to be the biggest one. So she was (wants) his second youngest brother come out of. Yeah, his brother is fun.

K: Okay.

L: He is a treasurer.

K: Ha, what a good book!

L: Yeah.

K: How many chapters are there?

L: Ten.

K: Okay. You said you're on Chapter 5. So you're half way done. Okay. And so is this something that everyone must do?

L: Yeah.

K: Or you just do some extra reading now.

L: No, that is our homework. Then you have to do it.

K: I see.

L: And that reading book is extra. And we are not done with the real reading book yet.

K: Okay.

L: So my teacher thinks that always better. So ...

K: Okay. Are you going to have a vacation soon? Easter vacation?

L: No.

K: No?

L: No.

K: What do you have?

L: We-we-we I don't know. Just stay home or something.

K: Just one week off?

L: No, four days.

K: Four days.

L: Yeah, and two is weekend.

K: That's not nice.

L: Friday

K: So Friday and Monday.

L: Yeah.

K: That's all?

L: Yeah.

K: Why?

L: Four days. I can't believe it.

K: Yeah.

L: That's our Spring recess.

K: Spring recess only four days.

L: My god.

K: Yeah. I would thought like my sister who is here today. She they have a whole week. So they went to Florida.

L: Yeah, this suppose to be a week. Last year we have a week.

K: Yeah. I wonder why. Hmm. Did you have any snow days yet? Where there was so much snow and ice, you could not go to school?

L: Yeah.

K: You do. How many?

L: Maybe five something. Yeah, sometimes.

K: Maybe that's why because you've already missed a lot of school.

L: No.

K: No?

L: Last year is more.

K: You've more last year? Hmm, I don't know I bet. Hmm. Well, so what did you do today? Play ball?

L: Oh, today I go to Chinese school.

K: You do?

L: Yeah, with Jack you know that friend, my friend.

K: Oh, yeah, he came here.

L: Yeah. He and he got go Chinese school because his Chinese less for watch. So he need learn some Chinese. But I don't have to go to.

K: Learning Chinese language?

L: Yeah. So I already in fifth grade. I mean in fourth grade in Chinese so I'm already good at Chinese. So I with his mom to go get him. And I just playing basketball right there.

K: Okay.

L: So we're going to play double.

K: Okay. So Jack has been in America for a long time?

L: Yeah, two years.

K: Two years. Okay. Hmm. So he has to go to American school during the week and then Chinese school on Sunday?

L: Yeah.

K: Boy, he has a lot of school.

L: And today you know when he is come back you know when he talking to me he talking to me that if he win the McDonald's price you know those price.

K: Right.

L: One million dollars

K: Oh, he might win.

L: Yeah.

K: [someone coming in] Okay. Well, what are we talking about? I don't really remember.

L: Oh, the-the Spring recess.

K: Oh, right. There're only four days.

L: Yeah. In China the Summer recess we have only two month.

K: That's it?

L: Yeah.

K: Why? But you want to have more vacation?

L: Yeah.

K: Yeah. Ha.

L: And we have many-many homework in those two months.

K: You have to do homework on Summer recess?

L: Yeah.

K: Like what?

L: Like every day write a paragraph no like five or something paragraph.

K: Right.

L: A story like that. Write a story.

K: Okay.

L: And it's hard in China.

K: Right.

L: Nobody like the-the Winter recess.

K: The Winter recess and Summer? How long is Winter recess?

L: A month.

K: Just one month.

L: We only have two recess: Summer recess and the Winter recess.

K: [someone coming in] Well, we have a funny tape this time, it's okay. So one month and two months. But why don't people like the Winter one?

L: Because we have same work same the same much work as the Summer recess.

K: Um-hmm.

L: So that's bad.

K: In one month you have to do the same amount you have to do in two months.

L: Yes.

K: That is bad.

L: Nobody like it.

K: You should not have any homework in the recess.

L: Yeah.

K: Maybe that's why you guys so smart though because you are always working.

L: And now we school we all play you know the 24 game. You know what I mean?

K: Un-un [shaking head]. The 24 game?

L: Maybe I could show you.

K: It's that a board game? Or is it ___

L: It's a good game.

K: A board game.

L: It's a card game. You want me show you this?

K: Um we'd better not. We might leave the tape again. We'll be in trouble or we can't do that.

L: Okay, that's a card.

K: We'll finish and then you'll show me. I'll get some ice cream and you'll go get it and then we'll eat ice cream.

L: It's a card. And you have four number on it. And you need use those four number to get twenty four.

K: Okay. You do it with school?

L: Yeah.

K: It's a kind of math game?

L: Yeah.

K: Okay.

L: Let's see ___

K: It's a fun game but you learn something too.

L: Yeah.

K: That's good.

L: Now we have the champion we have the final tomorrow final championship.

K: Um-hmm.

L: And then who win who win there is one people going to win. And if you win, then you can go to the Ohio State to play with those guys from the Cleveland something.

K: Okay, so it's-it's kind of like the game of equation? No?

L: What is equation?

K: Equation was a math game that we played I think I was probably in like the fifth grade. No, I was probably in the sixth grade when I played. And it was a board and you have to you have a bunch of different dices. You have to roll the dice and you have to make different equations and plug in different numbers and whoever has the best equation will win.

L: Yeah.

K: It was it was pretty hard. But I am not very good at math.

L: That's a good game. Now we have tomorrow we have the championship, me and my friend lost and dead.

K: Who is it?

L: I got do me

K: Um-hmm.

L: and my friend.

K: You play against your friend, ou-oh. Is that hard?

L: Yes.

K: Your friend is sad if you beat him?

L: Yeah, I was sad if I beat him.

K: Yeah. Is Jack's real name Jack? Or is it he go by Jack over here?

L: Oh, no. He go just his-his Chinese name is almost the same thing as that.

K: Yeah? What's his Chinese name?

L: His Chinese name is Zhang Ke.

K: Okay.

L: So look like same, right? His English Jack, Zhang Ke Jack, almost.

K: Okay. Do you have a Chinese name and an English name?

L: No.

K: No. All are the same. Okay, hmm.

L: How do you say my name?

K: /lan/. Is that wrong?

L: How do you say it's like this? [writing down *Langtian*]

K: /lanqian/. How do you say it?

L: I don't know. I don't want to say it.

K: But how do you say it in Chinese?

L: /langtian/

K: /langtian/. Okay.

L: So what you are going to say it?

K: /langqian/. [laughing]

L: Just saying in your language.

K: Um like, well ___

L: In American English.

K: It could be either way in English, could be /lanqian/ or could be /lonqian/. Depend on how you say the /a/.

Y: Stop.

K: Yeah.

L: We already stop three times.

---End of Conversation---

CONVERSATION 14: 3/16/1997

K: Did you have your recorder test at school yet?

L: Oh, yep, we-we don't have any we don't have the test now. But we have something to-to do with the recorder every week.

K: Oh, you do. You have to practice something new.

L: Yeah.

K: Okay. Hmm.

L: Oh, the 24 game I lost that boy.

K: Yeah.

L: And the teacher say before we only can go one people in other school. Now my teacher say we could go three more peoples. So I could go to that place to ____

K: Really.

L: Yeah.

K: Okay, when will you do that?

L: Twenty fifth.

K: Twenty fifth of March?

L: Yeah.

K: Tuesday.

L: Tuesday, yeah.

K: And you'll go to the Ohio State?

L: Yeah.

K: Okay. Wow, so you were second out of your whole school?

L: Yeah.

K: Shuway, it's good. Do you still practice a lot?

L: Yes.

K: Hmm.

L: This last page I got do.

K: For your recorder?

L: Yeah.

K: What's the name of that song?

L: E'S E JAMMIN'.

K: Hmm.

L: There is many e's in this.

K: Okay.

L: So I got do there and there.

K: Hmm.You'll be able to do it. Hmm. This book that you're reading is just for fun, not for school?

L: Un-un, for fun.

K: For fun.

L: We can learn something from there. Some words in there too.

K: Okay.

L: [going to get some books]

K: You got all those at the library?

L: Yeah. This is Clue Junior 2.

K: Oh, that will be a good book.

L: Yeah.

K: Do you like to play that game?

L: Yeah.

K: I do too.

L: Clue Junior?

K: Um-hmm.

L: I don't play that before.

K: That will be fun.

L: What you playing? Same thing as clue?

K: Um-hmm, yeah, yeah.

L: Is there any more? Like any more this kind of games?

K: Okay, of Clue?

L: Of Clue Junior.

K: Um I don't know. Well, this is a neat book. So you read it and you have to solve the mystery?

L: Yeah. This is a mystery.

K: What if you can't do it? Did they tell you what-what the answer is?

L: Yeah.

K: Hmm.

L: That is Clue Junior. And I got Clue books, sometimes.

K: Yeah. So you like mystery books.

L: Yeah, it's a fun.

K: What's this one?

L: This is number 3. This one give yourself some goose bumps, so you got choose twenty different endings. This is number 3, number 4, number 5.

K: Oh, you already read that one. Number 1?

L: Oh, there is number 5, number 6, number 7, number 8, and that's all I got.

K: Are there two number 1's?

L: Number, yeah, I already done with this.

K: Okay. Hmm, what about, oh, no. So you read these two?

L: Yeah.

K: Hmm.

L: I'm not done with these.

K: It's a kind of fun. So you read a lot.

L: Not a lot.

K: No? Quite a bit. Are you watching basketball? On TV? The-the college basketball?

L: No.

K: No.

L: Today not today. Today we have the-the real basketball, NBA.

K: Oh, the NBA is going on today.

L: So we're not watching the-the college basketball.

K: Hmm.

L: Now it's the final

K: Yeah.

L: college basketball.

K: Who do you want to win?

L: Ohio State. But they already lost.

K: Yeah.

L: The-the church (coach) of the Ohio State basketball is already fired.

K: The what?

L: Fired out.

K: Oh, right. They already lost. Hmm. Who do you think will win in the final four?

L: Kentucky.

K: Kentucky.

L: Kentucky or Duke. Duck, Duke whatever.

K: Yeah, Duke. Hmm.

L: You can say Duck. It's d-u-c-k.

K: D-u-c. No, it's d-u-k-e.

L: Oh.

K: Yep, it's Duke.

L: Duke.

K: Duck, ha like Donald Duck. You have to leave this in there because it says you've got to return it.

L: I don't need it because I could read all those books before that time.

K: Oh, so you'll take it back way before then. Like next weekend?

L: Um-hmm yeah, probably.

K: Looks like four weeks away.

L: Yeah, it is four weeks.

K: That's a long time. Hmm, when's your Spring break?

L: Um twenty eighth.

K: The end of March. You put that in today?

L: I just write this, Kelly will come.

K: Ah you can erase it now because I'm here.

L: This is very cheap.

K: Ha.

L: This is for only just a dollar

K: Okay.

L: fifty cents.

K: That's nice though.

L: Yeah.

K: Do you have a Saint Patricks Day party at school tomorrow?

L: Ah?

K: Do you have a Saint Patricks Day party at school?

L: Um we don't have a party.

K: No.

L: But you have to wearing green.

K: Yeah.

L: Now you got trouble.

K: Yeah, big trouble. Where did you get that?

L: Meijer.

K: Okay.

L: You can just erase with your finger.

K: With your hand.

L: Or this.

K: Or that works too.

L: Everything works.

K: Yeah.

L: That pen doesn't work. See. Is that how to spell your name?

K: Yeah, that's exactly right. Boy, you really surprised me, when I was talking to your answering machine and you picked up the phone. I thought, who's that? And that's your name?

L: Yeah, I can spell my name.

K: Ah-ha.

L: I can write something for you. I can write something for you.

K: Okay. That's pretty. Are you learning that in school? No?

L: Yes, probably.

K: You learned a long time ago probably.

L: You mean handwriting?

K: Yeah.

L: You mean cursive?

K: Hmm. Did you learn it a long time ago?

L: We still learn it right now, practice.

K: Hmm.

L: Yeah, I already know how to write e, b, something like that.

K: Yeah. I suppose you don't write in cursive like that in Chinese though.

L: No.

K: Because your letters are very different.

L: You could write like very fast.

K: Yeah.

L: Same thing cursive.

K: So they are connected.

L: Sometime you can, yeah.

K: Oops, where did you learn to do that? In art?

L: I learn it from my dad.

K: That's neat.

L: Yeah.

K: Hmm. Can you write my name in Chinese, too? Or is it hard to do?

L: Let me look in that. I don't know how to spell your name in Chinese.

K: Oh, the computer will tell you that?

L: Yeah.

K: Did you take that to school with you?
L: No, I can't. Too dangerous.
K: Oh.
L: There is your name in Chinese.
K: Oh, wow.
L: [making the computer to pronounce]
K: Ha, is that same in Chinese, too?
L: No, I don't think he could.
K: Oh.
L: Okay, I could write it.
K: Okay.
L: You want me write like this too?
K: It doesn't matter if you want.
L: Oops ... I never see that word before.
K: Hmm. So it's natural word. It's not just letters.
L: Yes, like letters. So that could be a letter.
K: Oh, yeah, the one line.
L: Yeah, every line could be a letter.
K: Ha, that's really neat.
L: There is many kind of letters like in English.
K: Okay. But they are all connected. That's neat.
L: Oops.
K: You just put one line in different places then you have different words.
L: Yeah. It's not the same thing as English.
K: Yeah, it's much harder.
L: For me, it's much easier.
K: So that one you put those extra lines in there? Does it make a different word?
L: You mean those lines?
K: Hmm.
L: No.
K: That's the shadow.
L: This just the shadow like a 3 D or something.
K: Okay. Because you know the stuff that is dark is the real
L: Yeah.
K: letters. Ha.
---End of Conversation---

CONVERSATION 15: 4/1/1997

K: Are you learning to type?

L: Yes.

K: You are! For school?

L: No.

K: For what?

L: For fun.

K: Hmm how often do you practice?

L: I just start it yesterday.

K: Ooh, okay. Where did you get the book?

L: Library.

K: You go to the library a lot, don't you? Hmm tell me about the Spring break.

L: Spring break?

K: Um-hmm.

L: Oh, today I go to um my mom work a baby-sitter.

K: Okay.

L: And today I go to help her.

K: Okay.

L: Um um there is two boys. One is two years old and one is three years old.

K: Okay.

L: Um I just saw this two-two child I got my mom got to look at those two guys. So she want me to help her to like just like get the look at the-the little one.

K: Um-hmm.

L: So she could like go to restroom.

K: I see.

L: So I could look at them like something.

K: Um-hmm. Do you play with them too?

L: Yeah.

K: Yeah. What you guys play?

L: They are boys.

K: Are they both boys?

L: Yep.

K: Yeah. Okay. Hmm so that's fun?

L: Yeah.

K: Will you go tomorrow too?

L: I don't think so.

K: No, wasn't that fun, huh.

L: Yeah.

K: What else? Have you been to McDonald's?

L: No.

K: No. Have you seen the TV commercials where the McDonald's at the end says: Fifty eight cents coming soon? Have you seen that?

L: Un-un [shaking head].

K: Something special, but I don't know what it is. Do you know?

L: For what?

K: I don't know. It just says: Fifty eight cents coming soon.

L: I don't know.

K: I hope it's chicken mcnuggents are fifty eight cents. I like those.

L: I hope a hamburger.

K: Yeah, you like those? You like the happy meal, don't you?

L: I like hash brown.

K: Oh for breakfast. Yep, hmm. Well, hey on Sunday you went shopping with Ping, where did you go?

L: Oh, Sunday?

K: Um-hmm.

L: Go shopping um we she trying to buy a roller blade.

K: Um-hmm.

L: She and her husband

K: Okay.

L: also want to buy a roller blade. And they want I to teach them how to playing.

K: Ah.

L: So they just tell me to go and bring my roller blade to go Rose Park to like learn how to do it

K: Okay.

L: learn how to play it. And that day is Easter Sunday. Nowhere is open.

K: Really.

L: We didn't even get down the car. Just get around, around and come back

K: Oh, so you just went for a car ride, you didn't go shopping.
L: Yeah.
K: Hmm where they want to buy them?
L: I think at Meijer's sport's shop.
K: Oh, the Galians?
L: Yeah.
K: The real big one.
L: Yeah.
K: Yeah. Hmm and you, are you going to get one?
L: A roller blade?
K: Um-hmm.
L: I already got one.
K: Oh, you already have one?
L: Yeah.
K: Oh, I thought those are Christine's.
L: Oh, I bought the same thing as hers.
K: Oh okay-okay. You know I have some just like that.
L: Cool.
K: Yeah, we should go sometime. Except for I left mine in Michigan. I have to go to get them.
L: Hmm.
K: Is that your Pepsi?
L: Yes.
K: What did you have for dinner?
L: Dinner I eat at his house.
K: Yes. What you have?
L: Um broccoli.
K: Yep.
L: Um
K: Just plain broccoli?
L: No, broccoli and-and ...
K: Chicken?
L: No, not chicken. Like meat ...
K: Hmm ...
L: Um pork, yeah.
K: Oh, pork, okay. Like pork chops?
L: Um like ah a-a big piece of pork like
K: Okay, yeah.
L: like we do like this

K: Um-ha.

L: and like this and it's like that big.

K: Okay. Yum, what else?

L: Um small fish.

K: Fish too? Fish and pork chop and broccoli. Was it good?

L: Oh, and soup.

K: And soup. What kind of soup?

L: Um I don't know how to explain.

K: Oh. The Chinese soup?

L: Um we eat we eat those in China a lot. It's like …

K: Chicken noodle?

L: It's like black.

K: Black soup?

L: No, like something is black. Looks like black and they put in the soup.

K: Okay, like beans?

L: No, like a paper.

K: You had black paper soup?

L: That thing like a paper. But it's not paper.

K: But you ate it?

L: Yes. It's not paper.

K: It's not paper.

L: It's just a thing you could eat it. But it looks like a paper.

K: Okay.

L: And you cut it when you get in the soup. And use this kind of thing to get them and you could eat. It's already separated.

K: Okay, hmm.

L: It's not paper, okay.

K: What's your drink?

L: Um water.

K: Water. Not Pepsi.

L: Ah-ah [shaking head].

K: What can you do now? It's dark out. Roller blade more?

L: No.

K: No.

L: Go to his house to play.

K: To play. Do you stay the night there?

L: No.

K: No. You can stay late because you don't have to go school tomorrow.

L: Yeah.

K: You are lucky kids you are on Spring break. Hmm.

L: Did you guys did you guys have Spring break?

K: Jos had Spring break last week. But I don't have Spring break.

L: Ah!

K: Oh, sad. But we went camping over the weekend. We went to West Virginia, in the mountain. It was fun.

L: Yeah.

K: Hmm. Hmm. Did your teacher give you any homework to take home for Spring break?

L: No.

K: Nothing. I bet you watched movies on Friday, didn't you?

L: Yeah, I do.

K: Like what?

L: Like Twister.

K: Really. I thought it was scary.

L: I know. The first part.

K: Yep-yep. What else?

L: Um the Hunchback of Notre Dame.

K: The Disney movie?

L: Yeah.

K: Ha.

L: And ___

K: Did you ever see Beauty and the Beast?

L: Un-un.

K: The Disney movie Beauty and the Beast.

L: Un-un.

K: They say that in the Hunchback of Notre Dame when the street of Paris scene comes on, you can see Belle, which is in Beauty and the Beast, in the street.

L: Cool.

K: You should look for her. Yep, she is like this old looking character. Yeah.

L: Oh and Oilary and Company.

K: Oilary and Company? Oh, Oliver and Company.

L: Yep, Oliver and Company.

K: Right, that's a funny movie with a dog.

L: Yep.
K: Yep.
L: And Jumanji. I don't know how to say it. Jumanji?
K: Juronamo?
L: No, Jumanji.
K: Jumanji?
L: It's a movie that Jumanji is a game, a board game. And there
    is a like a piece of like a piece that is look like a rhino
K: Um-hmm.
L: like a elephant. That high piece and if you just shake the dice
    and you can go by itself. And there is a middle there is a green
    part and you can write many letters in it. And sometimes um
    that guy shake and he is that-that place say those flying like
    those flying things are not good like will-will kill you will not
    good for you
K: Um-hmm.
L: And they can know what that means. And when the other guy
    shake it and she got something. And then that-that she-she
    starts a piece move.
K: Um-hmm.
L: And those things it's um like again he says um like some-
    thing. Then after that they the first he says those flyings those
    flying things are not good for you. And um in the TV many
    flying things are coming out. Very scaring.
K: Yeah.
L: And the other guy I think he is in the in the in the jungle. Um
    you must hide um I think so. Um and he that thing just let he
    flying. He just get in the scene. And he is in jungle.
K: Hmm. Did you like the movie?
L: I never saw the movie.
K: Oh, you're gonna watch it yet?
L: Yeah.
K: Okay.
---End of Conversation---

CONVERSATION 16: 4/29/1997

K: Okay, what're you going to do tonight? Tell me all about it.
L: Um we go we go everybody going to bring up-up some food.

K: Um-hmm.

L: Any kind of food, but we don't need drinks. Any kind of food like potato chips,

K: Um-hmm.

L: like some-some kind of vegetables,

K: Okay.

L: salads, something like that some food. And last year and this-this-this international night every like our principle our school want we to bring every kind like me bring Chinese food,

K: Okay.

L: like-like so we just see every country is different.

K: I see.

L: And we dress different kind of dress.

K: Okay.

L: Every country kind of dress. I'm trying get to see that I usually do in-in Chinese. Um in China I want my grandma maybe she will come. I want him bring three of them.

K: Okay.

L: We do that like the flag, you know?

K: Um-hmm.

L: Like if you get that um that's just like a class but it's not called a class. It's just a like when you-you have to get in first grade. You have to get in third grade I think. Then you can get that.

K: Okay.

L: Um that's very good. If you get that first, you're the best.

K: Okay.

L: So I got that in the second time. It's like you just get a thing every Monday in China

K: Um-hmm.

L: you have to get a flag. We put the flag up. Yeah, in Ame-America we do that too.

K: Right.

L: Get a flag off when every day begin. But in China we only do in the school we only do the first day, Monday.

K: Okay.

L: And we just get that. And we like this [drawing picture].

K: Okay. So with the flag?

L: Half to me and half to the flag.

K: Okay.

L: Then we just sing the song of the, our school song

K: Okay.

L: and the China song, the country song.

K: And you gonna do that tonight?

L: I'm trying to get that thing, but I didn't.

K: Okay.

L: I almost forgot.

K: Yep. So you go there you eat?

L: Yeah, I eat.

K: And you go home?

L: No.

K: No.

L: First grade last year just like we eat first. We have a and you can go to … After eat you can go to like my class, talk with my teacher and something like that.

K: Okay. So it's an open house internationally?

L: Yeah, last time it just called open house.

K: Okay. Um it starts at six o'clock?

L: [shaking head]

K: No, six thirty.

L: Six thirty.

K: Six thirty.

L: And everybody going to speak in their like every kind of language.

K: Yeah.

L: Like if I speak American I'm American, I speak English. Everybody knows how to speak English.

K: Right.

L: If like I'm a American, I speak English. Then I can say: Welcome to the to the international night. Um today we will have some food. Welcome to come. Something like that.

K: Okay.

L: And like if I'm in Chinese, I say I say in Chinese. I say that again. And then like Greece I say that again. Brazil say that again.

K: Okay.

L: So we every kind ___

K: How many how many different kinds of students do you have in your school? You have students from Greece?

L: Yeah. You see in my class we have almost ten.
K: Really!
L: See China,
K: Okay.
L: Korean, Brazil, Greece, um Russian,
K: Okay.
L: Puerto Rico,
K: Wow!
L: just speak Spanish,
K: Yeah.
L: um French.
K: Yeah, there are some from Europe?
L: Yeah.
K: Okay.
L: I think so. And we have Indians in our school, a lot of kind.
K: Wow, that's fun though.
L: I know. Some-some-some kids just come to our school my teacher tell them: our school is different than others because we have every kind of
K: Yeah.
L: every kind of peoples.
K: That's really neat.
L: It's like my last year teacher is in another elementary school now. Mrs. Harris teaching in another elementary school.
K: Um-hmm.
L: And those are all Americans.
K: Really. So it's only Cranbrook
L: I know.
K: that has such international mix.
L: And we have ESL and because we got international students.
K: Okay. Right. Um that's really exciting.
L: Yeah.
K: You can have fun tonight.
L: Oh, after we eat, and the first grade going to sing. I don't know what they going to sing. Ms.-Ms. Harris tell us they are going to sing, first grade.
K: Okay, but you're not in the first grade. You don't sing.
L: No.
K: Only the first grade.

L: Last year, we do Macrila.

K: Okay.

L: Everybody-everybody could go on there.

K: Okay.

L: I left when everybody go there.

K: What are you going to do this year then? If you sing with the first grade?

L: The first thing if I back I love it.

K: Okay, what's it?

L: The first thing I go to school playing basketball.

K: Oh, why am I not surprised, it's some kind of sport. What're you going to do all Summer? It's right around the corner. You have one month left in school.

L: My grandma maybe she will come.

K: Yeah!

L: She going to bring a she going to bring a violin.

K: Okay. You're going to learn to play it.

L: Yeah.

K: Okay.

L: And now I'm play the recorder. That's hard. You're going to play sixteen taps.

K: Yeah.

L: [playing] Oh, I'm not going to play it.

K: I remember you practice it.

L: I know. It's too hard.

K: Ha-ha it's fun. So will you go to violin school? In the Summer? Or go to someone's home?

L: We're going to someone like own teacher's house like I say I teach violin. If you if you want to come how much is a hour. Then just come to your house.

K: I see.

L: Jackie is learning to the-the piano.

K: Is he?

L: And Christine.

K: And Christine, too?

L: Yeah.

K: Okay. Are they related to each other?

L: Um ...

K: Jackie and Christine, are they brother and sister?

L: No.

K: No. They're just friends.

L: Yeah.

K: And they are your friends too.

L: Yeah.

K: You guys just do funny things when I was lying out there.

L: I know. That's the guy with Christine

K: You didn't know it was me at first.

L: I know.

K: I knew it was you guys though.

L: You know?

K: Yeah, you guys are fun. Ha so what else come out of your menu? You've torn something off it. What's that?

L: Oh, this?

K: What's that?

L: This. This are some coupons.

K: Hmm, is that good?

L: Yes, it's good. See sixty card for only 99 cents.

K: Oh wow, what kind of cards though? Like playing cards?

L: No, like those cards. Animal cards. Those are very good and what you do

K: Oh, it tells you about animals.

L: It's good.

K: So it needs to send only 99 cents to them?

L: No, they just give ___

K: Hmm, did the whole school have to buy it?

L: You don't have to buy it.

K: Um-ha here is a pizza coupon. That's good.

L: Where is that from?

K: Chuckey Cheese. Have you been there? Little bit like Magic Mountain.

L: You can playing there too?

K: What?

L: You can playing there too?

K: Um-ha. Yes with tokens and ski ball and all that stuff. When I was ___

L: Oh you can get free you can get free tokens for good grades.

K: Hey.

L: Yeah I did.

K: You can get free tokens.

L: Free tokens?

K: Yeah. Look at this. You can buy any large Pizza and fifty tokens for 20 dollars. Is that cheap?

L: No, it's not.

K: No. How much do tokens cost?

L: A-a quarter.

K: Oh!

L: I don't know in there.

K: So that's cheap then. Fifty?

L: Fifty is like a token times … Oh, yep, that's cheap.

K: That's pretty cheap.

L: Fifty times a quarter.

K: Yeah, divided by four. Are you doing division?

L: Yeah, I do it.

K: Hmm wow I don't know if Chucky Cheese is any good. You guys seem to like Magic Mountain a lot though?

L: Yeah.

K: Have you been there lately?

L: No.

K: No. Me either.

L: Yeah.

---End of Conversation---

CONVERSATION 17: 5/27/1997

K: Commercial?

L: Oh the commercial like you don't have to do a commercial because a commercial just like you do on TV and you could do a ad on a newspaper or on a poster too. So my teacher tell us to do this because she try to tell us to sell yourself as a friend.

K: Okay.

L: Sell yourself as a friend so I-I think a-a I think a newspaper or a poster is pretty good. So I just write a newspaper. Um so I just write like about myself. What I am good. And I say the title is Langtian Lang Great Friend For A Thousand Dollars.

K: For a thousand dollars, shuway.

L: And I down there I just write like um I'm a great friend. I can do things blah-blah-blah and so everything about me is very good.

K: Right.

L: So um the last part I-I write: "I think the price will be good."

K: [laughing] Oh, that's funny. Oh! What about two movies you watched?

L: Oh you know Ping right there?

K: Um-ha.

L: and his and her husband and me we-we went to AMC, the new theater

K: Okay.

L: to watch movie. The first we try to watch the-the Last World.

K: Yeah.

L: And when we go there, it's like um we just like um we okay after-after we watch that and

K: Oh, you saw this?

L: Yeah.

K: It's scary.

L: Yes.

K: It looks scary in the commercials.

L: I know.

K: Cool.

L: Dinosaurs eat-eat-eat a man like [imitating the sound]. And he was like this see-see this is a map. He said he want [imitating the sound]. And everyone do like [imitating the sound]

K: Yucky-yucky-yucky.

L: spread apart.

K: Yeah, go awful. Um what else did you see?

L: And we see another movie and I don't know the name. It's a hundred one hundred thousand something I don't know. And see that movie was funny. See it's about like just like Double O just like Double O Seven.

K: Okay.

L: Have you watch it?

K: Yap, yap.

L: See just like that. And there is a gun. Just like that. But it's not James Bond. It's another guy.

K: Hmm.

L: And he is getting like a guy is dead. Let's say who got it. That was in the White House.

K: Oh, Murder at 1600.

L: Yeah.

K: Yeah.

L: Have you watch that?

K: I haven't seen it. But it looks good.

L: I know. That's-that's fun.

K: Yeah.

L: And they fight like very like-like steal things like a guy.

K: Ha.

L: Yeah.

K: Yap.

L: And you suppose to watch one movie in the theater for three bucks, right?

K: Um-hmm.

L: And we watch the first one. We think it's very early. So we watch another one.

K: So you just stay there?

L: Yeah.

K: Nobody came to get you?

L: No.

K: You are kidding.

L: Because that theater is very small.

K: Oh.

L: That room is not too big. Just the smallest one.

K: Oh. Which one did you go to?

L: Um the second one we go to another little one. The first one we go to Room 12.

K: Right.

L: That's the middle biggest one.

K: Right.

L: Number 1 and Number 24 is the biggest.

K: Right.

L: That's cool in there.

K: Ha. Which movie theater did you go to? The brand new one?

L: AMC.

K: The one by the new Target store?

L: Yeah.

K: Okay. Did you like the seat?

L: Yeah.

K: They were comfortable, weren't they?

L: Yeah. And you know the-the sound in the I've watch um Star War in the number-number 1 room. It's cool. The sound is just like the sound is three D. It's cool.

K: Ha, sounds everywhere.

L: I know.

K: Wow, I didn't see I didn't see that movie. I didn't see Star Wars. So do you go to movies a lot?

L: No. I go to five times movie. One is Jack bring me, and four time with

K: Ping?

L: Yeah.

K: Hmm.

L: My dad don't want because they don't like watch movie only I like.

K: Oh.

L: So they just want to pay the money to Ping so every time she go she can bring me to.

K: I see.

L: They don't want the money. I don't know why.

K: [laughing] I think they like you. So you went shopping on Saturday and Sunday.

L: Yap, we go to Eddie Bower. Have you ever been there?

K: Oh, that's where

L: Warehouse.

K: you dad get the pants.

L: Yeah, the warehouse.

K: Yeah.

L: So it's very cheap.

K: Yeah.

L: Yeah.

K: Where is that?

L: Um

K: Eddie Bauer.

L: I know.

K: It's in Grandview?

L: No.

K: No.

L: It's Fisher Road. See you go have you go to the-the Meijer in the east?

K: Meijer, yeah. Where is it? It's far away?

L: See you see you go to Lane Avenue and all way down and go to Riverside

K: Lane Avenue, all the way down, okay, right.

L: Is that the way you go to?

K: Um sometimes we go there.

L: Okay,

K: Yeah.

L: There see you go

K: Is there a Walmart by it??

L: Yeah.

K: In the movie theater? Across the street?

L: Yeah.

K: Okay.

L: See that one go to the ... I can show you. See [drawing] See this is the way see this is the Riverside. This is Lane Avenue. So this is the way you go to, all way down and Meijer is just like right there. The first ___

K: Is this Fisher Road?

L: No, this is... I don't know what's that called. You know this is the Riverside and you turn that way to the Meijer.

K: Okay.

L: So this road you could turn um see the-the first railroad

K: Um-hmm.

L: you know train

K: Um-hmm.

L: like the first one you turn left.

K: Okay.

L: and that's Mac-Mac something I don't know. You turn left right there.

K: Um-hmm.

L: You go all way down. Um the first block is Fifth Avenue

K: Okay, right.

L: and the second one is Fisher Road.

K: Okay.

L: So you go you go there Fisher Road and you get across-across 270.

K: Okay.

L: And you see right there.

K: [laughing] How do you know all this?

L: Um.

K: You're so smart. This is Fish, this is …?

L: This is Lane Avenue.

K: Okay.

L: This is Riverside. [reading while writing] Riverside.

K: Hmm. What if I took what if I took Olentangy?

L: Yeah, yeah you could do that too.

K: You go like this.

L: You could do that too. But I think this one is better

K: Yeah.

L: and is faster.

K: Okay. Then what's this road?

L: This I don't know. If you go to Fifth Avenue, it's the last part.

K: It's the end.

L: Yeah, it's the end, right there. So ___

K: Oh, I know what that end because I have a friend that lives like right here. So when I go to visit her, I go on Fisher Road and I go under 270 and turn and that's her house. So she lives really close.

L: But, yeah. but you can't go 270 to this. There is no place you can go.

K: You just go underneath it.

L: Yeah.

K: Neat, okay. I have to go there. Jos needs some pants.

L: See this door in the warehouse. See like this big house.

K: Hmm.

L: See you go there first and you go left.

K: Hmm.

L: There is a place. There are a lot of things. But that's like a real store.

K: Okay.

L: And you go up right there up the restroom there. And you go up and go all the way down there and go left. And that's the cheapest place.

K: Really?

L: Yeah, like ___

K: What did you get there?

L: Like I bought a bag there for one dollar.

K: You are kidding?

L: Like ___

K: That's you got a book bag?

L: Yeah. And like um it's very cheap. Eddie Bauer.

K: I don't know how you spell it. Ha, I'll have to take Jos there. What else did you get?

L: And for you know you could go to my house later to watch those kinds of very big bags.

K: Um-hmm.

L: And you could put things out.

K: Hmm.

L: There is a wheel down there. You could just like this [showing].

K: Oh, yap.

L: You know that like that kind of thing. And you could like you could get your legs like this.

K: Right.

L: Like that. And this

K: Just for luggage.

L: Yeah, it's very-very big and it's only for ten dollars like that-that big. You can get a lot of things there.

K: Oh, my goodness, yes.

L: That's very cheap in there.

K: That's nice. You went there Saturday and Sunday?

L: Yeah.

K: Is there anything left?

L: Yes. You could oh when is June oh I could give you the-the-the schedule. It's about see if it's June and the-the last week of the month and the Saturday and Sunday. You got go there very-very-very early.

K: Um-hmm.

L: You know Ping. That day it's Sunday. I go with her.

K: Um-hmm.

L: She-she and her husband go there like eight thirty.

K: Um-hmm.

L: And she is the first one.

K: Really? What time is it open?

L: Twelve o'clock.

K: Eight thirty! Why did she go at eight thirty?

L: She just try to buy you know the-the thing that maybe I could show you later there.

K: Never mind.

L: So it's very-very cheap.

K: Ha.

L: And the best thing in there I think it's the bag. But there are a lot of bags there like that we will did too and we just have a ditch

K: Yeah.

L: We just have a ditch and we just gain everybody. And we go to there like ten thirty. So we ___

K: So you just wait in your car for an hour and half?

L: No, we got wait on the line.

K: You got on line?

L: Yeah, a line. You could sit down.

K: You wait in line for an hour and half to go shopping?

L: Yeah.

K: That doesn't sound like very fun.

L: But that guy is very fun.

K: But you get good deals.

L: Yeah. Next time you go there is June July. The last week of June and July. And Saturday and Sunday you should go there very-very like very early. It's very cheap. See you know a big bag you can get a lot of things in there. You could even see get your almost you could get a half of three fourth of the refrigerator in there. You know those kind of bags?

K: Yap.

L: You pay ten dollar for a whole bag no matter what you get in there.

K: Oh you can put stuff from the ___

L: Yeah.

K: Oh, I thought it was a big suitcase.

L: No.

K: But it's not you can pull it.

L: It's only for June and July.

K: It's crazy.

L: Yeah.

K: It's so crazy.

L: Like a very big coat. It's only like if you got sale 50 per cent sale it's like only like fifteen dollars.

K: Shu.

L: And if you got very big sale like that day we saw a coat is just like seven dollars.

K: Man, wow! That sounds good. Did you go swimming on Friday? Here? It was cold.

L: Actually, um you know Jack my friend

K: Um-hmm.

L: he is the first one get in there and I am the second one. He got a reward like this. First one in this swimming pool. Certificate reward to Jack for blah-blah. And the first single to swim in the pool.

K: That's crazy. It was so cold.

L: I know. I just get there [showing the sound of trembling] and get out of there.

K: Yeah, oh my goodness.

L: Jack got his back. He kicked my ball in the middle of the pool.

K: You have to go in to get it?

L: Yeah.

K: So what did you do? Get out of the pool and run up the stairs quickly to get a hot shower?

L: Yeah.

K: Oh, you guys are crazy. Have you gone since then?

L: No.

K: No, it's cold. It's warm today but not that warm.

L: I know.

K: I would sit out there in the sun. You'll have lots of time to swim in this summer. Are you going to go to the Summer school?

L: Yeah.

K: You are.

L: Yeah. I think for a month.

K: For one month, okay.

L: Because I think like I am boring in the house nothing to do.

K: Oh, there is nothing there.

L: I can do something in school.

K: Right. Ha, when are you out of school? Next week is your last week?

L: Um I think so.

K: Yeah, that sounds good. This week there is three days left. Next week there is ___

L: Friday we have no more class, Friday.

K: Friday is your last day?

L: Yeah, no, Sunday is our last day.

K: Okay, that sounds good. Then you will be on vacation. Then you will be in that pool a lot of times, don't you?

L: No, it's too cold.

K: No.

L: Oh, today I go to the skating party.

K: Tonight?

L: No, today I just in school.

K: Oh, you already went.

L: Yeah.

K: Okay.

L: My teacher bring us. Today we have fun a whole day. See we go there like nine thirty.

K: Um-hmm.

L: You get a bus to the place to skate. And you get back like twelve thirty. Then we lunch and we go out for play. When we come back, we watch video. And after that, we go home.

K: Why don't you go school? You didn't learn anything.

L: I know

K: You have a good day, ha?

L: Yeah.

K: What are you going to do tomorrow?

L: Um ...

K: More videos?

L: No.

K: No.

L: Like a month once video.

K: What did you do in your science project?

L: Um I'm just doing right now because I have to bring in tomorrow.

K: Oh, it's due tomorrow?

L: Yes.

K: Ou-oh.

---End of Conversation---

CONVERSATION 18: 6/29/1997

K: Okay. So what's Kelleys Island?

L: It's a island um near-near Cleveland I think.

K: Hmm.

L: It's like [going to the map to show it]

K: So it's far away.

L: right here.

K: Okay. Oh yep.

L: It's not very far.

K: It's on the Lake Eric?

L: Yeah.

K: What did you do there?

L: Um that island is not very small. It's not very big. And we use we use boat to go there. And the cool thing is you could drive your car on the boat.

K: You're kidding! So you took your car over to the island?

L: Yes.

K: Neat. What did you do on the island?

L: Oh island has many place. That island funny thing um …

K: What was it?

L: Oh see, this oh no.

K: Can you draw it?

L: Um we don't need to draw it.

K: Oh.

L: See there are many good places. There is people living in the island.

K: Um-ha.

L: And there is people like most people are visiting to the island.

K: Okay.

L: And that the next day to that day which is next day we already home. Next day there was a sports game.

K: Ohhh.

L: A jogging a jogging game.

K: On the island. It's that a race?

L: Yeah, a race.

K: Okay.

L: So there is going to be a lot of people.

K: Okay.

L: So that day we shu very lucky

K: Oh yeah, you go that day.

L: Yeah.

K: So there are a lot of shops?

L: On the on the island no. But you know on the on the land out there, there are shops. In right there the downtown is very-very small just like maybe just like three or five streets.

K: Hmm.

L: I mean shop the downtown is very small. But the outside is very big.

K: Hmm. It's historical or the forest there or ...? I don't know.

L: There is forest. There is no forest. It's not forest.

K: No.

L: It's just like Columbus. So more-more trees

K: Hmm.

L: People they just say this part is the island okay. And there are people, there are houses and there is the road.

K: Okay.

L: And there is the you know grass,

K: Um-hmm.

L: trees. And after that is the water.

K: Okay.

L: So they live there

K: So there is a lot of nature.

L: Yeah.

K: Can you camp there?

L: Um yep.

K: Um-hmm. Man, you went there for one day?

L: Yes, one day.

K: Did you swim there?

L: No.

K: No. Do you swim here every day?

L: Not today.

K: Now what time do you usually go swim?

L: Five thirty.

K: Yeah, five thirty? How come how come so late?

L: My mom say the sun is too big.

K: Oh, yep it will burn your skin.

L: [making some sound]

K: Yeah, I understand that. Hmm if we want to swim with you, we should go five thirty.

L: Maybe you go maybe you go I don't know.

K: Yep. You are not going today though because of the rain?

L: If five thirty the rain stop, yap.

K: Then you go. Does Jack go then too?

L: I think so. Christina going too.

K: Yap. What about um Summer school? You are going to regular school or you are going to Chinese school?

L: Regular school, only five weeks.

K: I see. So it's only five weeks? [Langtian gave her some ice-pop] Oh, thanks. Um it's still over in Cranbrook

L: Yeah.

K: Elementary? Is there a bus that comes to get you?

L: No.

K: No, you have to get there yourself.

L: That's the difference.

K: Do you ride your bike?

L: No.

K: No, it's too far.

L: Yap.

K: Yeah, that's good.

L: Oh, you like red.

K: Yeah, red is good.

L: Yeah. [separating the ice-pop] Ou-oh.

K: Huh, you'll have to get a dog in here to lick that up. Did you have any animals in China?

L: Un-un [shaking head].

K: Any pets? Do a lot of people have pets in China?

L: Un-un.

K: No.

L: Not at all.

K: It's not you can't have pets.

L: We don't we don't have pets.

K: No.

L: We don't used to have pets.

K: No cats or birds or fish or …?

L: Sometimes I get a little rabbit.

K: Um-hmm.

L: I could buy it. Like one buck you could buy a little

K: Um-hmm.

L: a little-little tiny-tidy duck.

K: Right.

L: Duck.

K: A duck, okay.

L: Yeah, a little one like that maybe.

K: Then what you do? Keep it in your bedroom?

L: Yeah. That's cool.

K: Then when it gets big, you eat it?

L: Un-un.

K: No.

L: Sell it when it get bigger.

K: You do what to it?

L: It's not going to get big.

K: Oh, just stay as little.

L: Un-un. They going to grow bigger but when they don't grow bigger yet, they are dead.

K: Then it's dead.

L: Yeah.

K: Oh, okay. Man, well, then nobody has dogs.

L: Almost.

K: No.

L: There was a wolf dog in a place. They say I don't know if this is true or not. That dog eat a kid's head.

K: Really?

L: I don't know.

K: Um you remember that alligator that ate that little boy? In Florida? Do you remember hearing about that?

L: Yeah.

K: A kind of like that. Um you miss your friends in China?

L: [Nodding head]

K: Yeah. Do you write them?

L: [Nodding head]

K: Yeah. Do you get letters from them? Yeah?

L: No, they never write me a letter.

K: No.

L: I write two letters to them. No-no one write me back a letter.

K: So you don't know what they are doing. Hmm, are you going to China sometime soon?

L: Yeah.

K: When are you going?

L: I don't know.

K: Um-hmm.

L: I hope I could. I love I like to ride airplanes.

K: Yeah?

L: Very cool.

K: How many times have you been on airplanes?

L: Um um one from China to

K: Here?

L: Chicago.

K: Okay.

L: Chicago to Columbus.

K: Okay.

L: And I think no more.

K: That's it.

L: That's it.

K: So you have to go Columbus to Chicago again? From Chicago to China?

L: No. You can go to Detroit and back to Tokio something

K: Hmm.

L: in Japan. Japanese capital and come back to China.

K: Through airplanes.

L: Actually you can also go from Columbus, Detroit, and back to China.

K: Hmm. Detroit is big. When Jos and I go to the Netherlands, we go from Detroit because Detroit is big. Yeah, ng-ng-ng. Let's see, what was I gonna ask you about? Oh, what's your favorite part on the airplane? The food?

L: [shaking head]

K: The drinks?

L: Un-un.

K: My favorite part is movie.

L: You mean the part I like?

K: Yep.

L: The part I like is like um I don't know. It's just cool I don't know.

K: Just being in the way of the height like that.

L: Yeah.

K: Just knowing man I am over the ocean right now.

L: Yeah. It's cool.

K: Yeah. Were you scared the first time?

L: No.

K: No.

L: But um but I don't like is there are only two bathrooms.

K: I know. Then in the morning everyone sleeps at night in the morning everybody goes to use it. Then have to wait.

L: They got a long-long line.

K: Yeah, too long, man-man-man. When your mom and dad first told you you were going to move to America, were you excited or scared?

L: Um some excited some I don't want to.

K: Really?

L: Yeah.

K: Because you have to say goodbye to your friends.

L: Yeah.

K: Ha. Are you glad you are here?

L: Um yeah.

K: You like to be here.

L: Un-un.

K: Does it have basketball in China as much as it here?

L: No.

K: No.

L: In America we playing basketball more than China.

K: I see. Where you played badminton then?

L: What?

K: Where you played badminton then?

L: At the Larkin's Hall.

K: Where?

L: Larkin's Hall. Maybe you haven't heard before. It is all sports in there. You can find like basketball,

K: Oh, I see.

L: swimming, something like that.

K: I see. Rusty scissors, huh? Ha-ha. So you go there like once a week?

L: Um this is this is the second time of the week.

K: That you went for badminton? Oh, you went there today?

L: Yeah.

K: Ah. Oh, yucky.

L: Oh, yes.

K: That's awful noise.

L: Just we just come back.

K: You played badminton? Did you play against your dad?

L: No.

K: Oh, you played against yourself?

L: No.

K: Are there other people there?

L: Yes.

K: Wow.

L: Sometimes before when it's not summer yet, there is a lot of people.

K: I see. Now everybody going outside doing stuffs.

L: Yep.

K: Hmm.

L: Damn, this is dirty

K: Um-hmm. What have you been doing in the library?

L: Oh, we have a summer-summer program.

K: Are you in Great Detective?

L: Um?

K: Are you in the Great Detective Program?

L: What's that?

K: You have to read so many books. Then you-you get prize and stuffs. Are you in that?

L: Yeah, I got prizes.

K: Yep. How many books have you read so far?

L: Thirty something.

K: Oh, my goodness. Still those choose your own adventure books?

L: Yep, choose your own adventure books.

K: Yep, you read those stuffs.

L: Yeah, I like those.

K: Anything else?

L: Um like chapter books I use to read it. I like to read it.

K: Have you been to movies lately?

L: Um yeah, The Lost World. Never mind.

K: You went through the last one?

L: You know that?

K: Yeah. Did you go to see The Saint?

L: [shaking head]

K: No. It's good. You ought to see that. Yep, it's good.

L: It is a action movie or something?

K: Yep. You know the guy that was in the old batman, Val Kilmer? That guy played the batman in the last movie?

L: Yep.

K: He is in it. He is he is a thief. And every time he goes to steal something, he puts on the different disguise. And the police and everybody can't find him because he is in disguise of something else. Very good. Very-very much action.

L: What was that called?

K: The Saint.

L: Yeah. I'll tell my mom to bring me there.

K: Yeah, it's at the cheap movie theater. It's only a dollar.

L: It is?

K: Yep. It's at the dollar theater. I'll write that down too. One dollar theater.

L: Movie 12, right?

K: What?

L: Movie 12, right?

K: Is that Carrage place? Movies 12? Yep, Movies 12. I'll write that down too. Movies 12. Well, Murder at 1600, did you see that one?

L: Yep.

K: That was good, wasn't it?

L: I know.

K: That was very good.

L: The first one is started [imitating the sound]. That guy was funny.

K: Yeah, crazy man. And what was the funny part was another guy. I forgot his name. But he goes up there and says: Can you fix my houses? They're trying to tear it down. And the guy was like you're crazy. That was funny. Ha-ha-ha.

L: And the part where you know the girl stole things from the place.

K: Yep, that was scary though. I thought she was going to get caught.

L: I know.

K: Yep, a kind of scary. Yep, I didn't like the part though, remember that they went to the bald guy's house to watch that video?

L: Yeah.

K: And then they started shooting and everything. And then the main character the black guy

L: Yeah.

K: he-he choke he broke the guy's neck. Remember that? He was in the kitchen and went [imitating the sound].

L: Yep.

K: Oh, I thought yucky-yucky-yucky. Don't do that. He is really awful.

L: Did you saw Ranger Walker?

K: Angel Walker?

L: Ranger Walker.

K: Ranger Walker, once every week?

L: Yeah.

K: Yeah, we don't have TV, but I heard of it.

L: You don't have TV!

K: Um-hmm.

L: I borrow you one, that little one.

K: Oh, that's okay. We don't need one. We watched it too much. And that will be bad. We could not get our work done. So tell me about Walker Ranger or Ranger Walker.

L: It's Walker Texas Ranger.

K: Yeah.

L: It's Texas.

K: You like it.

L: Yep, I like it.

K: There's big snakes in it, aren't there?

L: I don't know.

K: Sometimes?

L: Oh, maybe. I never watch that before.

K: Is it on Friday night?

L: Um Saturday night.

K: Saturday night.

L: Ten o'clock start, ten.

K: You stay that late?

L: Yep.

K: What time you go to bed?

L: Um eleven o'clock.

K: Oh, my goodness. That's so late.

L: Friday is ten thirty and-and Sunday is um um at um ten o'clock.

K: Ten o'clock. Monday-Monday through Thursday ten o'clock too?

L: Yes. Friday is ten thirty.

K: What time do you get up in the morning then?

L: Uh um Saturday is Sunday is nine thirty usually.

K: Nine thirty?

L: Yeah.

K: Lazy boy you! Get up. What about during the week? What time is your school?

L: Uh eight thirty.

K: Eight thirty. So you have to get up.

L: Eight o'clock.

K: You get up at eight o'clock and you are at school at eight thirty?

L: Yep.

K: How do you do that?

L: I don't know.

K: You can get ready and get to school in half an hour?

L: Yes. I could get ready liking-like eight-eight fifteen. And my dad drive me and Christina going. Tomorrow I don't have to my dad don't have to drive. Chistina's mom drive me.

K: Okay. Do you have Friday off?

L: Friday off?

K: Yes, because of the fourth of July.

L: Yes.

K: You will. No school?

L: Yep, no school.

K: No school. What are you going to do? What are you going to do on Friday?

L: Uh …

K: Watch fireworks?

L: Oh, there is?

K: Yep.

L: Yes, I forgot. Daddy, I want to watch fireworks on Friday.

K: No, there is on Thursday. Thursday night at ten o'clock.

L: Yes, yes, yes.

K: Write it down. Don't forget. You go to see it every year?

L: Yes.

K: To go downtown?

L: No.

K: Where did you go?

L: TV.

K: You watch on TV?

L: Yes. I don't like to watch it.

K: No?

L: My neck going to break.

K: Oh.

L: Tomorrow I go to school.

K: And your neck would be stuck like this. That's funny.

L: Even if you watch on the TV, it's better.

K: Yeah.

L: You can watch it more.

K: Because you have to go to bed.

L: That's from Kelleys Island.

K: Oh, yep. Tell me about these pictures. You went there with Ping. This is Ping, right?

L: Yep, this is Ping. This is my mom and this is our friend.

K: Okay. And who is that?

L: That's me.

K: How pretty there?

L: See I could I could tell you something. You see this is the island.

K: This is Jack?

L: Oh, yes. That is not the Kelleys Island.

K: Oh, that's not on Kelleys Island?

L: Let me show you the pictures. See this see this oh, I don't think so. Oh, never mind.

K: They are all wet.

L: See the Kelleys Island.

K: What is that? Hancock Wood Electric Cooperation Cooperated.

L: Yep.

K: Ha. So it's a nature park.

L: Yes. That's cool. This is one I made ___

K: Is that your bedroom?

L: Yep.

K: Oh, this is your assignment.

L: Yep, science project.

K: Oh, I thought that was your commercial: Buy Me and I Will Be a Good Friend.

L: Wait. Where is that picture?

K: Is this on international night?

L: No, that's when I graduated.

K: When you graduated?

L: Where is the picture? See this.

K: This is pretty, isn't it?

L: I know. I can't find the picture. Oh, see this is Canada, down there.

K: Okay, yep. What are you doing? Just stand in the water?

L: Yep. Just take a picture.

K: Is there any raining too?

L: No, water just getting up.

K: Just splashing. Oh, that's funny.

L: See.

K: Is this graduation from Cranbrook?

L: Yes, from fifth grade.

K: From third grade. Where you at ___

L: From fifth grade.

K: From fifth grade.

L: That is my mom. Look at look at that. It's cool.

K: It's beautiful, isn't it?

L: I know.

K: Your mom looks like a model.

L: Oh that's one they're fishing we just ask

K: Okay.

L: what you do and what kind of fish.

K: Yep. This is a good family picture. You guys look so cute, all of you. Let's let me see your project and hear what you are doing.

L: You can see it. I could let you see it.

K: Oh, you haven't it here?

L: Yes.

K: Oh, yep. Did Jack help you make it?

L: No.

K: He just watched you there.

L: Yep.

K: And what's this? This is a good picture you and Jack.

L: I know.

K: You should put that on the frame and put it in your bedroom. That's cute. Is Jack your best friend?

L: Oh, maybe. I don't know.

K: You don't have one, ha?

L: Look at Ping. Look at those pictures. Look at Ping.

K: She was not having a good day.

L: Look at Ping.

K: Where is Dioxin?

L: Um?

K: Where is Dioxin? Her husband. Do I say his name wrong?

L: You mean?

K: Ping's husband.

L: Oh, his name is Daoxin.

K: What was it?

L: Oh, I don't know how to say it.

K: Oh.

L: See like this

K: How do you say it?

L: You mean Chinese?

K: Yep.

L: Daoxin.

K: Daoxin. Oh, I guess I say it really wrong. I thought it was the Dioxin.

L: The Dioxin.

K: Yep, like the letter. All this time I've been calling him that. Oops. How do you say it?

L: Daoxin.

K: Daoxin.

L: Yep.

K: Daoxin.

L: Yep.

K: Daoxin.

L: You could call him Doctor Li.

K: Yep. I just call him Dioxin. Yep, I just thought that was his name. Whoops. He did not get to go though. He had work to do.

L: Yes, he do. He did go.

K: Oh, yep, he took the picture.

L: Yeah.

K: I see.

L: Oh, that's the day that we go to you know Lane Avenue. I mean in Fishinger.

K: Where did you go?

L: It's a lake. We go to it's another lake in Columbus.

K: This is this is in Kelleys island.

L: No. That's in another. We just xxx

K: Okay.

L: Yep, one by one, see. This is the father. This is the mother. See this is the father and the baby one two three four five and the mother.

K: Ohhhh.

L: You see they are just in the line.

K: Yep, they have the same order.

L: Look at this.

K: Yep, who is that? I know who that is. That is Ping's friend.

L: Yep.

K: Yep, I forgot her name but I know her.

L: Wen. His name is Wen.

K: Yep.

L: I mean her name is Wen. Oh, look at this.

K: What are they doing? Are you doing it to Ping though. Yep, that's fun. You guys did have a good time. Did you swim there?

L: No.

K: No, you just walked around. Was it hot?

L: No.

K: Not as hot as this week. Crazy-crazy-crazy. You look like you not like when Jack stands. You like: would you talk more, Jack? That's funny. This is in your bedroom.

L: Yep.

K: A kind of mess, don't you think?

L: Yes. At that time, yes.

K: You had to clean it up.

L: I don't used to.

K: You used to keep it nice and clean?

L: Oh, yep.

K: Try to anyway, ha. Look at your awards and stuffs on the wall. You're pretty amazing kid, ha? Is this your desk? You work at this desk?

L: No.

K: You sat here?

L: No.

K: No. What is that?

L: You mean this?

K: Yep.

L: I just put things in it.

K: You just put things in it.

L: I study in this desk.

K: Okay. You study a lot?

L: Um no.

K: Do they give you a lot of work at the summer school?

L: No.

K: No. What you do there? Just watch movies?

L: No.

K: Hanging out, go to recess?

L: No. Oh, I got a bunch of popcorns.

K: From school?

L: Yep. From my-my Spanish teacher.

K: Oh, you are taking Spanish?

L: Yep.

K: Should we talk Spanish a little on the tape?

L: Oh, no.

K: Yep, come on. *Hola*

L: *Hola*

K: *Como estas*?

L: *Muy bien.*

K: Ah, that's all I know. Yep, that's it. I can say like how do you say window?

L: I don't know. Never mind.

K: Table *la mesa*?

L: *La mesa?*
K: Did you learn that?
L: No. I didn't learn a lot yet.
K: How long have you taken Spanish?
L: Five weeks.
K: Five weeks. Now you're going to speak Chinese, English and Spanish. What's the next?
L: French.
K: Seriously you're going to take French too?
L: No.
K: You like to learn different languages? Yeah?
L: They are cool.
K: Is it easy for you to learn a new language after you have already learned English?
L: No.
K: No. They are all very different than Chinese, aren't they?
L: Yeah.
K: When I looked at that little Chinese book you have here
L: Yeah.
K: they are all looked same.
L: I know.
K: You know? They don't even look the same. But you can write it in what is this?
L: *Pinyin.*
K: If this is Chinese, what is this?
L: This is the sound of Chinese.
K: The sound of Chinese.
L: This like
K: So this is this is English. This is phonics. This is Chinese.
L: What is phonics?
K: Phonics is the other way of working sound.
L: Just like American, yeah.
K: Yeah.
L: This is Chinese those kind of things.
K: Okay.
L: Just like write my name.
K: Okay. Yeah, because you don't write your name.
L: I know. So I write my name in the sound.

K: Right. What if you write your name like this in Chinese on your paper? Would your teacher know it's you?

L: No.

K: No. But that's your name.

L: Yeah.

K: She should learn, shouldn't she?

L: Yes.

---End of Conversation---

CONVERSATION 19: 7/27/1997

K: Okay, did you go swimming?

L: Yep.

K: You and Jack?

L: Just after you left.

K: Yep, we saw you coming.

L: Why did you left?

K: I had to eat dinner. I was hungry. So, yep, besides it was raining.

L: We just swim in the pool like not a hour yet.

K: Yep.

L: Like forty five minutes and the pool is closed.

K: Oh, did the apartment guy come?

L: Yep.

K: Yep.

L: The Mike the Mike the manager come.

K: Hmm.

L: He-he get a sign and says: Pool close. And he says: "Hello, everybody. The pool is closed."

K: Because of the weather.

L: Yep.

K: Yep, I was there yesterday

L: Hmm.

K: with a friend

L: Hmm.

K: and he came and said: "You have to leave. It's going to rain."

L: Yeah.

K: I left.

L: So you know that when we just come-come back home

K: Hmm.

L: from the pool that-that the wind the very big wind and a lot of leafs get in the pool from the from the tree.

K: Oh, bad. Yep, ha. What did you do when this screen fell out?

L: I don't know when it's fell out.

K: Hmm. You weren't here.

L: No. I was swimming-s-swimming.

K: Oh, I see. Hmm.

L: I think it's on the way we go home oh we go back home because that's the time we have a lot big a very big wind.

K: Right. What did you think about last night?

L: Last night, rain.

K: Yep. It was a kind of scary.

L: I know. You know from Riverview Drive?

K: Hmm.

L: There is a part like it's a church or something like that? You know did you know where that-that the house get fired?

K: Um-hmm.

L: And there was a lot you know a

K: I don't know.

L: the street is like this. You know and that part there was a lot of water in there. You have to get your car like squeeze in there and get out.

K: Right. There was full of water last night?

L: Yes.

K: Ha.

L: A lot of cars got broken.

K: Were stuck? Ou-oh. Yucky. Where was Christina today?

L: She now um Christina was home.

K: Yep?

L: We go to church at one o'clock.

K: You went to church with Christina?

L: Yep.

K: At one o'clock?

L: [nodding head]

K: What church did you go to?

L: High Point.

K: High Point.

L: The Chinese church.

K: Where is that?

L: Henderson. You know Hen ___

K: Oh, yep.

L: Henderson.

K: Henderson on Olentangy?

L: No, Henderson you know on Bethel road something,

K: Um-hmm.

L: way back.

K: Okay, way back there. Do they speak Chinese?

L: [nodding head]

K: Really!

L: And English.

K: And English too.

L: We play a very funny game right there.

K: You do?

L: It's a card game. I think the name is Mafio or something.

K: Okay.

L: See the king you know the murder

K: Um-hmm.

L: is see we-we-we have like eight child there and we children there and a guy have bring cards and we need eight cards. The ace is a guy who-who you know who like speak who know everybody's card. And you get see your card. If you are a-a regular number like from two to from two to ten from one to ten I mean except ace from two to ten, you're a regular people just like us.

K: Okay.

L: If you if you are the jack, you are the police.

K: Okay.

L: See the jack is the cop.

K: Okay.

L: And-and if you are the king, there are two kings one police. If you are the king, you are the murder, the Mafio.

K: Okay.

L: So

K: You mean murder?

L: Yep.

K: Like you kill people?

L: Yes.
K: There are two killers?
L: Yes.
K: Okay.
L: See this card like you get see your card and no one else see it.
      So you know who you are and the ace they-they it is say he
      will say: "Everybody sleeping." And everybody get his head
      down. And then he will say: "Murders wake up." So-so the out
      the two murders now wake up. And the murders decide who to
      kill. So they kill people. The people they try to kill is the cop.
      You know you know bad people kill the police you know.
K: Right.
L: And if they didn't got it. They hope like if I am the murder I
      hope I can kill the cop right now.
K: Well, how do they kill them?
L: See I just we two decide we have to decide on one people.
      And ace he-he knows everything and he can't tell nobody.
K: Okay.
L: So the-the other people don't know anything. They can see
      nothing.
K: Okay.
L: You can't talk this game. And so-so the bad people the two
      murders they-they decide one people to kill like I decide like
      these five peoples I decide to kill you. And I told the ace
      we're going to kill. Then I like if you are ... point to him,
      okay. Then everybody go to sleep and the cop wakes up. And
      the cop try to try to find who is the murder. Okay then like
      he go to ask the ace and he say he can say nothing because if
      he say something and everybody know he is the cop, right?
      So he-he-he just um like say this is the guy he just point to
      him and if I'm the ace, I'm going to tell-tell him that if this is
      a murder or not.
K: Okay.
L: If it is a murder, the cop go to and the cop will be happy.
      They go to sleep. And the cop just point to after everybody
      wake up. And they try to decide one people to kill one body
      one people. See like-like the cop knows he is the murder, and
      he just point to him because he knows he is the bad guy. The
      good people just try to kill murders.

K: Okay.

L: And so he just try to ... he think we should kill him. And the other person let they decide. If the most people decide on him, and he is dead. No-no-no, wait. The first the murder will say will kill someone just like you are dead.

K: Okay.

L: Because two murders all decide to kill you and so you are dead you are out of the game the first round you know this time of the game.

K: Right.

L: And then-then everybody pick one people to-to you know die. And the police knows the murders just point to. So he just let everybody to point. If he is the murder and he is out

K: Okay.

L: and you know and he is out.

K: So the murder get caught, he is out.

L: Yep. There is one more murder. If this three more people these two murders, the murder wins.

K: Okay.

L: If both murders get-get caught, they are out. They are both lose.

K: Okay. Hmm.

L: That's fun.

K: And you did that at the Chinese church.

L: Yep.

K: Okay. Hmm how many people played?

L: Eight, I think.

K: Eight people. Did Jack go too?

L: Yep.

K: Okay.

L: Always there is a ace, one jack and two kings.

K: Were you ever the murder?

L: Yes.

K: Were you ever the cop?

L: Yes.

K: And the ace?

L: Not a lot. I don't want to be the ace.

K: The ace isn't a fun to be.

L: Yep, because she just talk like everybody sleep. Murders wake up. Murders decide who to kill. Murders you know

K: Go back to sleep.

L: go back to sleep. Cops wake up. Cops decide whether some- one is murder or not.

K: How does the cop know though?

L: He going ____

K: He's going to ask the ace.

L: Say you are the ace, okay?

K: Okay.

L: Let's see this is the murder and this is the murder and this is not the murder. Then if you [nodding the head]

K: Then I say?

L: Yep. If I point to this and you say.

K: Okay.

L: So I know this is the murder.

K: Okay.

L: And when everybody wake up and then I just want to finish.

K: I see.

L: That's fun.

K: And then nobody else knows you are the cop? But they listen to you anyway?

L: Um-nmm. Sometimes they don't.

K: Oh, they don't always listen. Hmm so that was fun.

L: Yeah, it is fun.

K: What else did you do there?

L: Um.

K: You go every week?

L: No.

K: No.

L: That's my first time.

K: Okay.

L: And Friday we go to someone's house.

K: Okay, to a party?

L: Yeah, a big party.

K: Ah-ha.

L: Like the shoes are a bunch of shoes you know that place where the door is

K: No.

L: is like the shoes can't even fit in this table.

K: Is the party here in your house?

L: No-no-no.

K: No.

L: At someone else's house.

K: But everybody leaves his shoes at the doors?

L: Yeah.

K: Oh.

L: So the shoes could fill this whole table.

K: Yes.

L: Maybe that's not enough.

K: Ha, that's fun.

L: Um-hmm.

K: Will your mom and dad go too?

L: No.

K: Just kids?

L: No. You could go too. But they-they don't want to and they-they have to study or something. And my mom have to work.

K: I see.

L: And they don't have time.

K: Is your mom still baby-sitting?

L: Um?

K: Is your mom still baby-sitting?

L: Yeah.

K: She is busy. You help her still? Sometimes?

L: Sometimes.

K: Are you going to baby-sit for me?

L: [nodding head]

K: Ah-ha, good.

L: Remember you said Jack baby-sit for you?

K: Oh, no.

L: Baby.

K: You know that's Jack. Jack is a little crazy. No, he is fun. What about the air show? Is that in Dayton?

L: Yeah.

K: Tell me about that. I know you went there.

L: Yes.

K: But I didn't know what you did?

L: Yes, I went there and the show is fun. There is a lot of you know airplanes.

K: Okay. So you sat outside and just looked at the sky?

L: Um yeah. They are not very high. The airplane is not high.

K: No.

L: They are very low like it's not in the first light yet.

K: Really?

L: It's like below the half from the first light and it's like as high as that tree.

K: Really!

L: Yeah.

K: So it doesn't even to the red lights out there?

L: No, that tree you see that big green tree right there?

K: Um-hmm.

L: It's like the top.

K: So very close to the ground.

L: Yeah.

K: So that's kind of scary then.

L: I know. Sometimes it just draw [imitating the sound].

K: Wow, hmm.

L: If they have some problems, then you're dead.

K: Yeah, I guess.

L: Yeah, a lot of trouble.

K: That's kind of scary.

L: You know the fun thing I like is a-a airplane he say you know those kind of airplane go like that now like the airplane for Channel Four you know those kind of planes.

K: Oh, yep.

L: What are those called?

K: Helicopters.

L: Yep, helicopters. They are not those kind of airplane. They are just regular airplane. But they could you know get the-the-the remember when the airplane start?

K: Um-hmm.

L: You know those kind of airplane that fight

K: Right.

L: that shoot guns.

K: Fighter planes.

L: Yep, fighter fight that window after there-there is a big you know what's that thing called? Air you know a lot of air coming out.

K: Oh, yep.

L: [imitating the sound] just ___

K: Like smoke.

L: Yep, those kind of things. And that airplane he turned that thing like you that thing used to go that way and the smoke go this way and they just fly. But he turned this in doing this way and the air just getting down like this. He could just do get up like that.

K: Okay.

L: You see it's almost the same as that.

K: Yep, wow, that's kind of neat.

L: I know.

K: [pointing to a guy who is doing *taji* in the parking lot] What do you think that guy is doing out there?

L: Ohh I don't know.

K: He do that a lot.

L: I know. I know how to say in Chinese, but I don't know how to say in English.

K: Oh really, it's something Chinese?

L: Yes. It's a kind of Chinese tradition.

K: Oh, really!

L: Yeah.

K: Ha.

L: He do that a lot. My grandma used to do that.

K: Really!

L: He she teach everybody. You know there is called *qigong*.

K: Okay.

L: Maybe you don't know what that is.

K: Yep, I've seen them a lot and I just don't know what they are doing. Looks like he is doing slow motion karate.

L: Yeah. And sometimes they got sword.

K: Yep.

L: Slow-slow motion.

K: Sometimes four or five

L: Yes.

K: out on the front that do it.

L: In another picnic table.

K: Yep, it's kind of fun. Did you get your haircut?

L: Um-hmm.

K: When?

L: Um I think yes-yesterday.

K: Yep, who did it?

L: My mom.

K: Really! Oh, let me see the back. Wow, that was really good.
     Does she have clippers?

L: What's that?

K: Those things /zzzzzzzz/.

L: Un-un.

K: No, she just does it with scissors?

L: [nodding head]

K: Wow, that's a good work. So you got your summer haircut.

L: I take haircut a lot of times.

K: You do.

L: My hair grow very ___

K: Very-very quickly. Hmm do you cut her hair then?

L: [shaking head]

K: No.

L: She won't let me.

K: No. Sometimes I cut Jos' hair but I do with buzzers.

L: Do you have one?

K: Yeah. Um I then asked him to cut mine but he doesn't never
     want to do it.

L: Because it's hard to cut you know that thing.

K: Like this kind of thing here?

L: Yeah-yeah. It's good like his kind of hair.

K: It's easy to /wuuuuuuuuuu/.

L: Yeah, that's how you get you know the height like that height
     and hair will all be like that height

K: Oh it's sticking up the same the same, yeah.

L: Man's hair like easy. Or you know get no hair.

K: Yep.

L: That's cool, like Michael Jordan. He never won't grow hair
     any more.

K: Never?

L: No.

K: He said that?

L: He just never going to grow any more.

K: Oh, 'cause he's got it.

L: See once-once you know there is a company that make you know things that make you grow hair and this kind just use Michael Jordan like Michael Jordan grow hair and that won't work.

K: It won't work for him.

L: They try to use him to make the commercial.

K: So is he bald?

L: Um?

K: Is Michael Jordan bald?

L: Yep, I think so. He will never grow hair any more.

K: Hmm, I wonder what happened to his hair.

L: He don't want any hair.

K: He doesn't.

L: Too hot.

K: Hmm.

L: He got be hot any day.

K: I suppose to play basketball it is hot. It's been so hot lately, it's been too hot to do anything.

L: You do that, you have to be very patient.

K: Really?

L: Yeah.

K: Do you know how to do it?

L: No, not that kind.

K: What do you know how to do?

L: *Qigong.*

K: Are they different?

L: Yeah, they are not the same. One is called *taijiquan.*

K: Okay.

L: I do not know how to explain.

K: That's what that is?

L: Oh, no. Yes-yes that is *taijiquan.* And the other kind of thing he do is you know you know with a sword.

K: Okay.

L: I think it's the same motion.

K: Just one's with the sword and one's without.

L: Yeah.

K: You know how to do with the sword?

L: No, never tried before.

K: Hmm. Did you do that often?

L: No.

K: No.

L: In China my grandma did a lot.

K: Yeah, is it exercise?

L: Yeah. it's kinda very, you know, a lot of old people do that.

K: [laughing] Old people.

L: Yeah, most-most old.

K: How old are there to be old?

L: Like sixty years old.

K: Oh, sixty?

L: Is old.

K: Oh, good. I thought you were gonna say thirty

L: [shaking]

K: No, sixty is old.

L: Thirty is not old.

K: No.

L: Thirty is middle.

K: Um-ha.

L: A half way to go.

K: What's the young?

L: Like twenty to thirty or something I don't know.

K: Yeah.

L: Thirty and below, yeah.

K: Is young. And thirty to sixty is middle?

L: Yeah.

K: And sixty over is old.

L: See that's very hard to do. You didn't see that.

K: Like he kicked very high.

L: Yeah. It's good.

K: Yeah. And you've to wear all white?

L: Used to the at least you know those kind of dress.

K: The pants and clothes too?

L: They used to wear white but you don't have to.

K: Okay.

L: But white is you know very good for it.

K: Yeah. A kind of amazing to watch, huh?

L: You know in the library in China in my-my city

K: Um-hmm.

L: And we living in a university just like same thing right now and the library is a very big library and in the front of the library there is a very big a little fountain.

K: Um-hmm.

L: You know little fountains? And some place for you to you know read or something you can play it. And every morning like six o'clock to eight o'clock there are a lot of people stand there to do like that.

K: Okay.

L: *Qigong.*

K: Good.

L: That's what my grandma did.

K: Say that again.

L: *Qigong.*

K: *Qigong.*

L: Yeah.

K: Hmm. Neat. Oh, are you going to look it up?

L: How to say it. Okay, whoops, yes, that's right.

K: So you're going to write in Chinese?

L: Yes.

K: You know how to spell it in Chinese?

L: Yes, that's not hard.

K: Now you don't forget Chinese?

L: Not a lot.

K: Because summer school was China Chinese school, right?

L: See this says effort, energy and strength.

K: Okay, that's what it means.

L: I think so. I don't know.

K: Effort, energy and strength. So it's a kind of like aerobics?

L: Yeah.

K: Here.

L: See what that means *taijichuan.*

K: What a neat thing! This is English-Chinese dictionary on a computer.

L: This is cool. No, there is no such thing on this.

K: There is no such thing. So you can told and you can read that?

L: Yeah. *Taiyangmen*, what is that? What's this? Okay, *taiyang-men*. I got it and exit.

K: Emergency?

L: Yeah. So you can use English to check Chinese too.

K: Hmm. That's neat.

L: [nodding head]

K: So if you went back to China right now, you would be able to read and talk normal.

L: Um-hmm.

K: Yeah, you would not mess up with words or?

L: But not-not-not write.

K: You couldn't write it?

L: Yeah, I could write it but I can't write as good as before.

K: Okay.

L: I can't talk like very like before I talk like that now is like that.

K: Okay. But at home you talk Chinese?

L: Yeah.

K: So you still get practice.

L: Yeah. Everyday I got write Chinese too.

K: You do.

L: [nodding head]

K: So you don't forget. Ha because when you go back there you have to go back all to Chinese. Are there a lot of people in China speak English?

L: No.

K: No. Most Chinese. What if they don't speak Chinese, what do they speak? Like in Jos' country, some people speak German,

L: Um-hmm.

K: some people speak Flemish. Does everybody in China speak Chinese?

L: Yes. But it's different kind of Chinese.

K: Like different dialects?

L: Yeah.

K: Okay.

L: Like maybe you are from someone else like you're from north

K: Um-hmm.

L: north-north China and I'm from south China. I talk my you know my you know what I used to talk in my place.

K: Um-hmm.

L: You know in my city and maybe you don't understand what I mean.

K: Okay.

L: Because it's a it's just --

K: So it's like here in America, people from the south they have accents.

L: Yeah.

K: They say things like "Yall come back now. Ya hear?" Like that they have funny ____

L: No-no-no.

K: No.

L: They have it's not just funny. It's ____

K: It's different.

L: It's just in another kind of language.

K: Really? So it's just not accents.

L: But read is the same.

K: Really? Ha.

L: Unless like-like-like we just have something special word like um like maybe you say in my in my, excuse me, in my city and maybe you don't understand what that mean in your city. That's kind of cool.

K: Yeah. It's funny though that you would not understand each other but you could read the same

L: Yeah.

K: words.

L: But there are two kind of words. One you could call cursive and the other is just regular words.

K: Okay. Where are you from in China?

L: *Wuhan.*

K: North or south?

L: Here I show you.

K: Ha-ha, oh yeah, that will tell us.

L: See this is the whole China, the yellow ones

K: Oh, my goodness! This is a big place, isn't it?

L: Yeah. See I'm from somewhere right here.

K: Okay.

L: But I don't think so it's on it.

K: So you're in the very east or you're in the middle.

L: Yes, here.

K: So you're from the mid-east. Have you ever been here in China?

L: No.

K: That's too far away.

L: Yes. I mean I don't like there.

K: No.

L: They speak exactly another kind of language.

K: Have you been up here?

L: No.

K: Where have you been in China? Oh, where is the Great Wall of China?

L: You see this, this little thing.

K: Yeah, oh yeah.

L: This is the Great Wall.

K: So it's have you been there?

L: Yes, I've been to Beijing, the capital.

K: Where is Beijing? And that's right where the wall is?

L: See Peking, you see.

K: Okay. That's the capital.

L: Yep. That's the start of the Great Wall.

K: Okay. Ha. Where does it end?

L: Oh, where does it end? It goes a long way.

K: Did originally the wall was made to go all the way across China?

L: No.

K: No, they never did.

CONVERSATION 20: 8/31/1997

K: So tell me all about your birthday party.

L: Um my birthday is on August 23.

K: Okay.

L: It's on Saturday.

K: Oh, good, yeah.

L: And that day um see Jack, Christina, Xuanxuan you know that little kid

K: Yeah.

L: used to with him. And Henry is another boy. He speak Chinese.

K: Lives here?

L: No, he lives in Upper Arlinton.

K: Hmm.

L: And who else? And a girl. Her name is Jane. He come to with me the same airplane from China.

K: The same airplanes from China?

L: Yeah, the same date, the same airplane.

K: Okay. Oh, okay. When you came to America

L: Yeah.

K: he was on airplane. Okay.

L: So we know we know like when we were in China because my dad and her dad they know when they're all in America. And my grandma, me and her we don't know each other. But my dad and that girl's dad they know each other. Whatever they say like my son going to come and my daughter going to come something like that. And they just like get the same plane. And that girl's dad and she change he change the-the air-airplane ticket change to another one so we two are on the same airplane.

K: Oh, how fun!

L: Because no that-that girl's mom is coming with her and she speak English you know better than I.

K: Um-hmm.

L: You know she speak some English but my-my grandma, her and-and me we don't speak any English. So maybe we're going to have some trouble. So we just want to go with her.

K: Right.

L: And-and I think that's all I have. And there is one guy he is about to come but he-he went back to a city is in Ohio is where is where like now like Columbus

K: Um-hmm.

L: is where Ohio State University is and that city is where Ohio University is.

K: Oh.

L: And his mom is back to there to-to study

K: Okay.

L: on-on Saturday. So he didn't get to come.

K: Hmm. What did you do in your party?

L: Oh we playing games.

K: Oh, it's here?

L: Yeah. And we-we playing video games.

K: Hmm.

L: And I got two-two new video games and a new little-little one.

K: Um-hmm.

L: And I got I got a game of it. It is like a little video game that you can control you have like that big screen.

K: A Game Boy you take with you?

L: Yeah, a Game Boy Pocket.

K: Wow!

L: It's smaller.

K: It's smaller.

L: It's smaller. And you know it shows better

K: Um-hmm.

L: than a Game Boy. But it use the same kind of you know those kind of card.

K: Right.

L: Yeah, the same kind of thing.

K: Neat. So you do that all the time now?

L: Oh, I can't because the battery is running out too fast.

K: Oh!

L: The first day like the first day my birthday because we play a lot because that's the first day you know. And the battery is for free because when I just bought the Game Boy they have battery in it. And that battery only use for two days.

K: Oh, no.

L: And now I change once already.

K: Can you recharge it or you've to buy a new battery?

L: Buy a new battery

K: Oh.

L: unless-unless you buy those recharge batteries.

K: Yes.

L: And one of those recharge batteries.

K: Yes.

L: But they are very expensive.

K: Oh, are they?

L: Yeah.

K: Cool, man, neat. So what else did you do? Play video games?

L: Yeah, playing that little thing.

K: Okay.

L: And we playing cards, some fun games.

K: Did you go swimming?

L: No, we don't go swimming. That day was cold.

K: Oh.

L: We did not go outside playing.

K: No.

L: No.

K: Did you have a birthday cake?

L: Um yeah.

K: Yeah.

L: That girl gave me the birthday cake

K: Okay.

L: for my birthday gift.

K: And ice-cream too?

L: Yeah.

K: And what else did you have? Did you get candles and blow them out?

L: Yeah. And we have a big pizza. We have two pizzas.

K: You did?

L: One is vegetable and one is pepperoni and sausage.

K: Oh, what kind did you eat?

L: I like I eat both. I like both.

K: You like both.

L: And the next day

K: Did you make it yourself?

L: No, we bought it from Pizza Hut.

K: Ah-ha.

L: And-and that day everybody was hungry because when my dad went he thought he would just get the pizza right away go back.

K: Um-hmm.

L: And then he go there very late. But when he go there and the lady there say you have to wait for a half hour to get the pizza. He wait there for a half hour for a half hour.

K: And then the pizza wasn't ready?

L: No, because we didn't order it. We-we-we trying go there and pick it up.

K: I see.

L: And we have to go tell her what we need first.

K: I see.

L: Like on the phone or on somewhere.

K: Right. So when you get there, it's ready.

L: Yeah. But that day we forgot that. And we just go there and we-we have to wait for like shu. It's only like dad go there not everybody else go there.

K: Right.

L: If everybody else go there, everybody has to wait for a half hour.

K: That will be funny. A lot of people standing around Pizza Hut waiting. Anything else happened in your birthday party?

L: Um oh let's see. Oh, on my birth in the day is my birthday you know Ping

K: Um-hmm.

L: she and her husband they went to their boss you know Daox-in's boss.

K: Um-hmm.

L: His boss has a ranch, a very big ranch.

K: Okay.

L: And they go there for a party.

K: Oh, wow.

L: It was cool.

K: You went too?

L: No.

K: Oh.

L: It was on my birthday.

K: Ah.

L: They say if it is not on my birthday, they will bring me there too.

K: Hmm.

L: It is big.

K: Yep. That's fun. So ___

L: So have you watched Jungle to Jungle?

K: No. Have you?

L: Yeah.

K: It's that with Tim Alan, the guy from Home Improvement?

L: No-no-no, it's Robin-Robin Williams or something.

K: Robin Williams okay. I haven't seen that. Is that at theater?

L: Yes. I don't know. No, it's only on the tape.

K: Oh, it's on video.

L: Yeah, it's only on video. You can borrow I don't know if you
      can borrow it or not borrow it. You can bought it.

K: Okay, they have it at the library?

L: Um?

K: They have it at the library or at the video store?

L: I think at the video store. I see it yesterday in-in Target.

K: Is it good?

L: Yes, it was good.

K: Yeah, you like it. I haven't seen any movies lately.

L: You should go see Air Force One.

K: Oh, we did see that.

L: I didn't see it.

K: That was good.

L: I know that was good. Have you seen Steel?

K: Un-un.

L: That was good too.

K: Yeah?

L: You know Shaquille O'Neal?

K: Oh, I don't like him. I met him once when I worked in Flor-
      ida. He was mean.

L: You met him?

K: Yeah, he was really mean.

L: Oh, my!

K: I didn't like him.

L: You met Shaquille O'Neal?

K: Yeah.

L: Did he give you did he give you, you know, his autograph?

K: No. I didn't ask for it.

L: Why don't you?

K: Well, because I worked for Disney World.

L: Yeah.

K: And he came to Disney World to like just come there

L: Hmm.

K: He was just really he thought he was really important and he kind of acted like a brat you know. He just wasn't very nice.

L: He is tall, huh?

K: Very tall. Probably double my size.

L: I don't think so. He is seven two.

K: He is tall.

L: I know. I know a guy in the NBA is seven seven.

K: Who?

L: Gheorghe Muresan.

K: What team he plays for?

L: Washington Bullet.

K: Hmm.

L: He is tall, man.

K: Seven seven, shuway.

L: But he look very ugly.

K: Yep.

L: His face is like-like down, stretch down.

K: [laughing] His face is bigger than my leg. So um were any girls at the party your girl friend?

L: No.

K: No. You don't have a girl friend?

L: No.

K: Not in middle school?

L: No.

K: No. You don't go to Cranbrook anymore?

L: No.

K: Are you sad?

L: Yeah.

K: You miss Cranbrook.

L: Hmm.

K: You know the bus that sits out there?

L: Hmm.

K: Why is it sitting out there?

L: I think somebody own it.

K: Just a regular person?

L: Yeah.

K: Not the school?

L: Like a school teacher.

K: Oh.

L: Sometimes they own a bus. See when they could they like they have ad and say: a school want any people to drive buses. Maybe they could you know.

K: I see. So they don't keep the buses in school though. They keep it here?

L: Oh I think that guy own it.

K: Oh.

L: You know he bought it the bus.

K: Right. Very strange very strange. It's nice though. I would not mind if I have one, would you? Thinking take all your friends everywhere you go.

L: And everybody yells stop, then you stop.

K: Yeah. Did you go back to school on Wednesday?

L: Yeah.

K: So you have been to school for ___

L: Three days.

K: Now you have tomorrow off.

L: Yes.

K: Do you think your teachers are going on strike?

L: Um I don't know.

K: No. They haven't talked about it much. Hmm I remember when I was in high school

L: Um-hmm.

K: I was a junior, so I was in high school.

L: What do you mean by junior?

K: I was there is like freshman, sophomore, junior and senior. So it was my third year in high school and had one more year to go.

L: Oh, okay.

K: That's junior. And the teachers went on strike and we had to miss school for two weeks. Yeah. Would you like that when teachers went out on strike?

L: [laughing]

K: Yep, you like to miss school. You know what happen afterwards? You have to go school in the summer to make up for it. So next summer, you would not get vacation. You have to stay in school.

L: Oh, my!

K: So no strike, no strike.

L: No, no strike.

K: Let's get school done now. Are you going to change your calendar?

L: [nodding head]

K: Today?

L: Yep, today is already September first.

K: No, tomorrow. Tomorrow is September first.

L: Oh, yep, today is thirty one.

K: Thirty one, right. Yeah. So you still go to church with Christina?

L: Over um Friday and Sunday.

K: Friday and Sunday you have two times a week?

L: Yeah.

K: It's just kids' church.

L: No.

K: No, it's adults' church.

L: It's called High Point. From there you know they have a regular a kid's club like two teachers.

K: Okay.

L: You know two-two regular people.

K: Um-hmm.

L: They are Christians. And one is American.

K: Really.

L: The teacher there for we are not playing. His name is Rob. He is very funny.

K: [laughing] Rob, okay. Do you know the people that live upper stairs?

L: Yeah.

K: Um Diana she is going to have a baby too?

L: Hmm.

K: They go to the same church you do.

L: High Point?

K: Um-hmm. But they go it's the same church building but they go to they go to different service.

L: It is?

K: Yep.

L: They do?

K: Because there is there is a Chinese church there, right?

L: Um-hmm.

K: And there is a regular like just

L: Oh yeah, beside it?

K: Yep, no, it's the same building, just they're different services.

L: Oh, okay.

K: They go to a different service than you, but it's the same church.

L: Oh.

K: That's kind of neat, ha? She was telling me about that. So what did you do at church this Friday night with Rob?

L: Yeah, his name was Rob. The first day Christina told me: "Hello Rob!" And I said: "Rob, are you going to steal something of mine?"

K: Ah!

L: Because I thought you know rob

K: Yep.

L: Rob you something.

K: Like a robber.

L: He is very funny.

K: Yep.

L: Yep. I played a lot of games on Friday.

K: You played the-the Killer game?

L: Mafia.

K: What was it?

L: Mafia.

K: Yep, oh, the Mafia.

L: The Mafia, yep.

K: That's it.

L: And we've learned another game from him. It's called it has a lot of names like Heart Attack, Killers something like that okay a lot.

K: Hmm.

L: The main thing is if you're the murder it's the same thing, okay.

K: Oh.

L: If you're the murder and you try to kill somebody and kill everybody else. That's not the murder.

K: Okay.

L: You kill a body then when even you see your card

K: Um-hmm.

L: only one murder, okay. You at least need like five people like a lot, okay.

K: Um too much Pepsi.

L: If you're the jack,

K: Um-hmm.

L: put your jack in the deck of cards.

K: Okay.

L: If you're the jack, you're the murder. And you kill people. You don't have to, though.

K: So why it's called Heart Attack?

L: You'll see.

K: Oh.

L: See I trying to kill people like if it were me, I'm trying kill you. And nobody see-see me. Like when-when you know your card, everybody going do like look at somebody.

K: Um-hmm.

L: Look at the eyes.

K: Okay.

L: And if I do [winking], you're dead.

K: Oh, because you wink at me.

L: Yeah. If I wink at you, you're dead. And I don't want anybody else to see it.

K: Um-hmm. ·

L: Because if they see it, they going to say: "He is the murder. He is the murder."

K: Right.

L: Then I'm dead.

K: Okay.

L: Okay, if they got wrong, then he is dead. Like if I guess you're the murder

K: Like just the person died right away as soon as you wink at them or they wait for a minute?

L: Like ten-ten seconds.

K: Um-hmm.

L: If I wink at you, and you're dead. And then you count ten more seconds, then you say I'm dead.

K: Hmm.

L: Then you're out of the game. What I'm trying to do is to kill everybody.

K: Okay. But if somebody wants to guess you're the murder, what they have to do?

L: If they say you're the murder, they can only have to say: "I say you are the murder." And then you say: "No, I'm not the murder." Then-then he is dead

K: Hmm.

L: right away because he guess the wrong people.

K: I see.

L: If he is not if he don't dead, he going to say: "I guess you're the murder. I guess you're the one." And finally he can get it.

K: Right, then he can get right eventually, ha-ha so you play. Why they call it Heart Attack?

L: I don't know.

K: Oh. I thought you said I'll see.

L: I don't know. They call it Killer, a lot of names.

K: Right. Where is your middle school? Far away from here?

L: No.

K: Where is it?

L: You know Olentangy?

K: Um-ha.

L: Till you know go that way.

K: Um-hmm.

L: The way to Meijer. You know that way.

K: Right.

L: To north and-and-and there is a Henderson. You know Henderson?

K: Um-hmm. It's on Henderson?

L: It's not on Henderson yet, and you turn left.

K: Okay. So it's close.

L: Yes.

K: You take a bus?

L: Yes.

K: And it comes right here to pick you up or go up to the road?

L: Go up to the road.

K: Hmm. And Jack and Christina go there too?

L: No.

K: Just you?

L: Yeah.

K: Oh, that's right. You're older than all of them.

L: Yeah, I'm in middle school.

K: You're old man.

L: I'm not old man.

K: So it's sad that they go to Cranbrook but you go to what's your school called?

L: Ridgeview.

K: Ridgeview. What's this?

L: That's ticket, meal ticket.

K: Hey.

L: If you use that, you only have to pay thirty cents.

K: Thirty cents, not bad.

L: If you don't have that, like you have to pay a hundred like no-no-no not a hundred okay like one dollar fifty for every meal.

K: One fifty?

L: Yeah.

K: Wow, that's expensive. But not really but you know it adds up after a while. And they have breakfast and lunch at school?

L: Yep. But you still have to pay for breakfast.

K: Oh, you do.

L: But that ticket could for breakfast and lunch.

K: Hmm.

L: You see there is a little-little thing right there.

K: Right.

L: See the little square with it?

K: Right. You mean to check it.

L: Yep, they going to check it and you can use it again for lunch.

K: Okay.

L: But if for lunch, they going just to get the ticket because you can't use it any more.

K: Right.

L: You can't use for lunch and use for breakfast.

K: Hmm. But it doesn't tell you what's to happen.

L: Un-un.

K: How do you know they have for lunch and breakfast?

L: I could check it on the Website.

K: You can find it on the computer?

L: Yeah.

K: They got an Internet?
L: Yeah.
K: Wow!
L: You could check it.
K: Yeah.
L: But sometimes you can't. They're going to say the number is wrong something-something like last time
K: Okay.
L: I trying to.
K: What if you get the school you can't find your ticket? You've to pay more then?
L: Yeah, then you have to owe them.
K: Hmm.
L: You owe them.
K: You owe them the ticket.
L: Yeah, no, you can't owe them a ticket. I don't think so.
K: You just owe them money.
L: Yeah.
K: That's a neat way to do it.
L: I think you can owe them a ticket. Oh, no.
K: Neat-neat-neat. So you eat there everyday you like it?
L: Yeah.
K: I liked it too. When I was in school I always bought my lunch because I didn't like to get up early in the morning and packed it.
L: But I still have to get up very early in the morning.
K: Yep, did your school start early in the morning?
L: Yeah.
K: What time?
L: Looks like you mean start
K: Yep.
L: or you mean I wake up?
K: Yep, what's your schedule in the morning?
L: Oh, six thirty.
K: Six thirty?
L: Yeah.
K: Why what time you have to be in school?
L: Oh, I have to be on the bus stop like seven fifteen.
K: Oh. Then the school starts at

L: Eight.

K: eight o'clock. Wow! I guess yep. I can remember I used to have to get up. I'd leave for school because I would drive with my sisters because they went to the same school. We would leave at a quarter to eight and the school starts at eight because we will drive we don't have the bus was slow you know. Your bus is slow? Yep, forty five minutes you have to ride the bus. What time you get home then?

L: Eight to three.

K: Three o'clock. Oh, that's a long day. And your school gets out at two fifteen?

L: No, two forty five.

K: How can you get home so early that takes a long time to get there?

L: I don't know.

K: Forty five minutes

L: Like sometimes we have to wait for like the buses is early I'm late. No, I'm almost late.

K: So you missed the bus?

L: I almost.

K: Oh, no.

L: The bus is already right here like I'm still here and they're gone and then the bus driver stopped the bus.

K: You ran up there and got on.

L: Yeah.

K: So do you have any friends in this new school?

L: [nodding head]

K: Yeah. Anybody lives here in Colony Square?

L: Yeah, no.

K: Oh, no, you're the only one.

L: You know the first day why I'm you know so late because my book-bag is so heavy. I can't put my books in my locker because the first day I don't have a locker.

K: Right.

L: So

K: You have a lot of books?

L: Yep, I have two books the first day and now I have three.

K: I see.

L: Math

K: Also the first day of the school you have to bring home all your stuff because you don't have the locker yet.

L: Yes. But somebody have lockers. Like if your name is very early, you going to have a locker. Like your name start with your last name start with A,

K: Then you'll have a locker.

L: then you'll have a locker.

K: Do you have one now?

L: Yep.

K: Good. Do you have a com.?

L: Yep.

K: You have to remember the numbers.

L: Yeah.

K: Did you have that in Cranbrook too?

L: No.

K: No.

L: We don't need a locker.

K: Not in Cranbrook. Wow, so you're in a big-time school now.

L: Because you could put your you could put your books in your desk

K: Um-hmm.

L: because your own desk. But in there you have to change classes.

K: Right. Is that hard to do?

L: Yeah.

K: Every hour you have to go somewhere else

L: Yeah.

K: got your locker and get your stuff.

L: No, you can't. So you have to bring your whole thing for the whole day.

K: No.

L: Yep.

K: No. Why can't you go to your lockers?

L: You only can go to your lockers when it's the first when it's morning. When-when you just go to school, you have to go to the what's that thing called? You know the thing where-where they have a big place?

K: Like a cafeteria?

L: No, not a cafeteria. It's a big place. And sometimes they sing the chorus. And sometimes they play the instrument.

K: The band's room?

L: No, a place.

K: Like the auditorium.

L: Yep.

K: Okay. You go there first?

L: You have to go there first.

K: Why? What you do?

L: Because-because the teachers maybe they come a little bit late.

K: Oh.

L: So you have to go there first. When the teacher tell you: "Six grade you could go now", go back to your home room. And when you go there, and you could go get-get all your things for the morning and you go to your home class.

K: I see.

L: And your home class and the teacher and whatever. And twelve-twelve is almost it's time to go to lunch. You get put your things in the last class you got for the morning and you got put it there. Put all your things there for the morning you know the morning things. And then you going come oh no-no-no you going get out things from the morning

K: Um-hmm.

L: in the locker room.

K: Okay.

L: And then just put it there and then go to eat lunch. When you come back from lunch from recess

K: Um-hmm.

L: and you going to get out all the things for the afternoon and go to class.

K: That's crazy. So what classes do you have? You go to auditorium, home room then locker.

L: You mean the number of class

K: Um-hmm.

L: um or you mean the subjects?

K: Um both.

L: Okay. So I go to home room

K: Um-hmm.

L: for Math and Health.

K: Okay, that's in the morning.

L: No, that's not all.

K: Oh.

L: Math and Health I go to Mrs. Baird.

K: So that's all in one room, Math and Health.

L: Yes.

K: Okay.

L: And then I go to Mrs. Farrow. What's the number? Let me show you this, my schedule.

K: Okay.

L: See this is my schedule.

K: Oh, my goodness. Look at that.

L: This is the season. It's Fall. This is the period one two three blabla. And this is the days Monday, Tuesday, Wednesday, Thursday, Friday.

K: Okay.

L: And this is the subject. Um this is room number, teacher. And this is I don't care.

K: Seat. You mean you have an assigned seat?

L: No, this only for the computer in the office.

K: I see.

L: They don't know who I am.

K: Look you get lunch every day. Is that nice?

L: That's not right. Tenth period I don't think so.

K: Oh that would be bad wouldn't it if you have lunch at tenth hour of the day. Okay, so first thing you do is go to Math in 204.

L: Yes.

K: This is how you say it?

L: Mrs. Baird.

K: Mrs. Baird.

L: See /aird/ /baird/ /d/.

K: Okay, /baird/. Okay, then after she teaches you that, she teaches you Health?

L: Yes.

K: And then she goes back and teaches you more Math?

L: No. I don't know what that Math Lab mean.

K: Yep, that's weird. Okay, so then third period you move to a different room with Mrs. Farrow and you have Reading?

L: Yes.

K: And then the third period you have

L: Computer Awareness.

K: Okay, so that's Theater in turn.

L: Yeah.

K: So first you have this then you have this then you have this.

L: Yes.

K: Okay.

L: I don't know what's going to have the fourth term.

K: What you

L: The fourth-fourth quarter.

K: Yep.

L: What going to have?

K: Then after that you going to have Theater.

L: No-no-no, this is the first quarter and this is the second and this is the third.

K: Right.

L: What's going to have the fourth?

K: The fourth there is no fourth because you have the summer vacation.

L: Oh.

K: Yep. So like you do Computer Awareness until Christmas and then from Christmas to

L: [shaking head] un-un.

K: No? From Christmas to Easter

L: For ninth week.

K: For nine weeks. So before Christmas you'll change.

L: Yeah, I don't know what that mean.

K: Ha I bet you like Art.

L: Yeah. What's Theater Art?

K: Theater Art I think that is drama

L: What's that?

K: like act on movies and stuffs.

L: Oh, movies.

K: Well, probably not. More like plays. You know like the phantom of the opera?

L: Um-hmm.

K: That kind of stuff.

L: Okay.

K: A kind of fun.

L: I'm going see in the Computer Awareness I don't have to bring all my things because it's not the different room. I only have to bring the things I need in Computer Awareness.

K: That says in different room

L: That's in library.

K: Oh. Mr. Brown.

L: Mr. Brown, yep. And see those two are the same room. So I could just leave my stuff right here and go there and bring out things I need for there and then come back because those two are the same room, 201.

K: And then after that you go to lunch?

L: Yeah.

K: After Computer Awareness?

L: No, I have to after this.

K: After Language Arts, you have lunch.

L: Yeah.

K: Okay. So then you leave all your stuff in Room 201?

L: No, you going-going to put your stuffs in your locker.

K: After Language Arts, you go to your locker and then go to lunch.

L: Yeah.

K: When you come back, you go to Mr. Brown.

L: No, I come back and then I go to the recess.

K: Okay.

L: And then I come back I go to the home room for Academic Assist.

K: What's that mean?

L: I don't know. Silent reading time.

K: Oh, okay. After what it say?

L: After Period five.

K: Before Period six. Okay.

L: Yeah, in the middle of that.

K: Eleven fifteen you have half an hour for lunch,

L: Half an hour for recess and half an hour for Academic Assist.

K: half an hour for recess and half an hour for Academic Assist

L: Then see after recess I go to my locker get my things to the home room for Academic Assist.

K: I see.

L: Then when the bell rings

K: Go to Science class. You go right to science you don't go to your locker.

L: No.

K: You take your AA stuff to locker to Science.

L: No-no-no, this AA stuff is like a-a time.

K: Oh.

L: Like recess is like a time.

K: Right. So you just read anything you want then?

L: Yeah.

K: Okay.

L: Or sometimes like your Math you are not done with your Math for the first period and then you have to do it now.

K: I see. Then you have

L: Oh I don't have. Tuesday and Thursday I'm going to have General Music and then on Monday, Wednesday, Friday I'm going to have Physical Education.

K: So you have both. On Wednesday you have Gym.

L: Yeah.

K: Then you have Music one day?

L: Yeah.

K: And you have Gym again.

L: Yes.

K: So when you go back you miss Gym you'll have Music.

L: Yes.

K: Which you like better, Gym or Music?

L: Gym.

K: What you guys do in Gym?

L: The first two days is boring because we don't do nothing.

K: Hmm. You have to take your clothes and change it too?

L: Yes, I have to take white shorts, and black shirt.

K: White shorts and black shirt?

L: Yeah.

K: And you have uniform?

L: Yep, we have to.

K: You have uniform for all day school too?

L: No.

K: Oh. And after that you go home.

L: Yes.

K: So this is at two forty five.

L: Um-hmm.

K: This gets over. Wow, it's a lot different than Cranbrook, huh?

---End of Conversation---

CONVERSATION 21: 9/28/1997

K: What-what's this? What're you doing?

L: Football.

K: Hey, are you into playing football these days?

L: Yeah.

K: Are you on the football team in school?

L: No.

K: No.

L: We don't have one yet.

K: No. You're in six grade. Yep? There is no six grade football team.

L: No.

K: Any sports teams?

L: Oh I don't know.

K: Oh.

L: We got a soccer team. It's like a seventh grade. You have to be like seventh grade or bigger or eighth.

K: Right.

L: You can't go there if you're a sixth. I don't know why. It's not fair.

K: And your school goes what grades? Sixth

L: Seven and eight.

K: Three grades. So seventh and eighth has sports.

L: Yes.

K: They have football

L: You don't have football. You don't have football teams.

K: They have basketball?

L: No.

K: Volleyball?

L: I don't know. I think they got a basketball team.

K: What do they have for the girls?

L: Cheer leaders.

K: Cheer leader for what? Soccer?

L: Yeah.

K: Ha.

L: They're just cheer leader(s) like-like I don't think so any such things like-like a soccer game. It's like in just like in Indianola and there is a basketball team home. I don't think there is ever going to be a schedule like that. But cheer leaders can go cannot go both you know.

K: I see.

L: You have to be like one place at once.

K: I see. Ha how many cheer leaders are there?

L: Like ten.

K: Any of them sixth grade?

L: No, I don't think so.

K: Only seventh and eighth.

L: Yeah.

K: Yeah, one more year. Then you can be a cheer leader?

L: No.

K: Only girls?

L: Yeah.

K: Yeah well okay. That make sense, yeah.

L: Girls can go to soccer game too.

K: Oh, they can?

L: Yeah.

K: But boys can't be cheer leaders.

L: Un-un I don't think so.

K: Maybe they can but they don't want to.

L: I know.

K: That probably is, huh?

L: It's kind of boring though.

K: Hmm.

L: That's what I think.

K: But September is almost over. One month of school gone.

L: Um-hmm.

K: How many more to go?

L: Yesterday the twenty

K: The twenty eighth.

L: Twenty eighth?

K: Um-hmm.

L: I think that's the date we started school. Wait, let me see this. It's on August some time I don't know.

K: Oh you mean when school started?

L: Yeah. Let's see. It's in August. It's on Wednesday.

K: August the twentieth the twenty seventh. So yeah one month gone. Shuway.

L: Come on. We already done.

K: Yeah.

L: *Hasta la vista*!

K: Bye-bye one month in school. So what you've learned in one month? Can you get your locker open now?

L: Yes.

K: Anything?

L: Yeah, it's pretty easy.

K: Yeah. You got your schedule done? Yon have to carry that piece of paper with you?

L: No.

K: You know where to go?

L: Yeah.

K: You have lots of homework?

L: Um like for this week yes.

K: Yeah, how come?

L: I have homework just like regular homework. But I have a book report I have to done on Monday.

K: Oh, tomorrow?

L: Yeah.

K: Are you done?

L: Yeah.

K: Oh good. You do your homework first thing Friday when you come home?

L: Yeah.

K: Yeah, good. So where you get your football?

L: I don't know. My mom gave it to me.

K: Oh, that's nice.

L: It was not brand new though.

K: Oh, that's okay. Actually they are better when they are already broken in.

L: I know.

K: Because when they are when they are brand new, they don't
    work very good.

L: I know. They are very sleepy something like that.

K: Yeah. A kind of hard too.

L: Yeah. Now this is I think a kind of better.

K: Yep. You play that with Jack?

L: Yep. At first I can't get used to it. But now I could.

K: Now you can throw it again?

L: Yeah.

K: Hmm. Are you allowed to throw it in the house?

L: No.

K: No. Jos his friends, he has friends from the Netherlands.

L: Yeah.

K: His friends is here right now.

L: Um-hmm.

K: Um they bought a football last weekend

L: Um-hmm.

K: They've being played with it. They can't throw it very good
    though. Maybe you better come to show them how.

L: [laughing]

K: Yeah. So what's happening in the neighborhood?

L: Oh, you mean that way?

K: Yep. Just here like with Jack and Christina.

L: Um Jack

K: I forgot your little friend's name.

L: Xuanxuan?

K: Yep.

L: I don't know about Xuanxuan because I haven't seen him for
    a long time.

K: Hmm.

L: But there is a girl. You know Charlene?

K: Ahhh.

L: She live close just like that just like that

K: Did I meet her one time?

L: I think so. You should, like in the swimming pool.

K: Um maybe.

L: She got like as long hair as yours.

K: Yep.

L: She is a mix or something.

K: Shuway I don't know.

L: Okay she-she just have a birthday yesterday.

K: So you had a party?

L: No, I don't went there.

K: You didn't go.

L: Because I have to go to take my piano class.

K: Oh, how is that going?

L: Okay.

K: Yep?

L: Yep.

K: You've learned how many songs now?

L: Oh, how many

K: [to the boy's mother, who is handing her a drink] Oh, thank you.

L: songs now? I don't know.

K: Twenty?

L: Um maybe.

K: Yep?

L: Um no.

K: No.

L: I have only like the teacher I know before because no teacher teach me so I have to learn by myself. And now some of them the teacher tell me you know like my new pieces

K: Um-hmm.

L: I already know how to play. I just have to do the fingers, the drop-downs, things like that.

K: Right. Hmm see you play with two hands.

L: Yes.

K: Like this hand does one and this hand does something different.

L: Yeah.

K: Hm when we're done talking, I want to hear.

L: Okay.

K: Yep.

L: [tapping on the table]

K: Wow, they are moving at different times. So do you practice in school at your desk?

L: No.

K: During

L: Yep, sometimes.

K: What's the class when you do have free reading time? No, Academic Reading?

L: Academic Assist.

K: Oh yep. Do you practice sometimes during Academic Assist?

L: I have a friend he play you know what's that thing called. The big thing then you do like with a stick bang-bang-bang-bang. Trumpet or something?

K: Oh, drums.

L: Oh yep drums. And he play drums and he always like [showing]

K: What's the Academic Assist to take?

L: Yep. You better stop now

K: Stop banging on the desk.

L: or it's going to break tomorrow.

K: Yeah. What you do for recess? Still go outside or it's too cold?

L: We still go outside even it's cold even it's snow.

K: At ten o'clock?

L: But not rain not on rain days.

K: What you do on raining days?

L: Um we go to the gym.

K: And do what?

L: Um talk.

K: Just talk?

L: Yeah. But seventh and eighth graders they have you know they get to play a game like soccer, kick ball, something like that.

K: I see.

L: And we could go watch it if you want to. But we could talk to like friend from in sixth-grade

K: Um-hmm.

L: If you want to.

K: Um-hmm. So you keep your football in that bag.

L: No.

K: No.

L: There is a special basket. It's like a cool design and you could go see after it.

K: The basket has a cool design?

L: The basket like I put all my balls in there,

K: Ah.

L: it's a cool design

K: Ha.

L: with the balls in there.

K: Yep you bet.

L: You could let me see it. I could let you see it later.

K: So you have all your balls there.

L: Yeah.

K: Not just football.

L: No, not all. Like there is one, one is like that green ball

K: Um-hmm.

L: like that I bought that ball the first time and that ball was under my dog. And the dog because if there is no one in there, he will like [showing the manner of drooping]. If there is a ball, he will like [showing]. So he looks better when he is like that. So I always put the ball in there.

K: Oh yep, that's nice. So do you still go to church

L: Yeah.

K: with Jack and Christina?

L: Yeah.

K: Do you like it?

L: Yeah.

K: What you do?

L: What I do?

K: Yeah.

L: I didn't went there a lot though. I didn't went there I went there I didn't went there last Friday, last last Friday and last last last Friday.

K: Why are not?

L: Because nobody will bring me.

K: They are busy.

L: Or something else happen. At first, it's Ping's last day in the in-in the America.

K: Ping's?

L: Yeah.

K: Where she go?

L: She went back to China.

K: Forever?

L: No.

K: Oh, just the visit.

L: Yeah.

K: Like she did last summer.

L: Yeah.

K: She stayed for a couple of months.

L: But this time may be longer because she go there and you know her sister maybe has some business and earn some money things like that.

K: I see. But her husband Daxin?

L: Daoxin.

K: Daoxin, yep.

L: He's still here.

K: He's still here.

L: Sometimes he came to our house to eat or something.

K: Yeah. I bet he's sad without Ping though.

L: I know. He is boring.

K: Oh, he's bored.

L: Yeah.

K: Not boring.

L: Bored?

K: Right. If you say he is boring

L: Um-hmm.

K: that means he's no fun.

L: [laughing]

K: Wow, so she went. You had a big party for her to go.

L: Yes. So I can't go that day. And the second day was oh we go the second Friday we go to Christina's house for a party. It's just like a regular party.

K: I see.

L: Like playing adults playing cards you know something like that.

K: I see.

L: And the third one nobody will bring me.

K: This past Friday?

L: And the fourth yeah no the one before that.

K: Okay.

L: And the fourth one I went there. But only we four were there. I mean we didn't went to church that day.

K: You mean you, Jack, Christina and

L: Zack-Zachary.

K: Zachary.

L: You know Zachary? You know that boy?

K: I don't know.

L: I know.

K: I only know you, Jack and Christina very well. The other ones I get mixed up.

L: He is Christina's friend. He go to church too. And I went with him. But that day only we four kid are there you know

K: Right.

L: except for the babies.

K: And there was no fun.

L: It's no fun.

K: How about Robb? He was there?

L: Yeah, he was there. You know Robb?

K: No, you told me though. You said,

L: Okay.

K: are you going to steal something from me?

L: [laughing]

K: Yeah. So what did you do?

L: Well last Sunday last it's last last Sunday,

K: Okay.

L: yeah, I went there. And we have you know Bible study.

K: Um-hmm.

L: After the bible study, we have we get play you know like play like we play frisbee golf frisbee football.

K: Oh, yeah.

L: You know how to play that?

K: Um-hmm. Um they call it ultimate frisbee.

L: I don't know.

K: Yeah. I study it at college. I took class with ultimate frisbee. You play just like football or frisbee?

L: No.

K: No.

L: It's different.

K: How do you play?

L: Like you know the first down in football it's not like how long is first down. You know like we throw to people. But when you catch it you can't run. You have to throw someone else.

K: Oh, yeah.

L: Like it's two hand touch. If I touch you, you have to sit there. First down is like

K: And you did this with four people?

L: Um?

K: You did this with four people?

L: Um four people six people it doesn't matter.

K: It doesn't matter.

L: You have to be like more than two or three or four.

K: Right.

L: Something like that. Two is not that fun though. Not that much people either.

K: Right.

L: Like fifteen or eighteen.

K: Ha so you played that. What was the bible story about?

L: Oh Jesus create you know Adam and Eve.

K: Ah-hmm.

L: And they create them because they want them to like protect the garden.

K: Um-hmm.

L: Or like you know guard the garden.

K: Okay.

L: So um Jesus create oh that day we talk about um like we have a study guide like a work sheet.

K: Um-hmm.

L: Um like [going to get those sheets]

K: Oh, they give you those.

L: Yeah. They give us those for you know learning still. And that day we study this. See this is like a work sheet.

K: Um-hmm.

L: This is the scripture today's scripture. See those like Jesus tell you know Adam and Eve

K: Right.

L: that they are special like guard you know the garden or things like that.

K: Okay.

L: And you read those and then you do those works.

K: And then you have to answer the questions.

L: Yes. And this is like-like you think this one is how you think. It's okay like ten like you say food like we have a lot of food. We have enough food.

K: Okay.

L: We don't need anymore so it's ten. But I don't think so it's like we have enough already

K: Right.

L: because some of them like living some place they have a lot of water some things like that and they don't have food, things like that

K: Right.

L: like Indian or something. And one way you have seen people like this use these things and throw them away like wasting.

K: Right.

L: And name one thing this class can do to you know like do better and tell them not to do that.

K: I see.

L: We can save money

K: Okay.

L: and buy the food. And this is air, birds like animals. Um I think is seven too.

K: Oh, you think land is only five? Why?

L: I don't know what you mean "land".

K: Um I think your answer is good. They throw trash on the street. That's not good.

L: I know.

K: Yep. All these though you can do tell people to stop tell people to stop tell people to stop tell people to stop. [laughing] Oh, that's good though. Yeah. Our bodies, oh smoking. Tell them not to smoke.

L: [laughing]

K: Yep. What do you think it means to "subdue" the earth?

L: To rule over the earth. To rule over the world.

K: Okay. "subdue" that's a weird word, isn't it?

L: I know. Okay this one is the one before that.

K: Oh, from the week before?

L: Yeah.

K: But you didn't go and they give it anyway?

L: No, I went there that time. I didn't go you know this weekend.

K: Right.

L: What the

K: You didn't fill any other answers in.

L: I know because they don't have any thing.

K: No. So this one was Genesis 1: 26 to 28.

L: We are all study Genesis.

K: Oh, yes.

L: We have no order. I don't know why.

K: You do all you don't do any new Testament only old.

L: Yep.

K: Yep. Trashing God's Earth. Hmm.

L: Waking up to Yourself.

K: Call the Rock

L: Yeah, the Rock.

K: middle school. So did Jack and Christine have different one

L: Yeah.

K: because they are not in middle school?

L: Yeah, they don't have the one like the little ones. Like Jeff and Stanley did I tell you about them?

K: Un-un.

L: Their real name is Jeffrey, Stanley and Jesstina. And but we call them Jeff, Stan and Jess.

K: [laughing]

L: And sometimes we call like-like we call them Jesstina to but we don't call them like Jeffrey or Stanley.

K: Um-hmm.

L: Sometimes we make Jesstina (some)thing like Jeffrey Stanley Jesstinaley.

K: Oh because ley at the end.

L: I know.

K: That's interesting.

L: Jeffrey Stanley Jesstinaley. You know they are sisters and brothers. Um Stanley is the biggest.

K: Um-hmm.

L: And Jeff and then Jesstina. Jesstina

K: But you call her Jess?

L: Jess.

K: How do you get Jes out of Jesstina?

L: It's j-e-s-s-t-i-n-a.

K: j-e-s-s-t-i-n-a. Oh, okay.

L: Jess.

K: So it's kind of like Jessica with t-i-n-a.

L: Yeah.

K: Okay.

L: So

K: Yep, neat. So the Rock?

L: The Rock ___

K: What's this? Just the layout. This one is about trashing trea-sure and this one is about waking up to yourself?

L: I forgot what's that to.

K: Ha it's about liking yourself?

L: No.

K: Oh. Read this.

L: And then you will know.

K: Read this scripture?

L: Yeah. Then God said: "Let us make man in our image, in our likeness, and let them rule over the fish of the sea and the birds of the air, over the livestock,

K: Um-hmm.

L: over all the earth, and over all the creatures that move along the ground."

K: Hmm. So it's about how man was created.

L: Yep. His image.

K: I see. Neat. So these are cool. You save all of them from every week?

L: Yeah.

K: Keep them in it.

L: You know Stan and Jeff they're like they're like you know just like teaching. They're all teachers.

K: Oh, they are not they are not little kids. They are adults.

L: No, they're adults. Yeah.

K: Stan, Jeff are just

L: But we play all the stuff just like kids.

K: Just like kids. How old are they?

L: Oh, they're not old. They are both you know young adults.

K: Okay.

L: One is seventeen.

K: Okay, that's teenagers.

L: One is seventeen and the other one is fifteen.

K: Okay.

L: Stan is seventeen. And they just like

K: Jess is how old?

L: Twelve I guess.

K: Okay.

L: Oh no-no-no, not twelve.

K: Oh, the same age as you.

L: Thirteen yeah thirteen.

K: Okay. So she can be your girl friend.

L: Maybe.

K: Maybe. You have a girl friend?

L: No.

K: No. We start talking something else?

L: Um?

K: Yep.

L: Yep. See so they're like those two are you know Jeff and Stan

K: Um-hmm.

L: they like you teach one this week and we I teach next week something like that.

K: Okay. And they played the frisbee football with you.

L: Yes.

K: Okay.

L: Because after you know the worship, then we call the children. They have I don't know what they have. Those adults I don't know what they do because we have to go over there.

K: Right.

L: And we want to go.

K: So you sing is that what you do for worship?

L: Um?

K: You sing songs?

L: Yep, we sing songs and we pray, things like that. And we read scriptures, things like that.

K: Okay. You sing songs out of the book?

L: Yeah.

K: Yeah.

L: A big book.

K: A big-big hymn book?

L: Like that big.

K: Yeah. That sounds fun. So you like to go?

L: Yep.

K: Good.

L: But I didn't go today.

K: I thought it's on Friday.

L: And Sunday.

K: Oh, and Sunday too.

L: This is Sunday.

K: Okay.

L: Those are on Sunday.

K: Yep.

L: Friday we do like-like-like-like Sunday. Adults going to learn the scripture.

K: Um-hmm.

L: And we Robb he is going to tell or Stan or Jeff they're going to tell us the scripture for like in another like in the in like kids' world.

K: Okay.

L: Now like seems that's hard to understand.

K: Right. So they're going to put in the words you understand.

L: Yep, just like telling stories.

K: Right.

L: It's it's fun.

K: It's fun.

L: Yep.

K: Good. Yeah. And did you go to the recreational building today? Sometimes you do that on Sunday. Where you go to play racket ball and

L: Oh, yep we went there today.

K: You went there today.

L: It's been closed for like-like a month or two.

K: Really?

L: Yep.

K: Why?

L: Because I think the air-conditioning or something.

K: Oh.

L: I don't know.
K: They put in something.
L: Yep, fixing something.
K: A kind of burden.
L: They don't have the air-conditioning but they have the warm air.
K: Right.
L: You know what I mean. You know those ones that come down from here.
K: Yeah. And it's too hot to let one in.
L: Yeah.
K: So you still play those cards that you put cards out there and whoever does the math problem quickest?
L: Oh, Challenge 24?
K: What is it?
L: Challenge 24.
K: Yep. Do you still play that?
L: Yep.
K: In school
L: No.
K: or just for fun?
L: For fun.
K: Do you have another contest, the big contest?
L: No, not yet.
K: Not yet.
L: Maybe in January.
K: That's nice you do it every year. Hmm so what else has happened? Okay, never mind. Go play piano now.
L: Wait.
K: [laughing]
---End of Conversation---

References

Aaronson, D., & Ferres, S. (1987). The impact of language differences on language processing: An example from Chinese-English bilingualism. In P. Homel, M. Palij, & D. Aaronson (Eds.), *Childhood bilingualism: Aspects of linguistic, cognitive, and social development* (pp. 75–119). Hillsdale, NJ: Erlbaum.

Abney, S. (1987). *The English noun phrase in its sentential aspect.* Unpublished doctoral dissertation, Massachusetts Institute of Technology, Cambridge, MA.

Adamson, H. (1988). *Variation theory and second language acquisition.* Washington, DC: Georgetown University Press.

Agnihotri, B., Khanna, A., & Mukherjee, A. (1984). The use of articles in Indian English: Errors and pedagogical implications. *International Review of Applied Linguistics, 22,* 115–129.

Al-Johani, M. (1982). *English and Arabic articles: A contrastive analysis in definiteness and indefiniteness.* Unpublished doctoral dissertation, Indianna University, Bloomington.

Andersen, R. (1977). The impoverished state of cross-sectional morpheme acquisition/accuracy methodology. *Working Papers on Bilingualism, 14,* 49–82.

Avery, P., & Radišić, M. (2007). Accounting for variability in the acquisition of English articles. In A. Belikova, L. Meroni, & M. Umeda (Eds.), *Proceedings of the 2nd Conference on Generative Approaches to Language Acquisition North America (GALANA)* (pp. 1–11). Somerville, MA: Cascadilla Proceedings Project.

Bailey, K. (1980). An introspective analysis of an individual's language learning experience. In R. C. Scarcella, & S. D. Krashen (Eds.), *Research in Second Language Acquisition* (pp. 58–65). Rowley, MA: Newbury House.

Bailey, N., Madden, C., & Krashen, S. (1974). Is there a "natural sequence" in adult second language learning? *Language Learning, 24*(2), 235–243.

Berry, R. (1991). Re-articulating the articles. *ELT Journal, 49*(3), 252–259.

Bickerton, D. (1981). *Roots of language*. Ann Arbor, MI: Karoma.

Bickerton, D. (1984). The language bioprogram hypothesis. *Behavioral and Brain Sciences, 7*, 173–188.

Bresson, F. (1974). Remarks on genetic psycholinguistics: The acquisition of the article system in French. *Problèmes actuels en psycholinguisticque/Current problems in psycholinguistics* (pp. 67–72). Paris: Editions de Centre National de la Recherche Scientifique.

Brown, R. (1973). *A first language: The early stages*. Cambridge, MA: Harvard University Press.

Bryman, A., & Cramer, D. (1990). *Quantitative data analysis for social scientists*. London: Routledge.

Butler, Y. G. (2002). Second language learners' theories on the use of the English articles: An analysis of the metalinguistic knowledge used by Japanese students in acquiring the English article system. *Studies in Second Language Acquisition, 24*(3), 451–480.

Cancino, H., Rosansky, E., & Schumann, J. (1978). The acquisition of English negatives and interrogatives by native Spanish speakers. In E. Hatch (Ed.), *Second language acquisition* (pp. 207–230). Rowley, MA: Newbury House.

Carroll, J., Davies, P., & Richman, B. (1971). *The American heritage word frequency book*. New York: American Heritage.

Celce-Murcia, M., & Larsen-Freeman, D. (1983). The article system. In M. Celce-Murcia, & D. Larsen-Freeman (Eds.), *The grammar book: An ESL/EFL teacher's course* (pp. 171–188). Rowley, MA: Newbury House.

Chalker, S. (1995). *The little Oxford dictionary of English grammar*. Oxford: Oxford University Press.

Chaudron, C., & Parker, K. (1990). Discourse markedness and structural markedness: The acquisition of English noun phrases. *Studies in Second Language Acquisition, 12*, 43–64.

Chen, P. (2004). Identifiability and definiteness in Chinese. *Linguistics, 42*(6), 1129–1184.

Chomsky, N. (1962). A transformational approach to syntax. In A. A. Hill (Ed.), *Proceedings of the Third Texas Conference on Problems of Linguistic Analysis of English on May 9–12, 1958* (pp. 124–158). Austin, Texas: The University of Texas.

Christophersen, P. (1939). *The article: A study of their theory and use in English*. London: Oxford University Press.

Cook, V. (1993). *Linguistics and second language acquisition*. New York: St. Martin's Press.

Corder, S. P. (1978). Language-learner language. In J. C. Richards (Ed.), *Understanding second and foreign language learning: Issues and approaches* (pp. 71–93). Rowley, MA: Newbury House.

Crookes, G. (1989). Planning and interlanguage variation. *Studies in Second Language Acquisition, 9*(14), 367–383.

Cziko, G. (1986). Testing the language bioprogram hypothesis: A review of children's acquisition of articles. *Language, 62*, 878–898.

de Villiers, J., & de Villiers, P. (1973). A cross-sectional study of the acquisition of grammatical morphemes in child speech. *Journal of Psycholinguistic Research, 2*(3), 267–278.

Du Bois, J. W. (1980). Beyond definiteness: The trace of identity in discourse. In W. L. Chafe (Ed.), *The pear stories: Cognitive, cultural, and linguistic aspects of narrative production* (pp. 203–274). Norwood, NJ: Ablex.

Dulay, H., & Burt, M. (1973). Should we teach children syntax? *Language Learning, 23*(2), 245–258.

Dulay, H., & Burt, M. (1974). Natural sequences in child second language acquisition. *Language Learning, 24*(1), 37–53.

Ekiert, M. (2004). Acquisition of the English article system by speakers of Polish in ESL and EFL settings. *Teachers College, Columbia University Working papers in TESOL & Applied Linguistics, 4*(1): Retrieved October 6, 2008, from http://journals.tc-library.org/index.php/tesol/article/view/42/49.

Ekiert, M. (2007). The acquisition of grammatical marking of indefiniteness with the indefinite article *a* in L2 English. *Teachers College, Columbia University Working papers in TESOL & Applied Linguistics, 7*(1): Retrieved October 6, 2008, from http://journals.tc-library.org/index.php/tesol/article/view/265/224.

Ellis, N. (1996). Sequencing in SLA: Phonological memory, chunking, and points of order. *Studies in Second Language Acquisition, 16,* 91–126.

Ellis, R. (1989). Are classroom and naturalistic acquisition the same? A study of the classroom acquisition of German word order rules. *Studies in Second Language Acquisition, 11,* 305–328.

Ellis, R. (1994). *The study of second language acquisition.* Oxford: Oxford University Press.

Emslie, H., & Stevenson, R. (1981). Pre-school children's use of the articles in definite and indefinite referring expressions. *Journal of Child Language, 8,* 313–328.

Epstein, R. (2002). The definite article, accessibility, and the construction of discourse referents. *Cognitive Linguistics, 12*(4), 333–378.

Fasold, R. (1975). The Bailey wave model: A dynamic quantitative paradigm. In R. Fasold & R. Shuy (Eds.), *Analyzing variation in language: Papers from the second colloquium on new ways of analyzing variation* (pp. 27–58). Washington, DC: Georgetown University Press.

Felix, S., & Hahn, A. (1985). Natural processes in classroom second-language learning. *Applied Linguistic, 6*, 223–238.

Garton, A. (1983). An approach to the study of determiners in early language development. *Journal of Psycholinguistic Research, 12*, 513–525.

Gass, S. (1979). Language transfer and universal grammatical relations. *Language Learning, 29*, 327–344.

Gass, S. M., & Mackey, A. (2002). Frequency effects and second language acquisition. *Studies in Second Language Acquisition, 24*(2), 249–260.

Geranpayeh, A. (2000). The acquisition of the English article system by Persian speakers. *Edinburgh Working Papers in Applied Linguistics, 10*, 37–51.

Goad, H., & White, L. (2004). Ultimate attainment of L2 inflection: Effects of L1 prosodic structure. In S. Foster-Cohen, M. S. Smith, A. Sorace, & M. Ota (Eds.), *EUROSLA Yearbook* (Vol. 4) (pp. 119–145). Amsterdam: John Benjamins Publishing Company.

Gorokhova, E. (1990). *Acquisition of English articles by native speakers of Spanish*. Unpublished doctoral dissertation, The State University of New Jersey, New Brunswick.

Grannis, O. (1972). The definite article conspiracy in English. *Language Learning, 22*, 275–289.

Greene, O. (1957). *The problem of the article in the teaching and learning of English as a foreign language*. Hartford, Connecticut: The Kennedy School of Missions.

Guella, H., Déprez, V., & Sleeman, P. (2008). Article choice parameters in L2. In R. Slabakova, J. Rothman, P. Kempchinsky, & E. Gavruseva (Eds.), *Proceedings of the 9th Generative Approaches to Second Language Acquisition Conference (GASLA 2007)* (pp. 57–69). Somerville, MA: Cascadilla Proceedings Project.

Guy, G. (1993). The quantitative analysis of linguistic variation. In D. Preston (Ed.), *American dialect research* (pp. 223–249). Amsterdam: John Benjamins.

Haan, P. (1987). Exploring the linguistic database: Noun phrase complexity and language variation. In W. Meijs (Ed.), *Corpus linguistics and beyond* (pp. 151–163). Amsterdam: Rodopi.

Hakuta, K. (1976). A case study of a Japanese child learning English as a second language. *Language Learning, 26*, 321–351.

Halliday, M. A. K. (1975). *Learning how to mean*. London: Edward Arnold.

Hatch, E. (Ed.). (1978). *Second language acquisition*. Cambridge, MA: Newbury House Publishers, Inc.

Hawkins, R., Al-Eid, S., Almahboob, I., Athanasopoulos, P., Chaengchenkit, R., Hu, J., Rezai, M., Jaensch, C., Jeon, Y., Jiang, A., Leung, Y.-K. I., Matsunaga, K., Ortega, M., Sarko, G., Snape, N., & Velasco-Zárate, K. (2006). Accounting for English article interpretation by L2 speakers. In S. H. Foster-Cohen, M. Medved Krajnovic, & J. Mihaljevi´c Djigunovi´c (Eds.), *EUROSLA Yearbook* (Vol. 6) (pp. 7–25). Amsterdam: John Benjamins Publishing Company.

Hawkins, R., and Chan, C. Y.-H. (1997). The partial availability of Universal Grammar in second language acquisition: The 'failed functional features hypothesis'. *Second Language Research, 13*(3), 187–226.

Hewson, J. (1972). *Article and noun in English*. The Hague: Mouton.

Hok, R. (1970). The concept of 'general-specific' and its application to *the/a* and *some/any*. *TESOL Quarterly, 4*, 231–239.

Huebner, T. (1983). *A longitudinal analysis of the acquisition of English*. Ann Arbor, MI: Karoma Publishers, Inc.

Ionin, T., Ko, H., & Wexler, K. (2008). The role of semantic features in the acquisition of English articles by Russian and Korean speakers. In J. M. Liceras, H. Zobl, & H. Goodluck (Eds.), *The role of formal features in second language acquisition* (pp. 226–268). New York: Lawrence Erlbaum Associates.

Jafarpur, A. (1979). Persian and English articles: A contrastive study. *English Language Teaching Journal, 33,* 133–139.

Jarvis, S. (2002). Topic continuity in L2 English article use. *Studies in Second Language Acquisition, 24*(3), 387–418.

Johnson, J., & Newport, E. (1989). Critical period effects in second language learning: The influence of maturational state on the acquisition of English as a second language. *Cognitive Psychology, 21,* 60–99.

Johnston, M., & Pienemann, M. (1986). *Second language acquisition: A classroom perspective.* New South Wales Migrant Education Service.

Jung, E. H. (2004). Topic and subject prominence in interlanguage development. *Language Learning, 54*(4), 713–738.

Kaku, K. (2006). Second language learners' use of English articles: A case study of native speakers of Japanese. *Cahiers Linguistiques d'Ottawa/ Ottawa Papers in Linguistics, 34,* 63–74.

Kaluza, H. (1963). Teaching the English articles to speakers of Slavic. *Language Learning, 13,* 113–124.

Kaluza, H. (1981). *Use of articles in contemporary English.* Schwetzingen: Julius Groos Verlan, Heidelberg.

Karmiloff-Smith, A. (1979). *A functional approach to child language.* Cambridge: Cambridge University Press.

Katz, S. L., & Blyth, C. S. (2007). *Teaching French grammar in context: Theory and practice.* New Haven, CT: Yale University Press.

Keenan, E. L., & Comrie, B. (1977). Noun phrase accessibility and Universal Grammar. *Linguistic Inquiry, 8,* 63–99.

Kharma, N. (1981). Analysis of the errors committed by Arab university students in the use of the English definite/indefinite articles. *International Review of Applied Linguistics, 19,* 333–345.

Krashen, S. (1977). Some issues relating to the Monitor Mode. In H. Brown, C. Yorio, & R. Crymes (Eds.), *On TESOL '77* (pp. 144–158). Washington, DC: TESOL.

Krashen, S. (1982). *Principles and practice in second language acquisition*. Oxford: Pergamon Press Inc.

Labov, W. (1973). *Language in the inner city*. Philadelphia, PA: University of Pennsylvania Press.

Lang, Y. (1989). *A comparison of the grammatical characteristics of different text categories in the Lancaster-Leeds Treebank*. Unpublished master's thesis, The University of Lancaster, Lancaster.

Lardiere, D. (2004). Knowledge of definiteness despite variable article omission in second language acquisition. In A. Brugos, L. Micciulla, & C. E. Smith (Eds.), *Proceedings of the 28th Annual Boston University Conference on Language Development* (pp. 328–339). Somerville, MA: Cascadilla Press.

Larsen-Freeman, D., & Long, M. (1991). *An introduction to second language acquisition*. New York: Longman Inc.

Lee, K., Cameron, C., Linton, M., & Hunt, A. (1994). Referential placeholding in Chinese children's acquisition of English articles. *Applied Psycholinguistics, 15*, 29–43.

Leech, G., & Svartvik, J. (1975). *A communicative grammar of English*. London: Longman Group Ltd.

Leopold, W. (1939). *Speech development of a bilingual child 1: Vocabulary growth in the first two years*. Evanston, IL: Northwestern University.

Leopold, W. (1949). *Speech development of a bilingual child III: Grammar and general problems in the first two years*. Evanston, IL: Northwestern University.

Leung, Y.-K. I. (2001). The initial state of L3A: Full transfer and failed features? In X. Bonch-Bruevich, W. Crawford, J. Hellerman, C. Higgins, &

H. Nguyen (Eds.), *The Past, Present, and Future of Second Language Research: Selected Proceedings of the 2000 Second Language Research Forum* (pp. 55–75). Somerville, MA: Cascadilla Press.

Li, C., & Thompson, S. (1981). *Mandarin Chinese: A functional reference grammar*. Berkeley: University of California Press.

Liao, T. (1985). A study of article errors in the written English of Chinese college students in Taiwan. (Doctoral dissertation, University of Colorado at Boulder, 1984). *Dissertation Abstracts International, 45–07*, 2017–2018A.

Lightbown, P., & Spada, N. (1990). Focus-on-form and corrective feedback in communicative language teaching: Effects on second language learning. *Studies in Second Language Acquisition, 12*, 429–448.

Liu, D.-L., & Gleason, J. L. (2002). Acquisition of the article *the* by non-native speakers of English: An analysis of four nongeneric uses. *Studies in Second Language Acquisition, 24*(1), 1–26.

Lu, C. F.-C. (2001). The acquisition of English articles by Chinese learners. *Second Language Studies, 20*, 43–78.

Lyons, C. (1999). *Definiteness*. Cambridge: Cambridge University Press.

Lyons, J. (1975). Deixis as the source of reference. In E. Keenan (Ed.), *Formal semantics of natural language* (pp. 125–143). Cambridge: Cambridge University Press.

Lyons, J. (1977). *Semantics 2*. Cambridge: Cambridge University Press.

Maratsos, M. (1976). *The use of definite and indefinite reference in young children*. Cambridge: Cambridge University Press.

Maratsos, M. (1983). Some current issues in the study of the acquisition of grammar. In P. Mussen (Ed.), *Handbook of child psychology vol. III* (pp. 707–786). New York: Wiley.

Master, P. (1987). Generic *the* in *Scientific American*. *English for Specific Purposes, 6*(3), 165–186.

Master, P. (1988, March). *Acquiring the English article system: A cross-linguistic interlanguage analysis*. Paper presented at the 22nd Annual TESOL Convention, Chicago, IL.

Master, P. (1990). Teaching the English articles as a binary system. *TESOL Quarterly, 24*(3), 461–478.

Master, P. (1995). Consciousness raising and article pedagogy. In D. Belcher & G. Braine (Eds.), *Academic writing in a second language: Essays on research and pedagogy* (pp. 183–204). Norwood, NJ: Ablex Publishing Corporation.

Master, P. (2002). Information structure and English article pedagogy. *System, 30*, 331–348.

Master, P. (2003). Acquisition of the zero and null articles in English. *Issues in Applied Linguistics, 14*(1), 3–20.

McEldowney, P. (1977). A teaching grammar of the English article system. *International Review of Applied Linguistics, 15*, 95–112.

Meisel, J. M., Clahsen, H., & Pienemann, M. (1981). On determining developmental stages in natural second language acquisition. *Studies in Second Language Acquisition, 3*(2), 109–135.

Nassaji, H., & Swain, M. (2000). A Vygotskian perspective on corrective feedback in L2: The effect of random versus negotiated help on the learning of English articles. *Language Awareness, 9*(1), 34–51.

Nation, P., & Waring, R. (1997). Vocabulary size, text coverage and word lists. In N. Schmitt & M. McCarthy (Eds.), *Vocabulary description, acquisition, and pedagogy* (pp. 6–19). Cambridge: Cambridge University Press.

Norusis, M. (1997). *SPSS: SPSS 7.5 guide to data analysis*. Englewood Cliffs, NJ: Prentice Hall.

Odlin, T. (1989). *Language transfer*. Cambridge: Cambridge University Press.

Parrish, B. (1987). A new look at methodologies in the study of article acquisition for learners of ESL. *Language Learning, 37*, 361–383.

Pavesi, M. (1986). Markedness, discoursal modes and relative clause formation in a formal and informal context. *Studies in Second Language Acquisition, 8*, 38–55.

Piaget, J. (1926). *The language and thought of the child.* New York: Humanities Press.

Pica, T. (1983a). The article in American English: What the textbooks don't tell us. In N. Wolfson & E. Judd (Eds.), *Sociolinguistics and second language acquisition* (pp. 222–233). Rowley, MA: Newbury House.

Pica, T. (1983b). Methods of morpheme quantification: Their effect on the interpretation of second language data. *Studies in Second Language Acquisition, 6*(1), 69–78.

Pica, T. (1985). Linguistic simplicity and learnability: Implications for language syllabus design. In K. Hyltenstam & M. Pienemann (Eds.), *Modeling and assessing second language acquisition* (pp. 137–151). England: Multilingual Matters Ltd.

Pienemann, M. (1984). Psychological constraints on the teachability of languages. *Studies in Second Language Acquisition, 6*, 186–214.

Pienemann, M., Johnston, M., & Brindley, G. (1988). Constructing an acquisition-based procedure for second language assessment. *Studies in Second Language Acquisition, 10*, 217–243.

Poesio, M., & Vieira, R. (1998). A corpus-based investigation of definite description use. *Computational Linguistics, 24*, 183–216.

Pongpairoj, N. (2007). Asymmetric patterns of English article omissions in L2A. In C. Gabrielatos, R. Slessor, & J. W. Unger (Eds.). *Papers from the Lancaster University Postgraduate Conference in Linguistics & Language Teaching (LAEL PG 2006), 1* (pp. 103–119). Lancaster, England: Department of Linguistics and English Language, Lancaster University.

QSR (1998). *NUD*IST 3.0.4d*. City Melbourne: Qualitative Solutions & Research Pty Ltd.

Quirk, R., Greenbaum, S., Leech, G., & Svartvik, J. (1985). *A comprehensive grammar of the English language*. London: Longman Group Ltd.

Robberecht, P. (1983). Towards a pedagogical grammar of determiners: A contrastive approach. *Papers and Studies in Contrastive Linguistics, 17*, 61–77.

Robertson, D. (2000). Variability in the use of the English article system by Chinese learners of English. *Second Language Research, 16*(2), 135–172.

Sand, A. (2004). Shared morpho-syntactic features in contact varieties of English: Article use. *World Englishes, 23*(2), 281–298.

Sarko, G. (2008). Morphophonological or syntactic transfer in the acquisition of English articles by L1 Speakers of Syrian Arabic? In R. Slabakova, J. Rothman, P. Kempchinsky, & E. Gavruseva (Eds.), *Proceedings of the 9th Generative Approaches to Second Language Acquisition Conference (GASLA 2007)* (pp. 206–217). Somerville, MA: Cascadilla Proceedings Project.

Schmidt, R. (1983). Interaction, acculturation, and the acquisition of communicative competence: a case study of an adult. In N. Wolfson & E. Judd (Eds.), *Sociolinguistics and second language acquisition* (pp. 137–174). New York: Newbury House.

Schumann, J. (1975). Affective factors and the problem of age in second language acquisition. *Language Learning, 2*, 201–235.

Schumann, J. (1978). The relationship of pidginization, creolization, and decreolization to second language acquisition. *Language Learning, 28*, 367–379.

Schumann, J. (1980). The acquisition of English relative clauses by second language learners. In R. Scarcella & S. Krashen (Eds.), *Research in second language acquisition: Selected papers from the Los Angeles*

Second Language Research Forum (pp. 118–131). Rowley, MA: Newbury House.

Selinker, L. (1972). Interlanguage. *International Review of Applied Linguistics, 10,* 209–231.

Shannon, J. (1995). *Variability and the interlanguage production of the English definite article.* Unpublished doctoral dissertation, The Ohio State University, Columbus.

Sharon, A. (1993). In search of the genuine article: A cross-linguistic investigation of the development of the English article system in written compositions of adult ESL students (Doctoral dissertation, The Florida State University, 1992). *Dissertation Abstracts International, 53–07,* 2352A.

Snape, N., Leung, Y.-K. I., & Ting, H.-C. (2006). Comparing Chinese, Japanese and Spanish Speakers in L2 English article acquisition: Evidence against the Fluctuation hypothesis? In M. G. O'Brien, C. Shea, & J. Archibald (Eds.), *Proceedings of the 8th Generative Approaches to Second Language Acquisition Conference (GASLA 2006)* (pp. 132–139). Somerville, MA: Cascadilla Proceedings Project.

Szabolcsi, A. (1983/84). The possessor that ran away from home. *The Linguistic Review, 3,* 89–102.

Tarone, E. (1985). Variability in interlanguage use: A study of style-shifting in morphology and syntax. *Language Learning, 35,* 373–404.

Tarone, E., & Parrish, B. (1988). Task-related variation in interlanguage use: The case of articles. *Language Learning, 38,* 21–44.

Taylor, I., & Taylor, M. (1990). *Psycholinguistics: Learning and using language.* Englewood Cliffs, NJ: Prentice Hall.

Taylor, L. (1990). *Teaching and learning vocabulary.* London: Prentice Hall.

Thomas, M. (1989a). The acquisition of English articles by first- and second-language learners. *Applied Psycholinguistics, 10,* 335–355.

Thomas, M. (1989b, March). *Use of English article by Mandarin-speaking second-language learners*. Paper presented at the 22nd TESOL Convention, Chicago, IL.

Thu, H. N. (2005). Vietnamese learners mastering English articles. Unpublished doctoral dissertation, University of Groningen, Groningen, the Netherlands.

Trenkic, D. (2002). Form-meaning connections in the acquisition of English articles. In S. H. Foster-Cohen, T. Ruthenberg, & M. L. Poschen (Eds.), *EUROSLA Yearbook* (Vol. 2) (pp. 115–133). Amsterdam: John Benjamins Publishing Company.

Warden, D. (1976). The influence of context on children's use of identifying expressions and references. *British Journal of Psychology, 67*(1), 101–112.

White, L. (2000). Second language acquisition: From initial to final state. In J. Archibald (Ed.), *Second language acquisition and linguistic theory* (pp. 130–155). Malden, MA: Blackwell Publishers Inc.

White, L. (2003). Fossilization in steady state L2 grammars: Persistent problems with inflectional morphology. *Bilingualism: Language and Cognition, 6*, 129–141.

White, L. (2008). Different? Yes. Fundamentally? No. Definiteness effects in the L2 English of Mandarin speakers. In R. Slabakova, J. Rothman, P. Kempchinsky, & E. Gavruseva (Eds.), *Proceedings of the 9th Generative Approaches to Second Language Acquisition Conference (GASLA 2007)* (pp. 251–261). Somerville, MA: Cascadilla Proceedings Project.

Whitman, R. (1974). Teaching the article in English. *TESOL Quarterly, 8*, 253–262.

Winford, D. (1990). Copula variability, accountability, and the concept of "polylectal" grammars. *Journal of Pidgin and Creole Languages, 5*(2), 223–252.

Wolf, Y., & Walters, J. (2001). Definite articles in the context of literary and scientific writings. *Journal of Pragmatics, 33*, 965–967.

Yamada, J., & Matsuura, N. (1982). The use of the English article among Japanese students. *RELC Journal, 13*(1), 50–63.

Yin, R. (1984). *Case study research: Design and methods*. Beverly Hills, CA: SAGE Publications, Inc.

Yin, R. (1994). *Case study research: Design and methods* (2nd ed.). Thousand Oaks, CA: SAGE Publications, Inc.

Young, R. (1986). The acquisition of a verbal repertoire in a second language. *Penn Working Papers in Educational Linguistics, 2*(1), 85–119.

Zdorenko, T., & Paradis, J. (2008). The acquisition of articles in child second language English: Fluctuation, transfer, or both? *Second Language Research, 24*(2), 227–250.

Zehler, A., & Brewer, W. (1982). Sequence and principles in article system use: An examination of *a, the,* and *null* articles. *Child Development, 53*, 1268–1274.

Zhang, D.-Z. (1978). *A practical English grammar*. Beijing: The Commercial Press.

INDEX

LaVergne, TN USA
30 January 2011
214470LV00003B/37/P